HOW TO READ HISTORY

HOW
TO READ
HISTORY

Archibald Robertson

FREDERICK UNGAR PUBLISHING CO.
NEW YORK

CONTENTS

CHAPTER I

WHY HISTORY?

"THIS," says Shaw in the preface to *Man and Superman*, " is the true joy in life, the being used for a purpose recognized by yourself as a mighty one; the being thoroughly worn out before you are thrown on the scrap heap; the being a force of Nature instead of a feverish selfish little clod of ailments and grievances complaining that the world will not devote itself to making you happy."

I take this as my starting point. For it expresses better perhaps than any other single sentence in literature the answer —or at least the beginning of the answer—to the question why we should study history. History is a link uniting each of us as an individual with a whole greater than ourselves.

If we consider man as an individual in isolation from his social environment, we are struck by his insignificance and futility. I hope to show presently that to isolate him in this way is an error. Nevertheless many thinkers have committed that error, and many who cannot be dignified with the name of thinkers commit it in their daily lives. It is a matter of common experience that the person who is habitually absorbed in his own immediate interests is apt to be utterly miserable, and a nuisance to others into the bargain. And naturally so; for the isolated interests of the individual do not appear on inspection to warrant the amount of trouble taken by himself and others to further them. To begin with, he has to be born and to grow up. To judge by the trouble entailed by that alone, one would think that some great end was surely in view. Yet to the immense majority of people born into the world life is a very doubtful bargain. The greater part of their energies are absorbed by the business of keeping alive. Then even that proves too much for them; and they die, leaving children to drive the same doubtful bargain with the same result. The minority who are called fortunate or successful owe their reputation, as a rule, to the degree in which they are able to cajole or coerce the majority into contributing to their power and comfort before they too die, leaving a name " to point a moral or adorn a tale." Few of those singled out as great men would qualify for a place in Virgil's Elysium:

> Those good poets and true, whose songs were worthy of Phœbus;
> Those who ennobled life by wise and useful invention;
> Those who by service done made names for some to remember.[1]

Traditional religion answers the question in its own fashion. For the traditionalist the futility of the life of the average individual is evidence of the existence of an eternal life in which the frustrations of the present are compensated. " Man," says Kant, " is conscious of an inward call to constitute himself, by his conduct in this world—without regard to mere sublunary interests—the citizen of a better. This mighty, irresistible proof . . . remains to humanity, even after the theoretical cognition of ourselves has failed to establish the necessity of an existence after death." [2] To those who can bring themselves to regard the present life merely as a preparation for eternity, history, in the sense in which we usually understand the word, is unimportant. The only history in which the consistent supernaturalist should be interested is " sacred " history, i.e. those events or alleged events which are relevant to the plan of salvation. That the universe is the creation of an almighty, all-wise, and all-good God; that man by wilful disobedience to God is alone responsible for the evil state of the world; that God in his wisdom and goodness revealed himself to man through the Hebrew prophets and in the life, death, and resurrection of Jesus Christ; and that man by accepting that revelation can win eternal life—that to the traditional religionist is what matters and all that matters. How civilization arose from savagery; how empires grew, flourished, declined, and fell; what poets have sung, philosophers thought, scientists in-

---

[1] *Æneid* vi, 662–664.
[2] *Critique of Pure Reason*, translated by J. M. D. Meiklejohn, p. 251.

vented, patriots struggled for, or statesmen achieved—that, to the traditionalist, if he is consistent, matters not at all.

But the traditional religionist seldom or never is consistent. Where practical life is concerned, he usually resembles the rest of us. He is as much taken up as the rest of us with the business of keeping alive and with the pursuit of fortune and success. He is as liable as the rest of us to become a nuisance to himself and others with his ailments and grievances. He may assent in so many words to the proposition that the present life is merely a preparation for eternity, but he does not act as if he believed it. His interest in " sacred " history is not noticeably greater than that of the Rationalist: it is often less. His interest in " profane " history is as great or as little as that of the average citizen. Judging by the criterion of behaviour, we are justified in concluding that traditional religion, for the majority of those who profess it, is more a convention than a conviction. That is not surprising; for the " truths " of traditional religion are in the nature of the case indemonstrable. Their chief effect, and indeed their chief function, throughout history has been to divert inquiry, which might otherwise be dangerous to the social order, into channels which, if fruitless, are at least harmless.

Since the dogmas of religion are indemonstrable and, as we have seen, unreal to the majority even of those who profess them, man has to find some other way out of the insignificance and futility which await him if he considers only his interests as an isolated individual. One way out is to realize that the individual and his interests are in fact not as isolated as they seem. This truth is constantly obscured by the bad metaphysics with which traditional religion has succeeded in infecting everyday language. We speak of man as composed of mind and body, as if mind and body were two separable and dissimilar things somehow joined together. We mean by the body the organism we see and touch, and we mean (or think we mean) by the mind an invisible, intangible, immaterial entity somehow inside the body, yet independent of it and other immaterial minds in other bodies. This view is antiquated and unwarranted. Man is not a mind joined to a body, but a " mind-body "—that is to say, an organism originating from other organisms, certain of whose functions are to perceive and think, just as other functions are to eat, digest, and reproduce. As a convenience of language, we give the name " body " to as much of the organism as we can perceive with our senses, and the name " mind " to the perceiving and thinking functions themselves. But the two are inseparably united. This functioning organism and nothing else is what we mean by an individual.

Once we grasp the fact that the individual is not a mind linked to a body, but an integrated organism with mental and bodily functions, it becomes impossible to isolate him from the society to which he belongs. He derives his being from that society through his parentage and ancestry. He returns part of his being to it through his children and descendants, if he has them. This continuity between the individual and the race applies to mental as well as physical traits, as every student of heredity knows. Further, the individual is physically and mentally dependent on society from day to day. We are not Robinson Crusoes; we eat food prepared for us, we wear clothes manufactured for us, we inhabit houses built for us, and we use transport provided for us by other people; and to adapt ourselves to a Crusoe existence would be to all of us an unpleasant and to many of us a fatal operation. The same applies to our mental life. In order to think at all we depend on language which we did not invent, but learnt from others. Our notions of right and wrong, truth and falsehood, beauty and ugliness are not innate, but derived from the society to which we belong, however much we may criticize and correct them in the course of our lifetime. All but an infinitesimal fragment of our knowledge of the physical world and of the past and present of human society is drawn from lessons and lectures, books and newspapers, talks and discussions embodying other people's experience, not our own. This social heritage—to sum it all up in a phrase—has made us what we are. The isolated individual is a figment of metaphysicians.

In a vague way man has always felt this. We do not start with the isolated individual and arrive at the notion of society by multiplication. Society in some form or other—the horde, clan, tribe, family, city, or what not—is there first. Accordingly, man has always been interested in the past of his race, even when he knew little or nothing about it. The oldest literary form is the epic or saga. In this man tries to fill up the blanks in his knowledge of the past by spinning yarns about real or imaginary ancestors. Every society has its ancestors, its mighty men of old, its heroes who, though they are dead, live on in their descendants. This biological continuity with the past is a commonplace to us, but is enormously important in primitive societies where dead ancestors are revered as the authors of fertility and plenty. Even though in the age before written records men know nothing whatever of their ancestors, yet by reciting wonder-stories about them to the assembled tribe they do them honour, enlist their aid, show from what a superior stock they themselves are sprung, and nerve themselves to new achievements. This seems to be the origin of the saga. Before there was history, there had to be myth. Myths may incorporate real events. We know, for example, that there really was a Troy and a Jericho, and that both were destroyed by enemies. But the genius of the myth-maker is not fettered by real events. Their reality is, as it were, accidental.

Then comes the age of written records, and the saga assumes literary form. As yet it occurs to no one to doubt that these wonder-stories are in fact true. At that stage the distinction between a well-told tale and a true tale has not yet been drawn. The saga-maker is—one can see—gifted above other men and, if gifted enough to tell the story, is gifted enough to know the truth of it. Some such rough-and-ready reasoning doubtless underlies the ancient idea that the minstrel or poet is divinely inspired—possessed by something greater than himself, a God or a Muse who will not let him lie.

The turning-point came when men of the trading cities of ancient Greece began to travel and to compare the myths of their own nation with those of others. The manifest inconsistencies between myth and myth awoke the spirit of criticism first in regard to theology, and a little later in regard to human history. The inauguration of critical science in the sixth century B.C. by Thales and Anaximander was followed by the

inauguration of critical history in the fifth century by Hecatæus, Herodotus, and Thucydides.

Of Hecatæus we know but little. Herodotus is the first
extant author who now and then instead of naïvely continuing the story professes uncertainty or even incredulity.
"Whether this account be true or whether the matter
happened otherwise, I shall not discuss further." "I think
that they say true." "I cannot say with any certainty." "I
am of a different opinion." "I think that Homer or one of
the earlier poets invented this." "My informant did not
seem to me to be in earnest when he said it." [1] Herodotus,
in short, tries, though with imperfect success, to be critical.

Thucydides makes a big stride forward. He knows what
scientific history should be, shows signs of recognizing its
materialist basis, and treats popular legends with scant ceremony. He even apologizes for following the usual practice
of ancient historians in composing speeches of which he had
no written record. He is the first Rationalist historian; and
his work is what he meant it to be—" an everlasting possession,
not the prize essay of a day." [2]

In Thucydides the historical science of antiquity reaches its
high-water mark. He had no successor worthy of him, with
the single exception of Polybius. The later Greek and Latin
historians are either pedestrian chroniclers, talented special
pleaders, or muck-raking scandal-mongers. Tacitus, the greatest of them all, professes to write " without bitterness or
partiality," but has in fact too much of both.

After that the twilight of the decline and fall descends on
the scene. With the coming of Christianity the Old and
New Testaments and the lives of the saints supply the place of
saga rather than of sober history. The chroniclers of the
Dark and Middle Ages often begin their work from the
creation of the world, invariably punctuate it with miracles,
and never rise to the level of Herodotus, let alone Thucydides.
The throne of historical science is vacant until the Renaissance
and Reformation.

Thenceforward the need of the Reformers to discredit the
Catholic Church, and the need of the Catholics to discredit the

---

[1] Herodotus, i, 5, 51, 57, 75; ii, 23, 28, etc.   [2] Thucydides, i, 22.

Reformers, together result in the revival of the critical spirit. The first-fruits of that revival are the demolition of the more obviously fraudulent claims of the medieval Papacy and the more obviously puerile lives of the saints, and the sorting out of genuine sources for the history of the past—a process which culminates in the eighteenth century in the great work of Gibbon. Since Gibbon's day the labours of archæologists, anthropologists, and innumerable documentary experts have accumulated such a wealth of material that it is now difficult for a student of history to see the wood for the trees. History has become less and less the affair of the gentleman of leisure, and more and more that of the endowed specialist rummaging among the archives of a chosen period and hoping, at best, to render its obscurity a little less obscure to the elect few who share his interests.

> That low man seeks a little thing to do,
>   Sees it and does it:
> This high man, with a great thing to pursue,
>   Dies ere he knows it.
> That low man goes on adding one to one,
>   His hundred's soon hit:
> This high man, aiming at a million,
>   Misses an unit.[1]

The trouble is that, while the " high men "—in other words, the historical specialists—pursue their great aim of knowledge for its own sake, we " low men "—in other words, the general public—get no benefit from it. The " little things" we do are for the most part concerned more with livelihood than with culture.. We are lucky indeed if they leave us with leisure, inclination, and energy to knock up a modest score in the field of general knowledge. Most of us grow to manhood misfed with the myths of yesterday, and never unlearn them. Even if we cease to believe them, the mischief is done; for the result is a widespread ignorance of history, and indeed indifference to it, at a time when its educative influence is supremely needed.

For modern man cannot do without literary links with his past. The function which the saga fulfilled for our barbaric

[1] Robert Browning, *A Grammarian's Funeral.*

ancestors, and the Old and New Testaments for those of more recent date, needs fulfilling in a fashion worthy of a scientific civilization. We, too, need our saga. The materials exist in abundance. The natural sciences, and the human sciences of anthropology and archæology, have provided a wealth of data on the origin and pre-history of man. More is known of ancient civilizations than has ever been known before; and that knowledge is still growing. Today we may examine the maladies of the ancient world and the causes of its decline and fall not with the detached complacency of a Gibbon, but as men conscious of our own social maladies and of the need of a prophylactic to avert a deeper decline and perhaps a final fall. For the diagnosis of those maladies and the discovery of their remedy we can draw on the detailed and documented history of our own civilization, much as a doctor utilizes the case-history of a patient. Last, but not least, the study of history will help us to a sense of proportion and of the insignificance of much to which pulpit, platform, Press, and radio conspire to attach exaggerated importance. It is not too much to say that a knowledge of history makes the difference between a man and a Babbitt. It is the greater pity that the history in which most of us have been educated should be a tissue of triviality, false emphasis, suppression of fact, suggestion of falsehood, and downright myth calculated to deter us, once we have done with examiners and their vagaries, from ever touching the subject again.

CHAPTER II

UNIVERSAL HISTORY

IT is usual to divide history into ancient, medieval, and modern periods. This is a convenient and, as we shall see, inevitable classification, but it has its disadvantages. It helps to generate that optical illusion which regards the ancients and the men of the Middle Ages as different varieties of men from ourselves and almost as different species, rather than as members of the same species, *Homo sapiens*, conditioned by a different social, economic, political, and cultural heritage. Man did not become a different creature when the Roman Empire declined and fell, or when Columbus discovered America. The changes which then took place were changes in man's way of life, not in man as a biological specimen. Moreover, they affected only Europe and so much of the rest of the world as interacted with Europe. The vast populations of India and China were not affected at all by the fate of Rome, and only in the course of centuries by the European expansion which began with Columbus.

To correct the illusion due to this tripartite division and the even more pernicious illusion created by the "nationalist blinkers" in which most history is taught, it is natural that attempts should be made to write a universal history. The most attractive and, on the whole, successful of such attempts is that of H. G. Wells in *The Outline of History*. Wells will have no half-measures: he begins his story with the origin of the earth and of life, devotes several chapters to biological evolution, brings man on the scene in his second book, reaches civilization in his third, and conducts us by way of Asia, Egypt, Greece, and Rome to the rise of Christianity, which comes half-way through the work; then by way of Islam, the Dark and Middle Ages, the Renaissance and Reformation, and modern power-politics to the First World War, leaving mankind at the end of the eighth book faced with the alternatives of world-union or catastrophe. It is nothing less than the saga of civilization which Wells undertakes to write; and he does it on an imposing scale and with marvellous readability.

It is easy to point to the pitfalls which beset any such undertaking. The anthropological, archæological, and documentary data necessary to write a universal history are more than one man can master in a lifetime, even with the expert advice which Wells called to his aid. There will inevitably be errors. Professional historians, jealous of the invasion of their province by a layman, were quick to pin-point those of Wells.

There is also the old trouble of the forest and the trees. When a man sets out to write a universal history, he probably already has a compelling vision (*kataleptiké phantasia*, as the old Stoics put it—an impression made by the thing itself) of history as a whole—say, Wells' vision of "life struggling towards consciousness, gathering power, accumulating will,"[1] until it accumulates the will to end confusion and war before *they* end *it*; or the more concrete Marxist conception which replaces "life" by man in society, "consciousness" by the mastery of nature, "power" by productive forces, and "will" by the class struggle. In so far as any such vision is based on scientific induction, it will be a key likely to fit many locks. The danger is that the historian may use his master-key as a substitute for the careful investigation of facts, and so fail to see the trees for the forest. Friedrich Engels had to warn his friends against using the materialist conception of history as " an excuse for *not* studying history."[2] Or the historian may fail to see the forest for the trees: he may get so immersed in detail that he omits to trace cause and effect, the general tendency in particular events, or the analogy between one historic process and another, so that the work becomes a mere chronicle, shapeless and uninstructive.

Nevertheless the enterprise is worth while. We should be poorer without such a work as Wells' *Outline*. On the whole

[1] Wells, *The Outline of History*, fifth revision, p. 5.
[2] Engels to Schmidt, August 5, 1890.

he avoids both the pitfalls of the universal historian. Some
of the hypotheses used in his prehistory are shaky: e.g. the
statement that " space is, for the most part, emptiness " is not
up-to-date. But he is generally accurate and always vivid—
at his best when he tells the tale of the Greeks and Persians,
Alexander, Mohammed, the medieval Papacy, the English,
American, and French Revolutions, Napoleon, and the development of modern science. And yet, while making the
past live, he never for a moment loses sight of his unifying
conception—man, the risen animal, evolving civilization by
accident in certain exceptionally fertile regions a few thousand
years ago; man paying in loss of freedom and equality for the
better technique taught him by his medicine-men and priests,
and becoming the serf or slave of the god, or the priest-king
who represented the god, or the lord to whom the priest-king
delegated his privileges; here and there man goaded by misery
and insecurity into some sort of protest and evolving a new
sort of God, a righteous God, to fight the discredited gods of
the priests; here and there man trading, travelling, inquiring,
and beginning to know his world and himself; and the " three
ideas of science, of a universal righteousness, and of a human
commonweal, spreading out from the minds of the rare and
exceptional persons and peoples in which they first originated,
into the general consciousness of the race, and giving first a
new colour, then a new spirit, and then a new direction to
human affairs." [1] Wells' emphasis on " rare and exceptional
persons " has too much in common with Carlyle's " great
man " theory to be wholly satisfactory. Even the rarest and
most exceptional minds must find people prepared to listen
to them if the seed is not to fall on stony ground. But Wells'
picture is nevertheless useful and educative.

The most important function of a universal history is to
give us a sense of historical proportion. The national histories which we learn at school take us back at most two
thousand years, of which the first thousand are a skimpy
prelude to the second, and the main interest is concentrated
in the last three or four hundred. Ancient history, if we
begin with Egypt and Babylonia, extends our knowledge of

[1] Wells, *The Outline of History*, fifth revision, p. 373.

the past a few thousand years farther. Compared with our school histories, those ancient civilizations seem antediluvian. But from universal history and its indispensable handmaids, anthropology and archæology, we learn that the antiquity of man is far greater than those few thousand years. The earliest sub-men are estimated to have stemmed off from the common anthropoid stock at least a million years ago. If we pass over early tool-users like Piltdown and Neanderthal man as no direct ancestors of ours, and confine our attention to *Homo sapiens*, we know from the evidence of fossils that our species has a history in Europe alone of thirty or forty thousand years, and therefore presumably a much longer history elsewhere before Europe emerged from the Ice Age and became climatically fit for habitation. Such an antiquity dwarfs that of the oldest civilizations much more than the antiquity of those civilizations dwarfs that of the English nation.

If the ages since the earliest sub-men began to chip flints into primitive tools may be likened to the lifetime of an individual, we may say that recorded history began about a year ago, that Greece and Rome rose and fell within the last six months, that America was discovered a month ago, that the industrial revolution began within the last twelve days, and that the problems of world war and world peace have forced themselves on our attention only since yesterday or the day before! It is important that we should keep some time-scale such as this at the back of our minds and that we should be able to refer to it when contemporary events get too depressing. Let us bear in mind that during far the greater part of our existence on the earth we were primitive food-gatherers or hunters using no tools or weapons other than the chipped flints or bones which we now see in archæological museums, and completely at the mercy of natural forces which we did not understand. Let us bear in mind that civilization with its arts and crafts and written records is something new on our planet, and that we have had, and still have, continually to adjust our traditional institutions and ideas to the changing environment which we ourselves have created. Then we shall be less surprised and disheartened at the difficulties of that adjustment, and at the same time we shall be assisted in making it.

It is not a question of science having outrun moral development. That is a defeatist cry raised by reactionaries with a vested interest in despair. It is a question of man's power over nature rendering antiquated his social, political, and religious institutions and ideas. It is not that we are bad at heart: it is that we are uneducated and woolly in the head. The forces which mould opinion—the pulpit, the political platform, the Press, the radio—devote a prodigious amount of time and energy to what can only be called the miseducation of the public by erecting into absolute values concepts like " Christian civilization," " king and country," " democracy," and so forth, which are not absolute at all, which are demonstrably the product of history, and which are to be assessed by their utility to the being who preceded and created them all— man, as old Protagoras said, " the measure of all things." Universal history at least provides an antidote to religious bigotry, national chauvinism, and journalistic claptrap.

To be sure, it can be put to another use. History, declared Gibbon, " is little more than the register of the crimes, follies, and misfortunes of mankind." Or, as Tennyson expressed it :

Raving politics, never at rest—as this poor earth's pale history runs,—
What is it all but a trouble of ants in the gleam of a million million of suns? . . .
Spring and Summer and Autumn and Winter, and all these old revolutions of earth;
All new-old revolutions of Empire—change of the tide—what is all of it worth? . . .
What is it all, if we all of us end but in being our own corpse-coffins at last,
Swallow'd in Vastness, lost in Silence, drown'd in the deeps of a meaningless Past?[1]

There is a certain arrogance in such judgments. The man who indicts mankind in the mass for their " crimes and follies " by implication sets himself on a pedestal as an exception to the rule. The criminal and foolish race at least had the grace to produce *him* to judge it. Either, then, he is a superman (a claim which nobody makes without qualifying for a mental

[1] Tennyson, *Vastness*.

institution) or the fact of common humanity should temper his judgment. The man who sees his fellow-men as "ants" by implication assumes that *he*, in contrast to them, is something more than an ant. Not only is this attitude arrogant, but it is fallacious. The needed correction was supplied by W. K. Clifford when he said: " I regard my fellow-men as animals in a menagerie, but I always remember that I am not their keeper, but one of them!"[1]

When we pronounce human history to be worthless and meaningless, we invite the question: " Worthless and meaningless to *whom*?" Worth and meaning are relative terms. They always imply a spectator or auditor. Traditional religion, by assuming a God as at once author, spectator, and critic of the cosmic drama, claims to invest life with absolute worth and meaning—whatever that may be—and then dogmatically denies that there can be any worth or meaning short of this. "Take away God," runs the argument, " and life is worthless and meaningless; and then where are you?" The answer is: just where we were before. Worth and meaning are human creations. Life has no *absolute* worth or *absolute* meaning, but it has a *relative* worth and a *relative* meaning to those who live it, and the more in proportion as they learn how to live. Its worth is the value *we* set on it; its meaning is what it means to *us*.

History, in telling the story of man, relates among other things the values and meanings evolved in human society. We learn from it what life meant and was worth to the Greek and Roman citizen, to the Epicurean and Stoic philosopher, to the Jewish, Christian, and Moslem visionary, to the medieval monk or burgher, to the merchant adventurer and empire-builder, to the Puritan and Jacobin revolutionary. We are the heirs of all the ages. We stand on the shoulders of all these people. It is because so many of us have been told nothing about it and do not know it that our purposes are petty and our meanings muddled. To correct this is the greatest function of universal history.

[1] This remark of Clifford was repeated to me by the late William Boulting, who knew him. It does not occur, so far as I know, in any published work.

But few have the time to study history as a whole, and fewer still the time to write it. Division into periods is inevitable for both historian and public. As I shall proceed to show, the time-honoured division into ancient, medieval, and modern history is not so artificial or so false to fact as it may seem on first inspection.

CHAPTER III

ANCIENT HISTORY TO HERODOTUS

THE conventional definition of ancient history applies that term to all that happened from the rise of the oldest civilizations to the fall of the Roman Empire. But, as we saw, the fall of the Roman Empire marks no break except in Europe and the Mediterranean lands. We need a re-definition of the term which will give it a world-wide application. We can obtain this if we define ancient history as that stage of social evolution, in any part of the world, during which society consists either of primitive groups based on common descent, such as the clan and tribe, or of simple aggregations of such groups, such as the tribal confederacy, the city-state, or the union of city-states in an empire of the ancient type. During this stage the tribal or civic basis of morality and religion, though it may wear very thin, never entirely disappears. The whole duty of man is duty to a social group; even the gods, as Jane Harrison shows, are projections of the social group and its needs. In the later stages of ancient history this basis gradually breaks down. Too many clans, tribes, cities, and confederacies have gone under in the struggle for existence, too many people have been carried into captivity and reduced to slavery or serfdom, too many gods have turned out to be no gods, or even to be devils, for the world any longer to seem good to more than a very few. A widespread conviction arises that the world is very evil. With that conviction comes a search for a new social basis, a new morality, and a new religion to replace the old tribal and civic foundations which have been cast down, and history passes into a phase which we may call medieval.

This breakdown of ancient social organizations is seen in its most acute form in the Roman Empire. Nowhere else is there such a complete removal of old landmarks; nowhere else is so large a proportion of the population enslaved. Elsewhere the breakdown occurs, and is accompanied by parallel symptoms of widespread pessimism and religious innovation, but the breach with the old is far less violent and complete. Buddhism never overthrew the older religions of Asia as Christianity did those of Europe. In India it modified them; in China it compromised with them. Hence those countries had, strictly speaking, no Middle Ages; their "ancient" history took on some "medieval" features and continued with no abrupt break to our own day.

The thing to remember about ancient history, and indeed about all past history, is that it relates to men and women of the same species as ourselves. The majority were occupied, as we are, in getting a livelihood in the day-to-day battle with nature, in courtship, marriage, and the rearing of children, and, when necessary, in defending themselves against enemies. They knew less than we about the world in which they lived, had less command over nature, and were less critical than we of tales of the marvellous; but their basic needs were the same as ours. In this way men had already lived through thousands of generations of prehistory, when a few thousand years ago in a few great, fertile river-valleys (the Nile, the Euphrates, the Tigris, the Indus) they unwittingly took a series of steps which launched them on the adventure of civilization. They invented pottery; domesticated animals; began to till the soil and clear the forests; produced a surplus of food above that necessary to maintain and propagate their kind; found that it paid better to enslave their conquered enemies than to kill and eat them; accumulated property in herds and slaves; and evolved a complex social organization, the city-state, ruled by priests or glorified tribal magicians, who were also the first kings.

Then began the long see-saw of empire-building and empire-breaking which priest-kings, after they had invented writing, recorded in detail on their monuments and which so dominates the written history of the ancient world that we are apt to regard those Pharaohs with sphinx-like features, those bearded Assyrian monarchs, and those plumed Greek warriors as typical men of their times. We depend for our knowledge of ancient history primarily on inscriptions and books written by the slave-owning minority. That helps to make ancient civilization seem more remote from us than it really is. Those empires, we feel, are as dead as the men who built them: what possible concern can they be of ours? Yet they were built and broken at the expense, and by the blood and sweat, of men of the same stuff as ourselves, who had to live and labour and keep the world going while carrying that imposing superstructure on their backs. This common material basis of life links the ancients to us no less effectively than the mathematics and astronomy of which Egyptian and Babylonian priests laid the foundations.

One of the turning-points in world history was reached in the seventh century B.C., when the Egyptians, in return for aid by Greek mercenaries in freeing Egypt from the Assyrians, opened their markets to Greek traders. From that time on Greek travellers like Thales of Miletus in the sixth century were at liberty to compare Egyptian institutions and ideas with their own, to learn what the Egyptians could teach of mathematics and astronomy, and to compare and criticize the theologies of Egypt, Greece, and other countries. That was the beginning of the Greek achievement in science and philosophy. It was a matter of time only before criticism was extended to the story of the human past. The critical spirit is already active, though in a fumbling and erratic way, in the first extant historian whose name we know, Herodotus of Halicarnassus.

Halicarnassus was a Greek colony on the south-west coast of Asia Minor, and in the youth of Herodotus was a dependency of the Persian Empire and governed by a " tyrant " in the Persian interest. Salamis was fought when Herodotus was four years old, but it did not liberate Halicarnassus. He was thus debarred from the political career normally open to a freeborn Greek. He spent his early manhood in travel, visiting different Greek cities, taking the Persian post-road from Sardis up to Susa, finishing his *Wanderjahre* with a long stay in Egypt, and everywhere collecting materials for his great work on the Persian invasion of Greece. In middle life he migrated to Athens, then at the height of her power and prestige under Pericles, and thence as a colonist to Thurii in southern Italy, where at last he found an abiding city to call his own. He lived to see the beginning of the death-struggle between Athens and her rivals in the Peloponnesian War, and died about the age of sixty with the issue still undecided.

In reading Herodotus, therefore, we look at the world through the eyes of a well-educated and well-travelled Greek in the most brilliant age of Greek history. His bias is such as we might expect. He has seen two civilizations at close quarters—on the one hand the far-flung Persian empire, heir of Babylonia and Assyria with their immemorial traditions of godship and kingship; and on the other hand the little Greek trading cities, upstarts in comparison, which, under the leadership of Athens, inspired by a new idea of equal citizenship and free criticism, scored in his own lifetime a wholly unexpected triumph over the Persian invader. Herodotus frankly prefers freedom, despises those Asiatic Greeks who tamely accept Persian rule (the Ionians are a continual butt), and honours Athens as a liberator even though " most men," he knows, " will mislike the opinion." [1]

He has been charged with credulity; and certainly his work does not satisfy our notion of a critical history. But it is an essay in that direction. History had but lately emancipated itself from epic; and we should wonder less at Herodotus' frequent adherence to epic convention than at his frequent breaks with it. I have already given some examples of his scepticism. While believing in the gods, he does not hesitate to reject what he considers " silly fables " about them. True, after a piece of criticism he pulls himself up with the words: " In saying this much, may I incur no displeasure either of god or hero! " [2] He tells us, on the authority of the priestesses of Dodona, that the early inhabitants of Greece had no distinct names for the gods; and he adds, as his own opinion, that " Homer and Hesiod were the first to compose pedigrees of the gods, and give the gods their epithets, to allot them their several offices and occupations, and describe their forms." [3] In this he is not so far from the truth; for a god is originally the projection of the need of a human group for

[1] Herodotus, vii, 139.   [2] Ibid., ii, 45.   [3] Ibid., ii, 52–53.

food and drink and fertility, and of the rites by which it tries
to win them: the individualized gods of saga are a later development, arising when man no longer whole-heartedly
believes in primitive magic and has to rationalize it how he can.

The quaint medley of history, legend, and travellers' tales
(often qualified with a wary caveat) which fills the first six
books of Herodotus leads up to a climax in the deathless
narrative of the remaining three. Here he is relating events
within his own lifetime—events of which he may have heard
from eye-witnesses; and even those who impugn his earlier
books accept the authority of the later.

Now and then something in the story makes us want to
know more. Why, for example, was the oracle of Delphi
on the eve of the Persian invasion so flagrantly defeatist?
Plainly because the priests *were* defeatist: they took the
common-sense view that Persia was irresistible. But in that
case did they really, as Herodotus says, counsel the Athenians
to trust in their "wooden walls," and hint at the victory of
Salamis before it occurred? The advice to embark is, no
doubt, genuine. In the desperate case in which Athens stood
after her unpardonable affronts to Persia, the best advice the
oracle could give was to abandon the city and flee. But the
"prediction" about Salamis looks as if it had been added
after the event—perhaps forged by the party of Themistocles
to glorify his statesmanship.

Again, why did Sparta send so small a force to Thermopylæ? The heroic end of Leonidas and his three hundred has
become such a legend as to blind nearly everyone to the fact
that they were to all intents and purposes murdered in cold
blood by their own Government. In military matters the
Spartans were no fools. True, Thermopylæ was a good spot
to make a stand; the passage between the mountains and the
sea was then only a cart-track wide, not, as now, about a mile
and a half; and the total Greek force numbered four thousand.
But Xerxes had, on the lowest estimate, some hundreds of
thousands of men to force it. The limitation of the Spartan
contingent to three hundred does not suggest that Sparta took
the operation very seriously.

Herodotus gives several explanations. The defending army

was, he says, a token force sent to induce the northern Greeks to fight till relief came; Sparta was busy celebrating her harvest festival (the Carnea) and could not move till it was over; also the oracle of Delphi had decreed that either Sparta or a Spartan king must perish. This " prophecy " was probably made up after the event. The festival might have served as a pretext for not defending Thermopylæ at all, but hardly for throwing men away. No doubt the first explanation is the true one. Thermopylæ was a delaying action. Sparta had to send *some* men to impress the other Greeks, but believed the position indefensible and took care to waste as few troops as possible. As for Leonidas, he may have had enemies. The two royal lines were often at odds. If we knew more of Spartan internal politics at that time, we might understand why he was sacrificed.

There are unforgettable touches in these last books of Herodotus. There is the warning said to have been given to Xerxes by the Spartan exile, Demaratus, as to the manner of men he is about to fight. " Though they be freemen, they are not in all respects free; law is the master whom they own; and this master they fear more than thy subjects fear thee." [1] There is the embassy of the Greeks to Gelon, the " tyrant " of Syracuse (who had made himself master there by putting down a slave revolt), to enlist that ancient *duce* as an ally against Persia; and his refusal to join unless they give him the supreme command; and the Athenian envoy's retort: " Greece sent us here to ask for an army, not for a general "; and Gelon's rejoinder: " Ye have, it seems, no lack of commanders, but ye are like to lack men to take their orders." [2] There is Xerxes' crucifixion of the body of Leonidas after Thermopylæ; and the chivalrous refusal of the Spartan Pausanias to retaliate in kind on the dead Persian commander, Mardonius, after Platæa. " Such doings befit barbarians rather than Greeks; and even in barbarians we detest them." [3] Other Greeks were not so particular, as we may gather from the grim story which ends the history. When Xanthippus the Athenian took Sestos, the last Persian stronghold in Europe, Artaÿctes, the Persian satrap (" a wicked and cruel man," says Herodotus

[1] Herodotus, vii, 104.   [2] Ibid., vii, 161.   [3] Ibid., ix, 79.

in extenuation), was crucified, and his son stoned to death before his eyes.

Let Herodotus sum up in his own words. " This I know—that if every nation were to bring all its evil deeds to a given place, in order to make an exchange with some other nation, when they had all looked carefully at their neighbours' faults, they would be truly glad to carry their own back again." [1] The conclusion of the whole matter, for him, is that which (after ringing the changes on the same theme in many places) he puts into the mouth of the Persian prince Artabanus, who vainly tries to dissuade Xerxes from the expedition. " Seest thou how God with his lightning smites always the bigger animals, and will not suffer them to wax insolent, while those of a lesser bulk chafe him not? How likewise his bolts fall ever on the highest houses and the tallest trees? So plainly does he love to bring down everything that exalts itself. Thus oft-times a mighty host is discomfited by a few men, when God in his jealousy sends fear or storm from heaven, and they perish in a way unworthy of them. For God allows no one to have high thoughts but himself." [2] A sentiment not, after all, very different from the early Christian : " He hath put down princes from their thrones, and hath exalted them of low degree."

The history of Herodotus is a perpetual inspiration to brave men who have to fight against great odds in a seemingly dark world.

The King with half the East at heel is marched from lands of morning ;
Their fighters drink the rivers up, their shafts benight the air.
And he that stands will die for nought, and home there's no returning.
The Spartans on the sea-wet rock sat down and combed their hair. [3]

---

[1] Herodotus, vii, 152.   [2] Ibid., vii, 10.
[3] A. E. Housman, *Last Poems.*

CHAPTER IV

THUCYDIDES AND HIS TIME

FROM Herodotus to Thucydides is a bare generation. Yet to turn from one to the other is to turn from confidence to disillusion. It is to turn from a historian proud of his civilization, mildly sceptical of its more childish superstitions, but sure of the moral government of the world and hopeful of the future, to a historian more deeply sceptical, sure of nothing but the operation of natural causes, and without faith or hope in a civilization which seems to be tearing itself to pieces before his eyes. Allowing for obvious differences, it is like turning from the nineteenth century to the twentieth—from Macaulay or Kingsley to Spengler or Toynbee.

After the defeat of Persia events moved quickly in Greece. Greek fleets under Athenian admirals swept the eastern Mediterranean, carrying the war into Persian waters and enriching Athens and other cities with Persian spoils and barbarian slaves. This age of achievement left its enduring message to posterity in the tragedies of Æschylus and the glories of the Parthenon. But the accompanying economic changes led to intensified class struggle and political faction. The saying of Abraham Lincoln that a democratic government " cannot endure permanently half slave and half free " was as true in ancient as in modern times. The peasants and artisans displaced from farms and workshops by slave labour had to be fed. At Athens this meant the corruption of democracy by doles at home and imperialism abroad, and everywhere a sceptical questioning of the traditional assumptions of civic solidarity on which the conduct of Greek affairs had hitherto been based. Professional lecturers or " sophists " went from city to city teaching such startling and subversive doctrines as that there are two sides to every question, that truth is relative, that the gods are unknowable, and that right and wrong are conventions laid down by groups strong enough to enforce them. Much of the teaching of the "sophists" sounds remarkably modern, and in a world cemented by real community of interest would make a good starting-point for social science. But in a world based on slavery and torn by class conflicts the conclusion suggested was that society would not bear thinking about and that too much thinking made bad citizens.

In 431 B.C. Corinth, the chief commercial rival of Athens, induced the somewhat reluctant Spartans and their Peloponnesian allies to declare war on Athens, so precipitating Greece into twenty-seven years of convulsion. Thucydides, the contemporary historian of the Peloponnesian War, was a wealthy Athenian connected with the noble Philaïd family, to which Miltiades and Cimon had belonged. He also owned gold-mines in Thrace. Interest, therefore, inclined him to conservative views. He was, however, steeped in the sceptical philosophy of his time. He is the first Rationalist historian—the first who systematically looks for natural causes in human affairs. In the opening chapters of his work he expounds something very like a materialist conception of history. He draws a distinction between primitive society, in which men scratch the ground for a bare living and have no surplus with which to trade, and civilized societies, which arise in fertile countries, and therefore occasion both internal strife and foreign invasion. But Thucydides is no mere theorist. "Men," he observes, "accept one another's reports of past events, even in their own country, without examination. . . . So impatient of labour are most men in the search for truth, and so prone to jump to ready-made conclusions." [1] He for his part has tried to verify his facts, though that is often difficult: even eye-witnesses differ owing to partisanship or bad memory.

He sees the Peloponnesian War as a clash not merely between rival city-states, but between two types of society— Sparta resting on landownership and appealing to the interest of landowners everywhere in securing their own dominance; Athens resting on money-power which can hire men to build

[1] Thucydides, i, 20.

ships, train and pay crews to man them, and appeal to the disaffection of the landless majority everywhere. In the speech put into the mouth of a Corinthian envoy urging Sparta to declare war, Thucydides effectively contrasts the two sides—Sparta conservative, slow in the uptake, too often a broken reed to her allies; Athens enterprising, restless, always ready to scrap old customs for new expedients.

The Athenian view of the matter is given in the famous speech of Pericles (which Thucydides may himself have heard and of which he probably preserves the substance) at the funeral of the Athenian dead in the first year of the war. Athens (says Pericles in words whose lofty idealism still has power to move us) stands for something new in the world. " We have a form of government which does not ape the institutions of our neighbours : we set an example to others; we do not follow theirs. The name of this government is democracy—so called because it looks to the interest not of the few, but of the many. All men are equal before the law where private interests conflict; but in public affairs advancement depends not on class, but on worth and on a man's reputation in his walk of life." [1] Thereby Athens has become the greatest city in Greece. " Everything from every part of the earth is imported into our city : the commodities of other nations are in as common use as our own." [2] Unlike Sparta, Athens does not suffer from spy-mania. Anyone may come and go as he likes. Yet she holds her own against all comers.

"We are artistic, yet economical; studious, yet not softened by study. Wealth to us is an opportunity of action rather than a matter of bragging. We hold it no shame to confess poverty, but a deep shame not to work to avoid it. Our citizens mind both their own business and the city's : even our artisans have a sufficient knowledge of public affairs. . . . In short, our city, take it all in all, is the school of Greece, and our private citizens, in my opinion, embody in their own persons versatility, grace, and refinement. . . . We have proved our power

[1] Thucydides, ii, 37.　　　　[2] Ibid., ii, 38.

by such evidence as shall make us the wonder of present and future ages. We need no Homer to praise us, nor any poet whose songs are sweet for a season, but whose report will not bear the light of truth. We have opened up every sea and land by our valour, and built everywhere everlasting monuments of our power to help or harm. Such is the city for whose preservation these men nobly fought and fell, and for which every one of us survivors should resolve to live and labour." [1]

Such was the picture of Athens in which patriotic Athenians liked to believe. We are irresistibly reminded of the encomia of modern British and American public men on the " western way of life." Thucydides puts it forward as the view of Pericles, not as his own. He seems to introduce this idealization of Athenian democracy early in his history, in deliberate and ironical contrast to the reality which emerges as he proceeds.

We for our part know that Athens was not the home of freedom and equality hymned by Pericles. One third of her population were slaves and formed no part of the citizen body. True, the life of an Athenian domestic slave was better than that of a Spartan helot. Plato, a generation after Thucydides, says satirically that in democracies slaves are as free as their owners; but as he goes on to complain of the freedom of domestic animals in a democracy, it is difficult to take him quite seriously. [2] Demosthenes, a generation later still, congratulates the Athenians on their mild treatment of slaves. The fact remains that slaves were liable to be bought and sold, to be flogged at the will of their owners, to toil under hard conditions on the land or in mines or workshops, and to give evidence under torture if a litigant required it and their owner agreed. No less excluded from citizenship were the many aliens who settled at Athens to trade, and who were debarred from naturalization by a law of Pericles restricting the franchise to men of Athenian descent on both sides. Such were the realities behind the eloquent claims of his funeral oration.

[1] Thucydides, ii, 40–41.   [2] Plato, *Republic*, 563 B.

It is naturally not on such grounds that Thucydides, himself an exploiter of slave labour in his Thracian mines, condemns Athenian democracy. It is rather that he has an intellectual contempt for shams—a contempt which in some ways anticipates Machiavelli. Thucydides genuinely admires Themistocles and Pericles, the architects of Athenian greatness, not because they were democrats, but because they had the ability (what Machiavelli would have called the *virtù*) to handle democracy as their instrument. Thucydides uses them as foils to set off the knavish incompetence of later demagogues.

These latter—Cleon and his kind—were not, as is often wrongly supposed, men of "advanced ideas" championing the poor against the rich. They were wealthy manufacturers, employers of slave labour in tanning and similar enterprises, and advocates of a narrow and ruthless imperialism. Old Athenian families hated them for their bad manners and their ruinous war policy. Thucydides voices this hatred in his history, Aristophanes in his comedies. Because of this, and because Thucydides and Aristophanes each had a personal grudge against Cleon, modern Radical historians such as George Grote have undertaken his rehabilitation. But the thing cannot be done. The facts speak too loud. One flagrant instance is enough. In 428, after Pericles had died of the plague, the important mercantile city of Mitylene revolted against Athens and put her to the trouble of a siege. After a year the common people of Mitylene, armed for war by their rulers, turned on them and forced them to surrender. Thereupon the rabid Cleon carried a decree that all adult citizens of Mitylene should be put to death and the women and children sold as slaves. This, as his opponents pointed out, meant massacring the friends of Athens as well as her enemies. Next day saner counsels prevailed, a ship was sent post-haste to stop the execution, and only the guilty were put to death. Grote naturally does not defend Cleon's savagery, but he tries to extenuate it as "nothing more than a very rigorous application of the received laws of war." [1] A politician who could not see an occasion when, if ever, "received laws" were out of place is past rehabilitation.

[1] Grote, *A History of Greece*, ed. Mitchell and Caspari, chap. XX.

Thucydides shows himself a thorough realist in his reflections on the revolutionary struggles incidental to the Peloponnesian War. The immediate occasion of his comment is a revolution in Corcyra (Corfu) beginning with the murder by the local oligarchs of sixty pro-Athenian democrats, and ending with the local democrats, reinforced by slaves and even women, massacring every oligarch on whom they could lay hands. The massacre of Corcyra, says Thucydides, was the first of its kind. But later "all Greece, one may say, was in commotion. Everywhere there were struggles between the democratic leaders, who sought to bring in the Athenians, and the oligarchs, who sought to bring in the Lacedæmonians. In peace-time they would have had no pretext, nor would they have been ready to call them in; but in war subversive elements on each side easily found occasion to bring in allies to put down their enemies and instal them in power. Many and grievous were the things which befell cities in these revolutionary struggles—things which occur now and will always recur while human nature remains the same, albeit with more or less violence and in different forms according to the particular turn of events. For in peace and prosperity both cities and private men are better disposed, since they are not under the constraint of necessity. But war is a violent schoolmaster: it robs men of their day-to-day margin of sufficiency and debases the character of most to the level of circumstances."[1]

This passage and the generalizations which follow on revolutionary violence have been much quoted. "Things which will always recur while human nature remains the same"—here, it seems to some, is this wise old Greek looking forward prophetically from the fifth century B.C. to eighteenth-century France and twentieth-century Russia, and pronouncing sentence in advance on all revolutionaries in all ages! But let us read him carefully. "War is a violent schoolmaster." Thucydides naturally is no Marxist: he does not see the cause of class struggles in the exploitation of man by man. But he does see the causal connection between war and revolutionary terror. He says in effect: "If you have the one, you will have

[1] Thucydides, iii, 82.

the other." There is no natural law obliging men to use violence against foreigners at the bidding of their Government, but debarring them from using violence against their Government at the bidding of economic necessity. There was no such law in fifth-century Greece; there was none in revolutionary France; there is none in twentieth-century Europe or Asia. Those who do not want violent revolutions should not set an example of violence by starting wars.

It is evident that in the Peloponnesian War slavery was the Achilles' heel of both sides. Sparta had ever before her the fear that her helots, normally kept down by terror, would see in her difficulty their opportunity. This fear was particularly acute during the Athenian occupation of Pylos in the Peloponnese (taken by Athens in 425 and not retaken till 409). Hence the Fabian caution which so often exasperated the allies of Sparta. Athens, for her part, having slaves of her own, never took full advantage of this Spartan weakness. It is remarkable that, while Sparta had ready-made " quislings " among the rich in every Greek democracy, no Athenian statesman, however bellicose—not Pericles, not Cleon—ever tried to organize a helot " fifth column." There was always, in fact, a pro-Spartan party at Athens which believed in the collaboration of the two states in defence of traditional institutions. In 461 this party had sent help to Sparta during a helot revolt. Pro-Spartan sympathies were naturally strongest among great slave-owners like Nicias, who hired out a thousand human chattels to work in the silver mines of Laurium, and at one time procured the conclusion of a treaty with Sparta providing *inter alia* that " if the slaves rebel, the Athenians shall assist the Lacedæmonians with all their resources." [1] Athenian statesmen were in a dilemma: to feed their people they had to hold their empire, to hold their empire they had to fight Sparta, and they could not fight Sparta decisively without endangering the economic basis of both states. This dilemma was their doom. Incapable of a revolutionary strategy, they fell back on a sterile imperialism which made enemies everywhere and friends worth winning nowhere.

[1] Thucydides, v, 23.

Thucydides was no mere spectator of the war. In 424 the Athenians sent him to Thrace to oppose Brasidas (one of the very few men of genius whom Sparta ever produced), whose diplomacy and generalship were winning city after city to the Spartan side. Apparently Athens hoped that the local influence of Thucydides would steady the situation in Thrace. It was an unequal contest; and the ill-success of Thucydides led to his impeachment by Cleon and banishment from Athens. He spent the next twenty years in exile, travelling and collecting materials for his history.

Meanwhile Nemesis overtook his enemies. Cleon crowned a bully's life by a coward's death on the field of Amphipolis. Athens made a temporary peace with Sparta, but could not refrain from adventure. She accepted the leadership of the super-demagogue Alcibiades, an unprincipled aristocrat who out-Cleoned Cleon, and after an unprovoked aggression and a horrible massacre on the island of Melos, staked her all on the attempt to conquer Sicily.

The two books devoted by Thucydides to this enterprise, in which Athenian imperialism over-reached itself, are of less philosophic interest than the earlier books, but are the most dramatic part of his work. We are shown the frenzied enthusiasm for the expedition, which was to make the fortune of every Athenian—the populace and the soldiery expecting a "perpetual income" from the conquest. Next, the embarkation—all Athens flocking to Piræus to see the start and joining in the public prayers for victory, and the high-spirited ships' companies "racing one another as far as Ægina." Then the pitiful panic in Athens over the nocturnal mutilation of the "herms" or phallic stone figures which served as boundary-marks or signposts. The mischief was probably done by "fifth columnists" who used the superstitions of the Athenians to create alarm and despondency. They succeeded only too well. A reign of terror began against those suspected of the sacrilege or of other impiety; and Alcibiades was recalled from Sicily to stand his trial on a charge of profaning the Eleusinian mysteries. What a comment on the funeral speech of Pericles with its boast of philosophic enlightenment and freedom from spy-mania!

Thucydides shows us Alcibiades giving the Athenians the slip and escaping to the Peloponnese, where he cynically gives away his country's war-plans and spurs the slothful Spartans to renew their struggle with Athens. Prompted by him, Sparta sends Gylippus to relieve Syracuse, invades Attica, and fortifies Decelea, a few miles from Athens and within sight of her walls. This is a deadly blow. "Not only were the Athenians deprived of the use of their land, but more than twenty thousand slaves deserted to the enemy, of whom the greater part were artisans. Moreover, they lost all their sheep and oxen." [1]

Meanwhile the wretched, dilatory Nicias leads the Sicilian expedition from disaster to disaster. The catastrophe is painted in masterly colours: the sea and land reverses before Syracuse; the inevitable retreat put off by the superstitious Nicias on account of an eclipse of the moon; the destruction of the Athenian fleet; the forlorn attempt to escape by land; and the last, horrible scene at the river Asinarus, when "the Syracusans (for the bank was steep) shot the Athenians from above, most of them drinking greedily and tumbling over one another down in the river. The Peloponnesians too came down on them and slew them, most of all those in the river. The water was soon befouled; nevertheless they drank it, defiled as it was with mud and blood, and the greater part fought for it." [2] Nicias is put to death by his Syracusan captors (very ungratefully, considering how much he contributed to their victory) and the rank-and-file prisoners are sent to a living death in the stone-quarries. "Army, fleet, and all perished, as the saying is, with an utter destruction. Few of many returned home." [3]

Still Athens fought on—her country in hostile occupation, her allies revolting right and left, her enemies now reinforced from Sicily and financed by Persian gold, her city riddled with treason, her back to the wall. She was able to fit out and man new fleets, to victual herself by sea, and to win more than one striking naval victory. Not until 404, nine years after the Sicilian disaster, did she surrender. Thucydides recounts only the first two years of this last struggle. He returned from

[1] Thucydides, vii, 27.   [2] Ibid., vii, 84.   [3] Ibid., vii, 87.

exile after the final *débâcle*, but seems to have found Athens little
to his taste, and retired to his Thracian estate.   There he came
to a violent end in unknown circumstances, leaving his history
unfinished.   Five hundred years later Plutarch saw his grave
in the Philaïd burying-place at Athens.

CHAPTER V

GREECE IN DECLINE

W AS there, it will be asked, no ancient Voltaire to flay with open scorn the iniquities and futilities which brought Greek civilization to its death-bed? If there was, his works have perished. One man's protest has come down to us—the protest not of a philosopher or historian, but of a poet.

Euripides was born of humble parents in the year (legend even says on the day) of Salamis, and died famous two years before the end of the Peloponnesian War. He therefore saw both the greatness and the decline of Athens. As a tragic poet he worked under severe limitations; for Greek drama was a solemn public ceremony, the handmaid of Greek religion, and in order to be produced at all had to conform at least outwardly to established ideas. It is all the more remarkable that Euripides should have succeeded in making it a vehicle for Rationalist criticism (albeit indirect) of contemporary politics and contemporary religion. He is not unpatriotic. His ideals are those of the Periclean funeral oration. He is proud of the contribution of Athens to Greek civilization, and in more than one play praises her enlightened humanity in contrast to her reactionary rivals, Sparta and Thebes. But his patriotism is not undiscriminating. His *Medea* is the noblest protest voiced in ancient times against the subjection of women. His *Ion* is a thinly veiled attack on the national mythology and the Delphic priesthood which fostered it. And when Athens outrages enlightenment and humanity, the rebuke of Euripides is unmistakable. Late in 416 B.C. Athens made her unprovoked attack on the island of Melos, massacred its men, and sold its women and children as slaves. A few months later, in the spring of 415, Euripides produced his *Trojan Women*, in which the horrors of the sack of Troy are painted with harrowing realism. It must have needed courage to hold up the mirror in this fashion to a city drunk with recent aggression and already fitting out her armament for new adventure in Sicily. We need not wonder that Euripides became unpopular. In the end he turned his back on a Greece torn by ruthless power-politics and finished his days at the neutral court of Macedonia.

Withdrawal from the struggle, political and religious, is the note sounded in Euripides' last completed (and most discussed) drama, the *Bacchæ*. This has for its subject the myth of Dionysus, the primitive fertility god of the Ægean peasantry. Euripides knew and respected the peasantry: in his *Electra* the one decent character is a peasant. The cult of Dionysus was late in winning recognition in polite Greek society. Homer mentions him only once and somewhat slightingly as " mad Dionysus." As against the dignified Olympians, he remained a crude, half-human, half-animal god incorporating many local tribal totems and worshipped by ignorant people, and especially women, with wild and uncouth rites. By the fifth century the struggle was over, and Dionysus had achieved respectability as the son of Zeus and patron of the drama. But in the *Bacchæ* Euripides depicts the conflict, as he imagines it might have been, between Greek officialdom and this cult of peasants and women. He ends by rejecting both sides. He is decidedly not with the persecutor, Pentheus. He tells us in matchless poetry all that Dionysus stands for—communion of man with man, and of man with nature, in time-honoured ritual; an end to greed, power-politics, and vexing problems such as occupy " the world's wise "; strength in persecution; escape, as of " a fawn to the greenwood," from the tempest of striving to a haven of happiness. Yet suppose " the simple nameless herd of humanity " could by revolutionary violence—by " doom and deed "—smite and destroy the oppressive State machine, what would follow? Horrors from which Euripides averts his eyes—like the tearing to pieces of Pentheus by his own mother. There is no way forward—there is only retreat from such a world.[1]

Euripides had genius enough to divine the direction in

[1] See Dr. Gilbert Murray's translation of, and preface to, the *Bacchæ*.

which his world was moving. In due course the worshippers, not of Dionysus, but of a new god (who, like Dionysus, offered rest to the weary and heavy-laden, underwent death and resurrection, fed his congregation on his body and blood, and preferred " the foolishness of God " to the " wisdom of the world "), did their part in bringing ancient civilization to an end. So aware were some Christians of the resemblance between the new saviour-god and the old that one of them, by stringing together lines from the *Bacchæ* and two other plays of Euripides, managed to fabricate a drama on the sufferings of Christ.[1]

The Rationalism of Euripides, then, ended in a retreat into mysticism. So, it seems, did that of his admirer, Socrates. Socrates was about ten years younger than Euripides and, like him, of humble parentage. In estimating him we are under the disadvantage of possessing no writings of his own, and we are dependent on three divergent accounts—that of a detractor, the comedian Aristophanes, and those of two disciples, the soldier-historian Xenophon and the philosopher Plato.

Aristophanes, our earliest witness, produced his comedy of the *Clouds* in 423 B.C., when Socrates was about forty-six years old. It is usual to dismiss the *Clouds* as a mere extravaganza—a skit directed not at Socrates in particular, but at " sophists " and intellectuals in general. The fact remains that Socrates is the central figure in it. A competent caricaturist (and no one will think Aristophanes incompetent) must be presumed to know whom he intends to pillory, and to base his caricature on *some* real features in his victim. When Aristophanes depicts Socrates as running a school of natural science and rejecting the gods, we need not take it all in sober earnest, but we must assume that Socrates had provided a handle for the attack. Now we know from Plato that Socrates was interested in natural science in his youth, but lost interest later and confined his inquiries to human affairs. We may be sure that, while his interest in science lasted, he discussed it with all comers. Whether he still did so in 423 or not, the fact would be within recent memory. Aristophanes

[1] This *tour de force* was once attributed to Gregory of Nazianzus. The real author and date are unknown.

spoke for the conservative landowners: everything new, therefore, came under his lash—the new demagogy, the new imperialism, the new science, the new scepticism. That the attack in the *Clouds* went home we know from the *Apology* of Plato.

Socrates took no part in politics. His only two recorded public acts (the opposition to the mass execution of generals in 406, and the refusal to carry out an illegal arrest under the Thirty) are those of a stickler for legality, not of a party politician. No doubt he shared the disillusionment of Euripides. But he had friends in both political camps— Chærephon and Lysias among the democrats, as well as Critias and Charmides among the oligarchs. This surely disposes of the contention that it was on political grounds that he was tried and executed in 399. Had it been so, the charge brought would have been political; for the Athenian democracy never pretended to tolerate attacks on itself.

The charge against Socrates was specifically religious. He was accused of propagating infidelity to the State religion—of " not recognizing the gods recognized by the city, introducing other and new divinities, and corrupting the youth." Xenophon, a superstitious conformist, is at pains to make out Socrates as pious as himself. But it is noteworthy that in the *Apology* of Plato (who witnessed the trial and may be presumed to do justice to his master's defence) the charge of infidelity is not met. Socrates deals at length with the " ancient " prejudice against him as a scientific sceptic, and calls the bystanders to witness that they have never heard him discuss science. He could utter this challenge, no doubt, more safely in 399 than in 423. But when he turns to the charge before the court, he does not rebut it by professing belief in the gods of Athens : he merely makes Meletus look silly and contradict himself. (It is hard to believe that Meletus was so incompetent, or that Anytus and Lycon sat by and let him make a fool of himself.) The remainder of the defence is a memorable plea for free discussion and a defiant refusal to abandon it. The only further reference to the charge of infidelity is the closing avowal: " I do believe that there are gods, and that in a far higher sense than that in which any of my accusers believe in them."[1]   Pious Athenians must have felt their worst suspicions confirmed.   Noteworthy, too, in the closing section of the *Apology* is the complete agnosticism of Socrates on the question of personal survival.   If this is authentic, the confidently affirmative position attributed to him by Plato in the *Phædo* is certainly fictitious.   " We go our ways," he concludes—" I to die and you to live.   Which is better, God only knows."[2]

The history of Greece after the Peloponnesian War is a sorry story told, on the whole, by sorry historians.   Xenophon, who begins where Thucydides breaks off, is superstitious, enthusiastically pro-Spartan, and without any conception of historical criticism.   His *métier* was soldiering; and his leadership of the retreat of ten thousand Greeks from Babylonia to the sea (which proved, as it were, experimentally the weakness of the Persian Empire) was more important to the world than his performance as a historian.   He deals in an entirely superficial way with the attempt and failure of Sparta in the fourth century to impose her policy on Greece in the teeth of democratic opposition, and the resultant stalemate between the rival democracies, Thebes and Athens.

To understand what was really happening we have to go to authorities other than historians.   Isocrates, a prosperous professional pleader and essayist whose long life lasted from the age of Pericles to the age of Philip of Macedon, tells of economic decay and chronic class and party warfare, loosing on Greece a mob of unemployed and " displaced persons " ready to sell themselves to any adventurer.   " It is easier," says Isocrates, " to raise an army, and a bigger and better army too, from vagabonds than from law-abiding citizens."[3]   He has his remedy, and consistently presses it on his countrymen over a period of more than forty years.   The adventure of the ten thousand has shown Persia to be easy game.   Let the Greek cities join forces.   Let Athens and Sparta set the example;   or if they will not, let some strong man impose his leadership.   Then let them invade Asia, loot the gorgeous East, and find homes for their surplus population.   One " man of destiny " after another raises his hopes.   First it is

[1] Plato, *Apology*, 35.   [2] Ibid., 42.   [3] Isocrates, *Philip*, 96.

Dionysius, the sinister tyrant of Syracuse. Then, after his death, it is Archidamus of Sparta. Then, Sparta being no longer what she was, Isocrates looks north and backs Philip of Macedon. His nationalism is qualified by one great thought. " The name of Greek denotes no longer a race, but a habit of mind : they are rather to be called Greeks who share our culture than who come only of a common stock." [1]

The sunset of the city-state had in fact come. It had failed to solve its problems, whether economic, political, or religious. In the fifth and fourth centuries the proportion of slaves to free citizens steadily increased, and with the growth of slavery the free peasant or artisan was impoverished. But if that growing mass of misery was to be held down, a welter of city-states, and especially of democratic city-states, was a wholly inadequate instrument. We have seen how in the Peloponnesian War both sides went in fear of a slave rising, and how Athens actually lost twenty thousand slaves by desertion. Finally the religion of the city-state, based on prehistoric magic and myth, even though rationalized by poetry and refined by art, would not bear criticism. Philosophers and " sophists " had done their work too well. A religion of the present was needed, not a religion of the past—one which would lend divine authority not to the fables of Homer and Hesiod, but to the tottering social order of the fourth century.

We meet this quest of a new theoretical basis for a slave society in Plato. " Man," says he, " is a troublesome animal, and therefore is not, and is not likely to become very manageable when you attempt to introduce the necessary division of slave and freeman and master." [2] Hence Plato's idealist philosophy, which denies the reality of the sensible world and therefore of the objects for which class and party struggles are waged; his justification of lying as a means to subordination in the State; his assertion of the divine right of the philosopher-king to dominate the common run of men; and his vendetta against democracy, against the " sophists," against experimental science, and against materialism and atheism—culminating in his advocacy of the death penalty for impiety. On this subject Plato becomes really violent. " Who can be

[1] Isocrates, *Panegyricus*, 50.   [2] Plato, *Laws*, 777.

calm," he exclaims, "when he is called upon to prove the existence of the gods? Who can avoid hating and abhorring the men who are and have been the cause of this argument?... How can anyone in gentle terms remonstrate with the like of them?"[1] Persuasion is difficult with the multitude and takes "a dismal length of time": therefore let the impious, who have not the excuse of "childish levity," be punished with death.[2] Anytus and Meletus would have agreed.

Parallels between ancient and modern historical figures are by their nature precarious, and should never be pressed. Otherwise it would be tempting to compare Plato and Thomas Carlyle. This will seem blasphemy to Plato-worshippers who see in their philosopher the author of a wellnigh perfect system of thought. Yet Plato is not so systematic a thinker as might be supposed. The thought of the *Protagoras* is not that of the *Republic*, nor the thought of the *Republic* that of the *Parmenides*. Allowing for the difference of circumstance between the Athenian aristocrat and the Scottish peasant-sage, they had a good deal in common. Each had a leaning to mathematics and mysticism and an aversion to inductive science. Each thought that the world was going from bad to worse. Each rejected the outworn mythology of his age, but was convinced of the necessity of religion and scornfully hostile to materialism. Each was revolted by a society abandoned to money-making, and contemptuous of those who made of the instruction of mankind a trade instead of a vocation. Each reinforced his exposure of contemporary evils by an idealization of the past—in Plato's case, a pre-historic Athens described on the imaginary authority of Egyptian priests; in Carlyle's, monastic life as recorded in a medieval chronicle. Each looked to a great man, a hero or a philosopher-king, to impose on his countrymen the discipline which he deemed necessary to their salvation. These like-nesses are obscured by the different media in which they worked. Whoever cares may speculate how Plato, had he been a historian, would have dealt with the Peloponnesian War, or how Carlyle, had he written philosophic dialogues, would have caricatured the false prophets of "gigmanity" in

[1] Plato, *Laws*, 887–888.   [2] Ibid., 890, 909.

verbal duels with Goethe, Emerson, or his imaginary Teufelsdröckh.

Whatever the vices of Athenian democracy, at least it went down fighting. No contemporary history of the last struggle with Macedon is extant. We are dependent on the orators —chiefly Demosthenes—and on second-hand narratives like those of Diodorus and Plutarch, compiled three or four centuries later. As always, contemporary evidence is the most worth study, provided we remember that no orator is an impartial witness, and that later writers had access to sources which have since been lost.

Demosthenes was the son of a rich Athenian manufacturer, but was impoverished early in life by fraudulent guardians who embezzled his patrimony. In spite of a successful action, he never recovered the money. He therefore started poor, and earned a living by writing speeches (as the custom then was) for litigants to deliver in the courts. He did not enter politics until his thirtieth year. The ancients told many stories of his difficulties in training himself to speak, of his stammer, of his taking lessons from an actor, of his practising with pebbles in his mouth, and so on. We need not believe all this, but we may accept the general impression conveyed —that Demosthenes made good under heavy disadvantages. Three years after his political *début* he began his unremitting campaign against the Macedonian peril.

In doing so he swam against the tide; for the most influential men in Greece (Isocrates, for example) saw in the invasion of Asia under some such leader as Philip of Macedon the only way out of their economic and political troubles. Such projects did not interest Demosthenes. He is no imperialist: his first political speech combats the idea of an aggressive war against Persia. He is—to use a modern idiom —a " little Greek " and somewhat of an idealist. Bit by bit he feels his way towards a reconciliation between Athens and her rival Thebes. He believes in democracy, in decent relations between Greek states, and in the dictatorship of none— not even of Athens. " Never begin an injustice," he cries, " in either word or deed.[1] ... Our city has always had one and

---

[1] Demosthenes, *On the Navy Boards.*

the same object, to protect the injured. . . . Circumstances change, Athens changes not."¹ Blind to the economic causes which compelled Greece to choose between imperial expansion and social overturn, he imagined that the punishment of corruption and the revival of antique patriotism would alone solve his problem. " There was something," says he of the old days, " in the hearts of the multitude then, which there is not now. . . . Whoever took money from aspirants to power or corruptors of Greece was universally detested: it was dreadful to be convicted of bribery. . . . But now . . . what? Envy where a man gets a bribe; laughter if he confesses it; mercy to the convicted; hatred of the denouncer." ²

Philip had come to the throne in 359 and had set to work from the first to make Macedonia a great power. The claim of the Macedonians to be Greeks was disputed in antiquity, and is disputed today. They seem to have spoken a dialect closely akin to Greek, but perhaps less intelligible to an Athenian than Highland Scots today to a Cockney. In the early years of Philip's reign he had made himself master of Amphipolis and other Greek cities on the Thracian coast, together with those gold-mines which had once belonged to the historian Thucydides, and which now served to swell Philip's revenue and to organize a party for him in every city of Greece. In 352 Athens awoke to find Philip in control of Thessaly. Until then Demosthenes had not meddled with the question: he was, we must remember, still a political beginner. But from now onwards in speech after speech he calls on Athens to shake off her lethargy; to remember her former prowess; to arm against Macedon before it is too late; not to leave her defence to mercenaries, but to grudge neither men nor money for the fray. He tries, in short, to re-create the Athens of Pericles out of its ashes. In the end, in 338, he manages to align Athens, Thebes, and other cities in a common democratic front against the invader. But it was then too late to avert defeat at Chæronea.

Hopeless though the battle was, Demosthenes towers above the orators who opposed him. Isocrates was not of their number: he was a man of the pen, not of the platform,

¹ *For the People of Megalopolis.*   ² *Third Philippic.*

and by the time Demosthenes entered politics, was in extreme old age.[1] As to the others—the theatrical Æschines, the venal Demades, and the rest—it is significant that in 330, when all was over, when the Greek city-states lay prostrate under Macedon, when Alexander had conquered the East, and when history seemed to have pronounced finally against Demosthenes, he was nevertheless able to win a verdict against Æschines in the Athenian courts and to drive his rival into voluntary exile.

The speech of Demosthenes on that occasion, the famous oration *On the Crown*, is a masterly vindication of all for which he stands. Athens, he says, has lived up to her heroic past and fought a good fight for the common freedom of Greece. He has done his best to further her war effort and to see that no class shirked its duty to the State.

> " At home, I never preferred the favour of the wealthy
> to the rights of the many: abroad, I valued not the
> presents or the friendship of Philip above the general
> interests of Greece."

Nor does he now repent.

> " To all mankind the end of life is death, though one
> keep oneself shut up in a closet; but it becomes brave
> men to strive always for honour. . . . Do not impute it to
> me as a crime that Philip chanced to conquer in battle.
> That issue depended not on me, but on God. . . . Never,
> never can you have done wrong, men of Athens, in under-
> taking battle for the freedom and safety of all! . . . By
> success we should have become incontestably and de-
> servedly the greatest of peoples. Even in failure the
> result is glory." [2]

Eight years later, after the death of Alexander, Athens and other Greek cities rose against the Macedonian regent, Anti-

---

[1] The story, immortalized in Milton's sonnet, that Isocrates died of grief at " that dishonest victory at Chæronea, fatal to liberty," rests on late authority and is inherently unlikely. Isocrates had backed the winning side, he was ninety-eight, and he may easily have died from natural causes.

[2] *On the Crown.*

pater. This time she was finally crushed, her democracy was suppressed, and Demosthenes and other patriots were condemned to death. Demosthenes took sanctuary in a temple and, when it was surrounded by soldiers, eluded his would-be captors by swallowing poison. According to Plutarch he staggered from his place of refuge, saying: " Gracious Poseidon, I quit thy temple while I yet live; Antipater and his Macedonians have done what they could to pollute it," and fell dead by the altar. So in his sixty-second year ended this Pericles born out of due time. Though his cause was lost, his stand for democracy lit a flame thousands of years later in men and nations of whom he had never dreamt. Clemenceau, the leader of France in the First World War, and Hyndman, the father of British Social Democracy, fighting for freedom, as they understood it, against a new Macedon in the shape of imperial Germany, both drew inspiration from the example and eloquence of Demosthenes of Athens.

Aristotle, the exact contemporary of Demosthenes, in his *Politics* (completed after 336), writes the epitaph of Greek democracy. For Aristotle, as for Plato, the slave basis of society is bed-rock. Those " capable of reflection and forethought "[1] are by nature masters: those not so capable are by nature slaves. True, accidents will happen; " slaves have sometimes the souls of freemen ";[2] there is the danger of revolt; and it is " very troublesome to keep upon proper terms with them." [3] But in general it is not unjust to enslave those fit for nothing better and, if they object, to go to war for that purpose. To be a complete citizen and share in the government of his city, a man should be free from any servile employment. " It is impossible for one who lives the life of a mechanic or hired servant to acquire the practice of virtue." [4] Now " democracy is government by men of no birth, indigent circumstances, and mechanical employments." [5] It is comparatively innocuous in a society of peasants or herdsmen, but if extended to mechanics it is very bad; " for their lives are wretched, nor have they any business with virtue in anything they do." Such democracy leads to " licentiousness in

[1] Aristotle, *Politics*, I, ii.   [2] Ibid., I, v.   [3] Ibid., II, ix.
[4] Ibid., III, v.   [5] Ibid., VI, ii.

slaves, women, and children." [1]   A landless free class is a great
evil, leading to demagogy and to predatory legislation against
the rich. If democracy there must be, the poor should be
assisted, " every one of them to purchase a little field, or if
that cannot be done, at least to procure the implements of
trade and husbandry." [2]   But in a really well-governed State
no citizen " should be permitted to exercise any mechanical
employment or follow merchandise, these being ignoble and
destructive of virtue; neither should they be peasants." [3]
Land should be concentrated in the hands of a military and
ruling class, and cultivated by " slaves, not of the same nation,
nor men of any spirit; for so they would be industrious at
their work and warranted not to attempt any revolution.
Next to these, barbarian servants are to be preferred." [4]   And,
in a sentence very topical at the time of writing, Aristotle
observes that " could the Greeks agree upon one system of
policy, they could command the whole world " [5]—and presumably have all the barbarian slaves they needed.

This was the idea which, as we have seen, had already
occurred to Isocrates; the idea with which Philip had conquered Greece; and the idea which Alexander within a few
years translated into practice.

[1] Aristotle, *Politics*, VI, iv.   [2] Ibid., VI, v.   [3] Ibid., VII, ix.
[4] Ibid., VII, x.   [5] Ibid., VII, vii.

CHAPTER VI

THE WEST GOES EAST

IT is extraordinary that we have no contemporary account of the conquests of Alexander the Great. Although authoritative histories of his campaigns were written by Ptolemy and other officers who took part in them, they have all perished. We are dependent on Diodorus, an incompetent compiler who wrote three centuries later; Quintus Curtius, equally incompetent and later still; Plutarch, who at least names his sources; and Arrian, five hundred years after the time, but a Roman governor and military commander who knew his subject, used contemporary evidence, and, though the latest of our ancient authorities, is also the best.

The military achievement of Alexander, though the most spectacular side of his career, is the least important. His victories had been thoroughly prepared. Two generations earlier Xenophon had shown that a small Greek force could cut its way through Persian armies and hostile tribesmen all the way from Babylonia to the sea. Ever since then Isocrates and half Greece had wanted to see the operation repeated in the reverse direction. Philip had built up the military machine with which to do it. The Persian Empire was a colossus stuffed with clouts, held together only by Greek mercenaries whom its gold could still buy. Against it were now thrown not only Greek troops fresher, more numerous, and better provided than those of Xenophon, but the seasoned fighters of Macedonia as well—in particular Alexander's own feudal cavalry, which had broken the Greeks at Chæronea and was to shatter the Orientals at the Granicus, Issus, and Gaugamela. Such a combination went through the Persian Empire like a knife through butter.

More significant than Alexander's victories is the use which he made of them. In the first place, the dream of Aristotle

was fulfilled : Greece was flooded with barbarian slaves. The
thirty thousand sold after the fall of Tyre must alone have
been a noble haul for the dealers.

In the second place, by assuming the heritage of the old
Oriental empires, Alexander transformed himself from a
Macedonian war-chief into a god-king. When the Egyptian
priests hailed him as the son of the god Amen, they did what
they had automatically done for their ancient Pharaohs.
Alexander, their deliverer from Persian oppression, was thus
proclaimed the legitimate successor of Ahmosi of Thebes,
their deliverer from Hyksos oppression twelve centuries
before.

In the Oriental empires the god-king was an immemorial
institution. Even in Greece the idea was not wholly alien.
Many legendary Greek kings (e.g. Agamemnon) had been
originally gods; and at the end of the Peloponnesian War,
when the need of a " saviour of society " was badly felt, some
cities had voted divine honours to the Spartan conqueror,
Lysander, even in his lifetime. But to the Macedonians, as to
other northern peoples new to ancient civilization, their king
was simply a war-chief, and the Oriental king-cult strange and
offensive. Hence the growing tension between Alexander
and his personal followers in the later years of his reign, and
the violent end of Parmenio, Clitus, Callisthenes, and anyone
else who ventured to cross the god-king. Alexander's last
years in fact show increasing symptoms of something very like
mania. His invasion of India was utterly unnecessary and led
to no solid results. When his army, after following him to
the Punjab, refused to march farther into the unknown, they
showed more sense of reality than he.

But the god-king had come to stay. Neither Alexander
nor his successors could govern an Oriental empire without
this business of deification. The Greek cities endorsed it. At
the end of Alexander's reign they sent to wait on him not
simply ambassadors, but *sacred* ambassadors (*theoroi*), such as
they would have sent to Olympian Zeus or Delian Apollo.
After Alexander's death, when his generals fell out and fought
one another for the spoils of empire, the temporary war-lord
of Asia, Antigonus, in 307 as a stroke of policy sent his son

Demetrius to Athens to expel his rival Cassander's Macedonian garrison and restore the democracy which had been suppressed fifteen years before. The grateful Athenians voted divine honours and the title of Saviour (*Soter*) to both Antigonus and Demetrius, changed the festival of Dionysus to one in honour of Demetrius, and chanted a hymn containing the lines:

> The other gods dwell far away,
> Or have no ears,
> Or are not, or pay us no heed.
> But thee we present see,
> No god of wood or stone, but godhead true.
> Therefore to thee we pray.[1]

But the day of democracies was over. Greek cities were now mere pawns in a strategic game and owed any liberty they had to the competition of rival dynasts. Three years later, when Demetrius was besieging Rhodes, the Rhodians owed their deliverance to Ptolemy of Egypt, who in his turn was voted divine honours and became a saviour. The baffled Demetrius earned the nickname of *Poliorketes*—the great " besieger " whose siege had not come off. Three years later again, Antigonus fell at Ipsus in battle with rival war-lords, Demetrius beat a retreat, Cassander reoccupied Athens, and no more was heard there of the new democracy or the new religion. Six years later, in 294, Demetrius recovered Athens, but by then he had forgotten about democracy. Rhodes was luckier: thanks to Ptolemy (a more efficient war-lord and therefore a more reliable " saviour ") she was able to remain independent and to grow rich on the roaring trade between East and West opened up by the conquests of Alexander. These incidents in an otherwise tedious series of dynastic wars illustrate the utter discredit which had befallen the old Greek religion, and its practical supersession by the cult of power-politics embodied in the god-king.

The third important feature in the policy of Alexander and his successors was the Greek colonization of the East. Alexander dotted his empire with numerous Alexandrias, from the famous one in Egypt to the remote outpost which

---

[1] Frazer, *The Golden Bough*, abridged edition, p. 97.

perpetuates his name in the still recognizable form of Kandahar. His successors left their mark on the map in such new cities as Antigonia in Asia Minor, which after the death of Antigonus was renamed Nicæa and, as such, was fated to be famous in ecclesiastical history; Seleucia in Babylonia, planted by the founder of the Seleucid dynasty; Antioch in Syria, named after Antiochus, the father of Seleucus; Apamea in the same region, named after Apama, his wife; Laodicea on the Syrian coast, named after Laodice, his mother, and still flourishing today as Latakia; another Laodicea in Asia Minor (that mentioned in the New Testament) named after a later Seleucid queen; and many similar dynastic foundations. These cities were peopled by discharged soldiers or fortune-seekers from Greece, who formed the citizen body and ran the place, while natives of the country provided the hewers of wood and drawers of water. The Greeks had found their Eldorado. Rich inhabitants of Alexandria, Seleucia, or Antioch lived in a luxury unknown to the fellow-citizens of Pericles or Demosthenes; and art, literature, and science found more lavish patrons in the Ptolemies and Seleucids than they could ever have found in the little states of the Greek homeland.

But what of the conquered populations? The richer natives adopted the Greek language and way of life. There was no bar on intermarriage: Alexander and his successors alike encouraged it. The Hellenization of the upper classes is shown by such cases as those of Manetho, the Egyptian, and Berossus, the Babylonian priest, each of whom compiled from native records a history of his own country in Greek. Unfortunately neither survives except in fragments quoted by Josephus and later writers. Other examples of Hellenization are provided by the Jews of Alexandria, who had to have their sacred books translated into Greek, and by the priestly aristocracy of Jerusalem, whose transgressions of the law contributed to the Maccabean uprising. Hellenization, however, seems to have been an affair of the cities and, within the cities, mainly of the richer classes. In the countryside the peasantry continued to speak their native tongues—Phrygian, Lycaonian, Aramaic, Egyptian, Iranian, as the case might be; and the populace in the cities was, at most, bilingual. To the native masses the Greek rulers were foreigners who taxed them and fought wars over their countries, but whose language and culture were alien to them, and to whom they felt no obligation and no loyalty. We have but little popular Oriental literature of the period to set against the wealth of Greek historical, poetical, philosophical, and scientific writing which has come down to us. But it is significant that, in the little we have, the chosen symbol of the conquering power should be a wild beast—"terrible and powerful, and strong exceedingly; and it had great iron teeth : it devoured and brake in pieces, and stamped the residue with his feet: and it was diverse from all the beasts that were before it." [1] Still more eloquent than the imagery of the Jewish visionary are the facts of history—the speed with which, within two centuries of Alexander, Greek conquests east of the Euphrates fell to the Parthian invader; and the completeness with which, after a few more centuries, even the Greek language in the Middle East was swamped by Syriac, Coptic, and Arabic. The final verdict on Hellenistic civilization was pronounced by its subjects, who, when it came to the point, lifted no finger to save it.

Not only exploited Orientals felt the new imperialism to be vanity and a striving after wind. Among those banished from Athens on the suppression of her democracy in 322, and restored to citizenship by Demetrius in 307, was a self-taught philosopher of modest means named Epicurus. We have only fragments of his writings. Our knowledge of his system comes mostly from Lucretius; of his life, mostly from Diogenes Laertius' *Lives of the Philosophers*, a late and uncritical work which has the redeeming merit of preserving three priceless letters of Epicurus himself. This greatest of ancient freethinkers turns his back, as it were, in contempt on the power-politics of his time and on the philosophies which try to justify them. In his garden, where men and women, freemen and slaves join in equal discussion, he preaches the gospel of contentment with little. In conscious reaction against the "golden" Plato and in studiedly lucid language, Epicurus declares sensation to be the test of truth and

[1] Dan. vii, 7.

metaphysical speculation superfluous. Sensation tells us that matter exists: nothing tells us that anything else does. Pleasure by this test being good and pain evil, the wise man will cut out of his life those pleasures, such as drunkenness, gluttony, and debauchery, which are purchased only by disproportionate pain. He will eschew the pursuit of power, the only purpose of which is to win illusory security and to procure satisfactions that never satisfy. As to the gods, impiety consists not in denying the gods of the multitude, but in affirming of them what the multitude believes. As to death, it is "nothing to us, seeing that, when we are, death is not come, and when death is come, we are not."[1] It is permissible to wonder whether Epicurus was not nearer to the spirit of Socrates than the latter's professed interpreter, Plato. He had his reward. In the suffering Greek world of the third century B.C. men flocked to hear him. "Friends," says Diogenes on the authority of an earlier biographer, "came to him from all parts and lived with him in his garden,"[2] notwithstanding the extreme simplicity of his entertainment. Few who joined the school were ever known to leave it.

Epicurus declined political problems which in the conditions of his day admitted of no satisfying solution. His rival, Zeno, the founder of the Stoics, was more pretentious. Zeno was a Hellenized Phœnician of Cyprus who settled in Athens towards the end of the fourth century and embraced the Cynic gospel of voluntary poverty, which he afterwards developed into a more systematic philosophy of his own. None of his works are extant; and it is difficult to disentangle his original teaching from the matter added by later Stoics. Zeno, like Epicurus, was a materialist and, on paper at least, equally contemptuous of the conventional values of Greek civilization. In an ideal society, he teaches, there would be neither temples, ritual, law-courts, money, nor marriage; men and women would live free and equal citizens of the world. But since most people are not reasonable, the Stoic compromises and accepts, while reserving his private judgment, the prevailing forms of property, marriage, government, and religion. For him God is another name for

---

[1] Diogenes Laertius, X, 125.   [2] Ibid., 10.

nature; the gods of the State, rightly understood, are but aspects of natural law; and the enlightened, whatever their outward circumstances, are free in a world of slaves. This detached acquiescence in the world as it was did not prevent Stoicism at its best from making notable contributions to human progress. But it made Stoicism at its worst a rather repulsive kind of cant, and exposed it to justifiable gibes on the part of Epicureans who took their anti-religious propaganda seriously.

CHAPTER VII

ROME TAKES OVER

To the average European or American the outline of Roman history is only a little less familiar than the history of his own country. There is ample reason for this. The civilization of modern Europe and America is derived from that of Rome. The law of most European countries is based on Roman law. Latin remained an international language for considerably more than a thousand years after the fall of the Roman Empire. It forms the basis of many of the vernaculars which have replaced it in common speech, and is an important ingredient of others, including our own. It is still the official language of the greatest of Christian Churches. It is natural that we should regard the ancient Romans as cultural ancestors rather than as complete foreigners, and their history as a prelude to our own rather than as an alien story with which we have nothing to do.

It is curious, therefore, to reflect that we are without any contemporary record of the process by which Rome rose from a small Italian city-state to be a great Mediterranean power. No Greek historian of the late fourth or third century B.C., the formative period of Roman greatness, has come down to us. The Romans themselves did not begin to write history until late in the third century, when they had become acquainted with Greek literature. Their early histories, written in Greek, were based on a mass of fable and on meagre temple records, and have mostly perished. Polybius, the last great Greek historian, who wrote in the second century B.C., when Roman predominance in the Mediterranean was an accomplished fact, is our first extant contemporary witness (and an invaluable one) to Roman affairs. Livy, the only other extant ancient historian of the rise of Rome, wrote almost at the date of the Christian era, and for the early period relied on the largely fabulous works of his predecessors. Most of his history has perished; and the portion which survives, while brilliant in style, shows partiality, inaccuracy, and an entire incapacity to criticize his sources. The gaps in Polybius and Livy have to be supplied by Plutarch, who is later than either and is in any case a biographer first and a historian second.

It follows that for early Roman history—that is, for the period prior to the first direct contact between Rome and the Greek world—we are obliged to distrust our literary sources. Romulus and the other early kings are conventional saga-heroes. We know from archæology that Rome was a walled city as long ago as the sixth century B.C. This takes us back to a time when, according to Greek historians, the Etruscans were the dominant power in northern and central Italy, and corroborates the tradition that at that date Rome was ruled by Etruscan kings. But the traditional designation of those kings (Tarquin) is a title, not a personal name; and the stories told of them are fabulous—some being lifted bodily by Roman annalists from incidents related by Herodotus of Greek or Persian worthies. We know that about the end of the sixth century Etruscan power declined; and it is probable that Rome and other Latin cities then won their independence. But the exact date, 509 B.C., assigned to the expulsion of the Tarquins may be due to no more than a wish to synchronize the foundation of the Roman republic with that of the Athenian democracy. The early history of the republic is little more reliable than that of the kings. On Livy's showing most of the temple and other records, including the famous Twelve Tables, perished when Rome was sacked and burnt by the Gauls in 390 B.C.[1] The earlier narrative, therefore, cannot be regarded as more than an ingenious romance, containing perhaps here and there a nugget of factual tradition, such as a well-known war or the consecration of a temple. Once the catastrophe of 390 is behind us, Livy's account of the establishment of Roman power in central Italy during the fourth century may be accepted with the reserve which we

[1] We have no guarantee that the Twelve Tables later in use were an exact reproduction of the law of the early republic.

inevitably attach to a historian for whom his country's wars are always just and always in the end successful.

In the opening years of the third century we reach the first long gap in the text of Livy. A little later Rome becomes inextricably involved in the affairs of the Greek cities of southern Italy. In default of Livy we are dependent on Plutarch for the story of this dramatic encounter between the old and the new.

A generation has passed since the death of Alexander the Great. His empire has been finally partitioned between Ptolemy in Egypt, Seleucus in Asia, Lysimachus in Thrace, and Demetrius the Besieger in Macedonia and Greece proper. But Demetrius has the misfortune to possess a restless young brother-in-law and rival in Pyrrhus, king of Epirus. In 288 Pyrrhus and Lysimachus drive out Demetrius and partition Macedonia between them. Two years later Lysimachus drives out Pyrrhus, and the latter's dream of becoming a successor to Alexander is momentarily ended.

Hardly, however, is the door banged, barred, and bolted against Pyrrhus in the east, when an apparently unlimited opportunity of adventure opens to him in the west. In 281 he receives an embassy from Tarentum, the wealthiest and most powerful of the Greek cities in Italy. Tarentum has long had trouble with the half-civilized Italian tribes of the interior. To cope with these she allied herself twenty years ago with Rome, the rising new power in central Italy. But Rome's price proves to be too high : in return for protection she now demands submission. No self-respecting Greek democracy will stand for that. In fact, the Tarentines have already answered the question by attacking a Roman fleet which entered their harbour uninvited. Will Pyrrhus, a Greek in race and language, kindly intervene to save Greek freedom in Italy?

Here is a chance indeed for Pyrrhus. Neither Alexander nor any of his successors ever crossed the Adriatic. By accepting the Tarentine invitation Pyrrhus hopes not only to defeat Rome, but also to push on into Sicily, champion the Sicilian Greeks against their hereditary enemy Carthage, conquer both Carthage herself and her dependencies in Africa,

Sicily, Sardinia, Corsica, and the Balearics, and end up with as mighty an empire in the West as any of Alexander's successors in the East.

Leaving the eastern war-lords to their feuds, Pyrrhus in 280 crosses to Italy with his army and his elephants—since Alexander, an indispensable arm in first-class war and as great an innovation then as the tank in our day. He garrisons Tarentum and, thanks to his elephants, defeats the Romans at Heraclea. All the Greek cities of Italy now join him; and in 279 he advances on Rome. But the Latin alliance holds firm; and Pyrrhus (since he does not want to waste time and men in Italy before striking west) offers Rome terms. She is to leave southern Italy alone and to be content henceforth with her hegemony in Latium. To his amazement the senate, rallied by old Appius Claudius (first of the authentic Roman empire-builders), rejects his terms and demands his unconditional evacuation of Italy. In 278 Pyrrhus again routs the Romans at Asculum; but still they keep the field. Heraclea and Asculum have been "Pyrrhic" victories; the novelty of elephants is wearing off; and Pyrrhus cannot afford to go on losing men. He patches up a truce and moves on to Sicily to fight Carthage. But the Sicilian Greeks do not welcome him, and Carthage concludes an alliance with Rome against him. Foiled here, too, he returns to Italy in 276 (leaving Sicily, in his own words, to be "a prize-ring for Rome and Carthage"), finds his allies disgusted by his desertion, and next year is catastrophically defeated by the Romans at Beneventum. He returns to Epirus, leaving Rome mistress of Italy; tries to repair his losses in Macedonia and Greece; and in 272 is killed, like the Biblical Abimelech, by a tile hurled by a woman in the streets of Argos.

It is said that no less a judge than Hannibal reckoned Pyrrhus a general superior to himself and second only to Alexander. If so, his military ability was nullified by a political folly which amounted to megalomania. "To one thing constant never," he failed in every one of his undertakings and, for sheer futility, beats all contemporary war-lords—not excepting his brother-in-law Demetrius.

The predicted prize-fight in Sicily was not long in coming. For most of the period of the Punic Wars we enjoy the inestimable guidance of Polybius—the first extant historian after Thucydides to approach his task in a scientific spirit. Born at Megalopolis in Arcadia not long before the end of the Second Punic War, he grew up during the first stages of Roman intervention in Greece proper, and was himself a leading advocate of collaboration with Rome against Macedon. He spent the middle years of his life in Rome as a hostage for the good behaviour of his countrymen, and became the friend of leading Roman statesmen. Released in due course from this merely nominal captivity, he lived to be an eye-witness in 146 B.C. of the final destruction of Carthage and to see Greece too, after a last vain revolt, pass under direct Roman rule. The purpose of his history (completed after 146) is to demonstrate to his fellow-Greeks, in the spirit of a Stoic philosopher, the chain of causes and effects by which a little-known Italian state had in a short space of time become mistress of the Mediterranean world. Unfortunately only fragments survive of his later books, and we have to make do with the far less trustworthy Livy.

Between the two protagonists, Rome and Carthage, Polybius tries to hold an even balance, and on the whole succeeds. It is not an easy task; for no civilized man, not himself a Carthaginian, could have desired the victory of Carthage. The Phœnician founders of *Kart-hadasht* (" new city ") had brought to it from their homeland a tradition of daring commercial enterprise coupled with ruthless cruelty (" at Carthage," says Polybius, " no one is blamed however he may have acquired his wealth ") and a religion of which a regular feature was the burning of children in sacrifice to the fertility god, Baal-Hamman. Late in their history the upper class at Carthage seem to have acquired a veneer of Greek culture; but it was never more than skin-deep. The invective of Jewish prophets against Tyre, " the renowned city . . . strong in the sea, she and her inhabitants, which caused their terror to be on all that haunt it," which traded her merchandise for " the persons of men," and profaned her sanctuaries with a multitude of iniquities, may be transferred without alteration

to her daughter-city, Carthage.[1] The Greeks of the fifth
and fourth centuries and the Romans of the third century B.C.
who arrested Carthaginian expansion in the West undoubtedly
won a battle for future civilization.

On the other hand, Rome did not enter the struggle with
clean hands. She had not hesitated to ally herself with Carthage
to secure her empire in Italy. Once that end was achieved,
Rome in 264 B.C. turned on her ally and seized Messana
(Messina) with a cool perfidy which sheds a curious light on
the charges of " Punic faith " levelled at Carthage by Livy and
other Latin writers. The First Punic War was an act of naked
aggression on the part of Rome. It succeeded because the
mercenaries of Carthage were no match for the citizen-
soldiers of Rome, and because there was nothing about
Carthage which could induce her subjects to make any sacrifice on her account. The most famous episode of the war is
the all-but-successful invasion of Africa by Regulus in 256
and his defeat and capture by the Carthaginians a year later.
It is significant that Carthage had to employ a Greek mercenary,
the Spartan Xanthippus, to cope with Regulus. The story
(immortalized in an ode of Horace) of Regulus' peace mission
to Rome, his heroic sabotage of the negotiations, and his
execution by torture on his return to Carthage rests entirely
on Roman authority. It may be true, or it may be an early
example of atrocity propaganda. Nothing known of Carthaginian or Roman usages excludes either alternative; but the
silence of Polybius makes the tale suspect. Rome emerged
from the First Punic War in 241 mistress of Sicily and richer
by a handsome indemnity, while Carthage had to face a formidable mutiny of her unpaid mercenaries, and was unable to
stop Rome from occupying Sardinia and Corsica two years
later.

For the Second Punic War we are able to compare the
detachment of Polybius with the partiality of Livy, whose
history is again extant from this point onward. The impression we get is that of a one-man war doomed to failure
from the start. Hannibal was one of the greatest soldiers of
all time. The idea of marching through Spain and Gaul,

[1] Ezek. xxvi, 17; xxvii, 13 ; xxviii, 18.

taking Rome in the rear, and raising Italy against her seems to have been entirely his own, and might have succeeded if he had had a national army and an honest and competent government behind him. But the Carthaginian merchant-princes fought their wars by proxy. Hannibal set out in 218 with an army of African and Spanish mercenaries, half of whom were lost by the time he had crossed the Alps. Success depended on his receiving the necessary reinforcements from Carthage and winning the Italians to his side. But Carthage gave him little or no support; and though the southern Italians joined him in 216 after Cannæ, Rome's allies in central Italy remained faithful. Hannibal had to hold out in isolation for thirteen years while Rome put her last man into the field and slowly wore him down. His final hope disappeared when his younger brother, Hasdrubal, who had marched overland from Spain to relieve him, was cut off and killed in 207 at the river Metaurus. Meanwhile Rome threw up a leader of genius in Scipio Africanus and, unlike Carthage, had the sense to back her man when she had found him. Applying Hannibal's strategy in reverse, he drove Carthage out of Spain, carried the war into Africa, forced Carthage to recall Hannibal, and at Zama in 202 ended her as a great power and turned the whole western Mediterranean into a Latin lake.

From that day onward Rome was the foremost power in the ancient world. But, as the sequel showed, she paid a formidable price for victory. During the long war Italian agriculture went to pieces, and Rome escaped starvation only by importing food from Sicily, Sardinia, and Egypt. The Italian peasantry never recovered from the blow. When agriculture revived, it was on a basis of slave labour, which was imported into Italy *en masse* during a series of victorious campaigns. Thus the population of Italy and of Rome itself gradually changed its composition. The situation in fourth-century Greece was reproduced on a magnified scale in second-century Italy. Instead of Latin, Sabine, or Etruscan peasants or artisans tilling their own land or plying their own craft, Italy was flooded with Greek, African, Spanish, Celtic, and Oriental slaves who tilled large estates and discharged all the menial offices for the Roman plutocracy, while the native peasantry sank deeper and deeper in debt and finally were squeezed off their farms to drift to the cities or seek their fortune in the legions. And with the influx of Oriental slaves began the infiltration of Oriental religions. In the last years of the Second Punic War, in obedience to a conveniently discovered Sibylline oracle, the cult of the great mother-goddess of Asia Minor was introduced into Rome. That this was not just panicky superstition, but calculated policy, is shown by the fact that Roman citizens were forbidden to take part in the cult. The intention was evidently to conciliate the mass of slaves, freedmen, and other aliens who formed a growing part of the city's population and whom it was important to keep quiet at a time when Rome had a foreign invader on her hands in Italy. But this was an unusual step. Some years later, in 186 B.C., the senate prohibited the worship of Dionysus (or Bacchus) at Rome even by private persons. As in Greece, so in Italy, the best people were reluctant to tolerate the worship of alien gods with its possibilities of unlawful association. Only in a war crisis was the embargo relaxed.

Of Roman history in the second century B.C. we have no contemporary account except for fragments of the later books of Polybius, which do not carry us beyond 146. The extant books of Livy peter out in 167, the year in which Rome conquered Macedonia and augmented her labour-force in Italy by the sale of one hundred and fifty thousand slaves. After that we know Livy only through the work of epitomizers who wrote centuries later. For further knowledge we are dependent on Plutarch and Appian, who lived two to three hundred years after the events, but are valuable in so far as they embody contemporary material inaccessible to us; on miscellaneous allusions in other late authors; and on the not unimportant evidence of inscriptions and coins. The essential facts which emerge are the transformation of Rome from an expanding city-state into a bloated slave-empire; the growth of corruption at home and extortion abroad; the destruction in one year (146) of Rome's two principal commercial rivals, Carthage and Corinth, and the sale of their surviving inhabitants into slavery; the sharpening class struggle in Italy between the rich landowners and the impoverished peasants; and the violent opposition of the senatorial nobility to any attempt at reform—an opposition which, in the case of the two Gracchi and others, did not stick at murder and which, as time went on, made revolution inevitable.

CHAPTER VIII

THE ROMAN REVOLUTION

NOT until the last century B.C. are we again able to read Roman history in the light of contemporary sources. Chief among these are the speeches, letters, and other writings of Cicero, supplemented by the *Commentaries* of Cæsar, the two short tracts (slightly later, but still contemporary) of Sallust, and the life of Atticus by Nepos.

Cicero was born at Arpinum of well-to-do parents in 106 B.C. He spent his youth, like most wealthy Romans of that age, in studying as much Greek philosophy, rhetoric, and general literature as he could put to practical use, and at twenty-five began to practise in the Roman courts. During these years the class struggle in Rome and Italy was at its height. The senatorial nobility, after disposing of the Gracchi, had been forced to utilize the services of the democrat Marius to see them through two serious military crises and to replace the citizen-army, which had decayed with the decay of the peasantry, by a long-term professional soldiery. A few years later an uprising of their Italian allies forced the senate to extend Roman citizenship to the free population of most of Italy. Next year (88 B.C.) Mithridates of Pontus profited by the hatred provoked by Roman oppression in Asia Minor and Greece to make himself temporarily master of the eastern provinces. In this extremity, sooner than see Marius again at the head of an army, the senate gave the command to his aristocratic rival Sulla. There followed seven years of civil convulsion, in which Marius and Sulla alternately massacred each other's supporters, followed in 81 by the dictatorship of Sulla in the senatorial interest. Even after his retirement and death it was clear to all who had eyes to see that the Roman republic had ceased to exist save by leave of the army.

It is a striking example of the blindness which can go with a purely literary education that Cicero to the end of his life never learnt this lesson. During the years after Sulla's death, when Cicero was building up his reputation at the bar, the senatorial régime was protected by the legions of Sulla's lieutenant, Pompey. For five years Pompey was engaged in fighting the revolutionary Sertorius in Spain. How near the régime was to utter overthrow was revealed in 73–71, when, in Pompey's absence, the gladiator Spartacus, at the head of seventy thousand runaway slaves and impoverished peasants, kept the troops of Rome at bay in Italy for two whole years. Finally Spartacus was killed in battle with Crassus, leaving six thousand of his men to line the Appian Way on crosses. Yet Cicero seems never to have doubted the possibility or desirability of that minority of well-to-do Italians, to which he himself belonged, continuing indefinitely, under republican forms, to dominate and exploit the Mediterranean world by such methods as these. His first political speech, in 66 B.C., in which he supports the transfer to Pompey of the supreme command in the war against Mithridates, together with unlimited authority in all the eastern provinces and the right of declaring war and concluding alliances at his discretion, betrays no consciousness of the fact that he is actually making Pompey a dictator. But, while indifferent how much power is given to a man deemed (wrongly as it turned out) to be loyal to the senate, Cicero reacts with the ferocity of his class everywhere and always against any sign of unconstitutional action by the left.

A naïve acceptance of Cicero's version of events led to the popularization, from the Renaissance to the nineteenth century, of a distorted view of the revolution which put an end to the Roman republic. On this view, sedulously propagated by Cicero and perpetuated by later writers who took their facts from him, the revolution was a tragic triumph of vice over virtue. As late as the eighteenth century "Catiline" was the synonym for a murderous conspirator, "Cæsar" for an ambitious and crafty tyrant, "Cato" for a disinterested defender of liberty, and "Brutus" for a heroic tyrannicide. Under the cross-examination of modern scholarship this story dissolves into a legend. Cicero can be called in evidence against himself. Besides making speeches, he wrote three treatises on the art of rhetoric. Among the qualifications which he considers necessary in an orator, strict veracity does not figure; and he certainly did not practise it. If we are to believe his speeches of 63 B.C. against Catiline, that opponent was an inveterate profligate and cut-throat who, as the climax to a career of crime, plotted to burn down Rome and came to a bad end which he had merited many years earlier. Yet we know from Cicero's letters that as late as 65 B.C. he thought of defending Catiline in court and even of running in double harness with him for the consulship. In a speech made when Catiline had long been dead, Cicero tells us that he had the makings of a very fine man, that that very fact made him dangerous, and that he had all but deceived Cicero himself. So versatile a witness should not be taken too seriously.

The fact was that with Pompey, their only general, away in the East, the senatorial nobility were in a shaky position and knew it. The recent revolt of Spartacus had shown them on what a volcano they were living. The land of Italy was being ruined by slave cultivation. The last free peasants were being driven to the wall and starved off their holdings. The danger was that the two classes of the oppressed, the slaves and the free, would join to make an end of the land-grabbing nobles and usurious financiers who called themselves the "republic." Something had to be done to redistribute property and to broaden the basis of citizenship if Rome was to survive. A minority of the ruling class tempered their self-interest with enough enlightenment to see the need of anticipating revolution by reform. But on the whole the men in possession, the "army of the well-to-do" as Cicero complacently calls them,[1] were resolved to do nothing. Naturally enough, the consequence of their obstruction was first an abortive and finally an actual revolution. In 63 B.C. Cicero, having been elected consul over the head of Catiline, successfully opposed a bill for the purchase and distribution of land among the poorer citizens. We still have the speech in which he denounces the commissioners who were to

[1] *Letters to Atticus*, i, 19, 4.

superintend the scheme as "ten kings."[1] Constitutional reform being blocked, people turned to desperate remedies. Catiline stood for the consulship again and rallied the poorer classes in Rome and Italy by proposing the cancellation of debts. The history of the last seventy years had shown that the authors of such projects were apt to come to violent ends; and Catiline was prepared to give blow for blow. He was narrowly defeated at the poll and, assailed by Cicero in the senate with a whirlwind of invective, fled from Rome to join the small army of discharged soldiers, impoverished peasants, and slaves which he had collected. His chief partisans in the city, left to themselves, lost their nerve, and in less than a month were arrested and executed by order of the senate. Early in 62 Catiline fell fighting bravely at the head of his men.

So ended the abortive revolution. For a little while Cicero was able to posture as the man who had saved Rome, and even to write a poem (the loss of which we need not regret) on his exploits as consul. But Nemesis was swift. In 61 Pompey returned from the East. In five years he had added more territory to the Roman Empire than any general since Scipio Africanus. We have no contemporary account of Pompey's campaigns; and their history has to be pieced together from the geographer Strabo, who wrote at second hand, and from such later sources as Josephus, Plutarch, Appian, and Dio. Pompey had put Mithridates to flight and founded new Greek cities in his dominions; he had carried the Roman arms to the Caucasus; he had annexed Syria; he had intervened in a Jewish civil war, stormed Jerusalem, and penetrated its Holy of Holies; he had accepted money and homage from Ptolemy XI of Egypt, the last successor of Alexander now left on a throne; and with it all he had amassed treasure by the million, slaves by the hundred thousand, and a prestige which dwarfed that of all the god-kings added together since Alexander. He came back to find his demands for the resettlement of his veterans and the ratification of his acts in Asia blocked by the senate. Pompey was no revolutionist. He had done the senate good service,

[1] On the Agrarian Law, ii, 6, 15.

and he would do them good service again. But first he would show them who was master. To this end he took into his counsels two men whom he thought he could use. One was his old colleague and rival Crassus, whose enormous wealth, derived from speculation in land, houses, and slaves, made him a useful ally. The other was Gaius Julius Cæsar.

As with all great men, so with Cæsar we must carefully distinguish fact from legend. Ancient and modern historians, writing in the light of the event, have been apt to view Cæsar's whole career as one long preparation for the dictatorial power which he eventually wielded. Plutarch and Suetonius, for example, writing more than a century and a half after Cæsar's death, attribute to Sulla an impossible prophecy that there were "many Marii in Cæsar," and this at a time when Cæsar was at most twenty-one years old.[1] Obviously it is the kind of prediction which gossip would invent in after years. The fact is that until middle life Cæsar must have been less interested in power than in personal survival. In the words of Guglielmo Ferrero (a severe critic of Cæsar), "the man whom almost all modern historians naïvely regard as resolved from his earliest youth to undertake, single-handed, the government of the world, and whose life is described as a continuous and calculated effort towards the supreme goal of his ambition, had . . . more than any other distinguished man of his time been exposed to the merciless buffeting of events."[2] He was suspect to the ruling party from the very start as the nephew of Marius and the son-in-law of the Marian Cinna. That a young man so circumstanced should have defied the command of Sulla to divorce his wife proves both his conjugal devotion and his courage. When we add that on his first military campaign he was awarded the "civic crown" (the Roman equivalent of the Victoria Cross), that on later campaigns his physical endurance was notorious, that his soldiers were fanatically devoted to him, and that not even his worst enemy denied

---

[1] According to the traditional chronology Cæsar was born in 100 B.C.; but there are good reasons for dating his birth in 102. The alleged prediction was in 81.

[2] Ferrero, *The Greatness and Decline of Rome*, vol. I, chap. xviii.

his temperance in diet,[1] we shall rate at their true value the
charge of sexual inversion and the taunt, " every woman's
man and every man's woman," hurled at him by a rancorous
senator in the heat of debate.[2] The senate had no Speaker
to call honorable members to order. Such stories tell us
nothing of the character of Cæsar, but much of the venom of
party passion in the last years of the Roman republic.

Up to his thirtieth year, Cæsar, apart from his scrape with
Sulla, was chiefly engaged in military service and in the study
of Greek oratory and Greek science. His rhetorical training
placed him, by the admission even of his rival Cicero, second
to none among the public speakers of the day. Disinterested
scientific curiosity was a far rarer trait in the Roman world.
The great age of ancient science, the age of Euclid, Aris-
tarchus, Archimedes, Eratosthenes, and Hipparchus, was
over. Scientific progress depends on experiment; and a
society in which all manual work is done by slaves is more
favourable to armchair philosophy than to physical discovery.
Cæsar is one of the few Romans recorded to have taken any
interest in Greek science. Perhaps we may attribute to that
the total absence of superstition which Suetonius numbers
among his leading traits. It was certainly calculated to make
him impatient with men who could let a military operation
depend on the look of a victim's entrails or could stop public
business by hauling down a flag. Nevertheless there is no
contemporary evidence that before his consulship Cæsar had
any thought of dictatorial power. The senatorial party, who
hated him as he never hated them, would have been glad to
see Cæsar involved with Catiline. He opposed the execution
of the revolutionary leaders at considerable risk to himself,
but otherwise kept in the background. In fact during these
years Cæsar was only in the second rank of politicians, less
powerful than Crassus and far less powerful than Pompey.
Had the two older men deemed him capable of becoming

---

[1] Cato is said to have described Cæsar as " the only man who undertook
to overthrow the State sober." Suetonius, *Julius*, LIII.

[2] Suetonius adduces as evidence for the charge a bantering song sung
by soldiers at Cæsar's triumph. Such evidence will impress no one
acquainted with the sort of songs soldiers sing even in our refined age.

their rival, they would assuredly themselves have taken the consulship in 59 instead of putting him forward.

The events of 59 turned Cæsar into a revolutionist in spite of himself. They showed him, firstly, that the senatorial nobility were impervious to reason on the question of land reform and, secondly, that they were helpless when tackled by a man without superstition and with the army on his side. He began his consulship by enacting that the proceedings of the senate and the popular assembly should be published from day to day. This record, posted in public places in Rome under the title of *Acta Diurna*, was the first newspaper known to history. Having thus ensured the maximum publicity for his measures, he brought in a bill, very similar to that rejected in 63, for the purchase and distribution of land to discharged soldiers and poorer citizens. The senate, as usual, resorting to obstruction, Cæsar called in Pompey and his veterans and carried the bill over the heads of the senate by a vote of the people. The other consul, Bibulus, who declared the omens unfavourable to the conduct of public business, and the proceedings, therefore, null and void, was contemptuously ignored; and further measures agreeable to Cæsar, Pompey, and Crassus were voted by popular acclamation. The senate found itself prisoner to a " three-headed monster " against which there was no appeal.

Cæsar had now taken his first revolutionary step. He could not count indefinitely on the support of two such natural conservatives as Pompey and Crassus. To avoid the fate of the Gracchi and of Catiline it was necessary that on quitting office he should have an army behind him. This Cæsar achieved by having the proconsulship of Gaul[1] voted to himself. It was further necessary to prevent the senate from upsetting these arrangements behind his back. Cæsar there-fore allied himself with the raffish young aristocratic dema-gogue, Clodius, and through his agency introduced the free distribution of corn to the poorer citizens. Further, they were allowed to combine freely in guilds (*collegia*), thus creating

[1] I.e. Cisalpine Gaul in northern Italy, plus the transalpine province of Gallia Narbonensis (modern Provence and Languedoc). The rest of Gaul was not Roman until conquered by Cæsar.

a permanent democratic organization in opposition to the senate. Finally, Cicero having refused Cæsar's offer of a place on his staff in Gaul, Clodius was allowed to drive him into exile and outlawry for his illegal execution of the Catilinarians four years before. Having thus robbed the senate of its authority and its ablest leader, Cæsar in 58 left for his province.

Cæsar has himself told us the story of his conquest of Gaul and of the events which led to his dictatorship. The *Gallic War* is the simple, unadorned, impersonal narrative of a seven years' war by the chief actor in it. If Cicero had had the telling of it, we can imagine how he would have embroidered and embellished it, how he would have lauded himself and disparaged his adversaries. Cæsar at least paints himself, as Cromwell would have said, "warts and all." He left the work unfinished, the last of the eight books being added by his officer Hirtius. In many respects it is not a pretty story. We cannot help recoiling as we are coolly told that fifty-three thousand of the Aduatuci (a Belgic tribe) were sold as slaves to the dealers who accompanied the army; that the people of the Veneti (round the modern town of Vannes) were similarly treated; that a rebellious chief of the Senones (round Sens) was flogged to death; that at Avaricum (Bourges) the entire population was massacred; and that at Uxellodunum (Puy d'Issolu), where the Gauls made their last stand in 51, all prisoners had their right hands cut off. This last we learn from Hirtius. Cæsar was not more cruel than other ancient conquerors. Alexander and many other empire-builders had been as bad. But in Cæsar's case his generosity to opponents at Rome contrasts violently with his ruthless application of the rules of war in Gaul. The fact is that we are here faced with one of the salient contradictions of Roman history. Italy was being ruined by slave labour. Cæsar knew, as every enlightened man knew, that the future of Rome depended on the revival of free agriculture. It was one of the chief objects of his domestic policy. Yet he could not afford to be less successful in the West than Pompey in the East. For a century and more the main criterion of success at Rome had been the acquisition of new lands, new loot, and new human chattels. So in the course of his Gallic campaigns Cæsar flooded Italy, just as Pompey and earlier conquerors had done, with hundreds of thousands of slaves, whose importation made the revival of free agriculture impossible.

In extenuation we must remember that Gaul, when invaded by Cæsar, was not a free country. The aborigines, the little dark people known as Iberian, whose blood still flows in the veins of most Frenchmen and whose language may survive in Basque, had centuries before been reduced to serfdom (except in the extreme south-west) by tall, blonde Celtic and Belgic invaders from over the Rhine. The aristocracy treated their serfs as barbaric aristocracies usually do; and, while the nobility were quickly civilized and Romanized, the peasant mass (apart from those sold into slavery) were probably no worse off for the change of masters. We may doubt, indeed, whether the status and way of life of the Gallic peasantry altered very much from Cæsarian times to the Revolution of 1789. They changed their lords, their language, their religion, and their name, but not their serfdom.

Of special interest to us is Cæsar's account of his invasion of Britain. In the course of conquering Gaul it came to his notice that British tribes were sending help to their kinsmen across the Channel. He therefore led two punitive expeditions to the island, and on the second occasion (54 B.C.) penetrated north of the Thames. Considered as a military operation, the expedition was a fiasco; for the tribute which he imposed was never paid or enforced. But it established regular contact between Mediterranean civilization and Britain, which until then had been barely " on the map." [1] Cæsar therefore writes of Britain not as a conqueror, but as an explorer and with the disinterested curiosity of a student of Greek science. He tells his readers of a country even more barbaric than Gaul. Only the south grows corn and has a veneer of civilization. The midlanders are hunters and herdsmen, ignorant of agriculture and clad in skins. As to marriage, "ten or twelve men, usually the brothers of a

---

[1] The voyage of Pytheas of Marseilles in the time of Alexander had never been followed up.

family, or fathers and sons, have wives in common; the children, however, are reckoned to belong to him who first cohabited with the mother."[1] The similarity of this ancient British custom to the *punaluan* or group marriage discovered by Lewis H. Morgan in Hawaii in the nineteenth century is obvious, and renders inexcusable Andrew Lang's doubt whether it ever existed as an institution.[2]

The Roman upper class were far less interested in such matters than in the chances of freeing themselves from the grip of the " three-headed monster." So long as Pompey and Cæsar held together there was no hope. " The two ' in-laws ' (*socer generque*) have ruined everything," ran the saying in the smart set, in allusion to Pompey's union with Cæsar's daughter Julia. We have a miniature picture of Roman society at this time and its attitude to its rulers in the lyrics of Catullus, all written between 62 or 61 B.C. and his death in 54 at the age of thirty. They include some of the loveliest and some of the filthiest verses in all literature. Nothing could be lovelier than his lyrics to " Lesbia " (in real life Clodia, the dissipated sister of the demagogue Clodius), the elegy on his dead brother, or the poem which celebrates his home-coming from provincial drudgery to his beloved Sirmio on the lake of Garda, and which in its turn inspired one of the loveliest poems of Tennyson.[3] Nothing could be more disgusting, less poetical, or less witty than the lampoons of Catullus on his rivals. One feels that a society which could enjoy such dull garbage did not deserve freedom. His choicest abuse is aimed at Cæsar and his engineer officer Mamurra, who, besides making a pile in Gaul, seems to have crossed Catullus in some love affair. It is characteristic of Cæsar that he rewarded this young gentleman of Verona, who had lampooned him in the language of the stews, with an invitation to dinner.

A more measured attack on the power-politics of the day is found in the didactic poem of Lucretius, the great Epicurean, who was some years older than Catullus and died a

---

[1] Cæsar, *Gallic War*, v, 14.

[2] *Encyclopædia Britannica*, thirteenth edition, article " Family."

[3] Tennyson, *Frater Ave Atque Vale*.

little before him. We know no details of the life of Lucretius. The silly story that he wrote his poem in the lucid
intervals of insanity induced by a love-philtre can be dismissed with the contempt which it deserves. Though a
Roman and probably a patrician, he is significantly silent on
the subject of Roman greatness. His poem *On the Nature of
Things* breathes a horror of war and cruelty, and a burning
hatred of the religion which was used to justify them. His
nearest approach to a faith is a natural piety towards the life-
process, which he personifies as *Alma Venus* in the opening
lines of his poem. But on priestcraft, as a prompter of evil
deeds, he declares uncompromising war. Those who think
his denunciation of the legendary sacrifice of Iphigenia strained
and rhetorical must remember that in his time human sacrifices were still offered in some parts of the Roman Empire.
Against official religion he pits the Epicurean doctrine that life
is of natural origin and death, its necessary end, not to be feared.
From ignorance of this simple truth arises the mad struggle
for power.

> Pitiful souls of men !   O hearts all blind and unseeing !
> Lo, how deep is the darkness of life, how great are the dangers
> Ringing your fill of days !   Why see ye not that for nature
> One thing alone is needful, that pain be kept from the body
> And that the soul rejoice and be free from sorrows and terrors? . . .
> Nor will the body the sooner be quit of a fiery fever,
> Tossed on a purple couch with rich embroidery woven,
> Than on a humble bed with a threadbare coverlet o'er thee.
> Since, then, for bodily weal no hoarded treasure availeth—
> No, nor the pride of rank can avail, nor the glory of empire—
> Think not by such toys that the soul is profited either.
> Say that before thine eyes the field is alive with legions
> Aping the pomp of war and marching in mimic manœuvre—
> Strong reserves in the rear, and on each flank cavalry stationed—
> Marshalled in goodly array and moving as one to thy order :
> Canst thou, for all this show, thy soul from religion deliver,
> Scaring its ghost from thy heart?   Art free from fear of thy ending?
> Hast thou a care-free breast and a mind all empty of terror,
> Seeing thy fleet sail forth and deploy itself on the waters?
> Nay, but we know these shows are a mockery all and a plaything.
> Truly the fears of man and the cares that shadow his pathway
> Yield not to clashing of arms or to lethal onset of arrows,
> Neither regard they the king on his throne nor the master of empire,
> Neither the glitter of gold nor the shimmering glory of purple :

Freedom of soul, be assured, is achieved by nothing but reason.
Is not the whole of life, moreover, a struggle in darkness?
Even as in black gloom do children tremble at all things,
Fearing to go in the dark, so we ofttimes in the day-time
Shrink back afraid from things that are no whit more to be dreaded
Than those bugbears false that in darkness terrify children.
All this terror of mind and all this darkness of spirit
Neither the rays of the sun can dispel nor the shafts of the daylight—
Only the shape of nature herself and the law of her being.[1]

Lucretius probably died in 55 B.C., and Catullus in 54. In
the latter year also died Julia, Cæsar's daughter and Pompey's
wife, and with her the last obstacle to Pompey's reconciliation
with the senate. In 53 the defeat and death of Crassus in
Parthia left the two masters of the Roman world face to face
without an intermediary.

Our two contemporary authorities for the ensuing years
are Cicero's later letters and Cæsar's *Civil War*, each of which
can be used to check the other. For filling in the gaps Plutarch, Suetonius, Appian, and Dio are useful, provided always
that we remember their late dates. From 52 to 50 the two
sides manœuvre for position. Pompey, the political heir of
Sulla, aspires to the rôle of saviour of society from all subversive movements, of which in the existing state of Italy
there are plenty to fear. The senate, *faute de mieux*, is ready
to welcome him in that capacity. To that end it is essential
that Cæsar, the revolutionary of 59, shall be disarmed. But
for Cæsar to disarm is to put his head in a noose. He refuses
to disarm unless Pompey does so too. So the manœuvring
goes on, until in 49 the senate forces the issue by an ultimatum,
Cæsar crosses the Rubicon, and civil war begins. In appearance it is a struggle between Rome's oldest and most honoured
military hero, standing for law, order, and the rights of
property, and a revolutionary general leading an army of
peasant-soldiers to the plunder of the rich. The rich make a
pitiable exhibition. Pompey, the senate, and a long train of
terror-stricken property-owners abandon Rome in a panic;
and Cæsar and his legions move in. But there is no plundering. Cæsar is a masterly opportunist. He has won the devotion of his soldiers by addressing them as " comrades," sharing

[1] Lucretius, II, 14–19, 34–61.

their hardships and dangers, and letting them loot freely in Gaul; but he has them well in hand. In the hour of victory Rome is astonished at his moderation. He sets his prisoners free, invites Cicero and other runaway senators to return, and does nothing more revolutionary than promise doles to the poorer citizens. He thus makes sure of Italy while he defeats first Pompey's officers in Spain (who are forced by their own men to surrender) and then Pompey himself in Greece. At Pharsalus, seeing the enemy routed or dead, he exclaims: " They would have it so! "[1] Pompey escapes to Egypt and is murdered there. Cicero, out of his element in a civil war and shocked by the ferocious threats of the beaten party, profits by Cæsar's clemency and returns to Rome.

Cæsar is now dictator—but dictator by grace of his legionaries. He uses his victory to extend Roman citizenship to Cisalpine Gaul, where many of his soldiers were recruited; to relieve economic distress in Rome and Italy by remitting a year's rent to poorer tenants; to distribute gratuities to his officers and men, and doles to common citizens; to reorganize finance and local government in Italy; to encourage free agriculture by obliging graziers to employ one free labourer in three; and to plant colonies overseas. Most of these measures are palliatives and, for reasons already indicated, without lasting effect. Of more permanent importance than any is the reform of the calendar. Here we see the student of Greek science at his best. The old Roman calendar, ascribed by tradition to the mythical Numa, was based on the lunar month and had to be brought into line with the solar year by periodically intercalating an extra month. The priests responsible for the intercalation followed no strict rule, and by the time of Cæsar had got the calendar into an indescribable muddle. Cæsar called in the Greek astronomer Sosigenes to bring order out of chaos, and with his help instituted the Julian calendar—an improvement on any method of time-measurement previously known. It was to be sixteen centuries before mounting discrepancies necessitated closer adjustment.

The story of Cæsar's end is so coloured for English readers

[1] Suetonius, *Julius*, XXX—citing Pollio, who was there.

by Shakespeare's play that we have difficulty in adjusting ourselves to the real facts. The genius of the poet has painted in masterly fashion the picture of a pompous, posturing old gentleman without an idea in his head, who for some obscure reason has managed to become the uncrowned king of Rome; of the lean and hungry Cassius, the noble Brutus, and their friends stabbing him to death for his ambition; of the wily Antony fooling these amateurish tyrannicides into letting him harangue the mob at Cæsar's funeral; of a typical Shakespearean mob veering from side to side and throwing up their sweaty night-caps now for Cæsar, now for Brutus, and now for Antony; and of Brutus and Cassius riding "like madmen through the gates of Rome," with Antony, Octavius, and Cæsar's ghost hard on their track, until they fall on their own swords at Philippi.

What Cæsar really was and really did we have seen. The plot against him was hatched partly by members of the beaten senatorial nobility and partly by disgruntled careerists of his own party. Cassius, the ringleader of the conspiracy, was typical of the former. Lean he may have been; but we may be sure that this competent and rapacious soldier never went hungry. His brother-in-law, Marcus Brutus, is one of the most undeservedly idealized characters in history. No one could be less like the real Brutus than Shakespeare's "noblest Roman of them all." He was one of Cicero's circle and, like Cicero, posed as a philosopher and moralist. That did not prevent him from lending money to provincials at the lucrative rate of forty-eight per cent, and stickling for repayment to the uttermost farthing—a fact which makes the tirade against extortion, put into his mouth by Shakespeare, read like a bad joke. Both Cassius and Brutus had submitted to Cæsar after Pharsalus and had been rewarded with office and honour. They drew into their counsels men like Trebonius and Decimus Brutus (a relation of Marcus), who had held command under Cæsar, but had now become jealous of his power; and others to the number of at least sixty. Such was the company who on the Ides of March, 44 B.C., hemmed in and despatched with twenty-three daggers an elderly man armed only with a *stilus*. The story of his last words to

Brutus is plain invention. Cæsar was probably past utterance, if not dead, before Brutus got in his blow. If any words escaped the dying man, who would remember them in the scuffle?

Two opposite reactions to the assassination—one of privileged, the other of common folk—are worth noting. On the one hand we have Cicero's short, delighted letter to a conspirator. "Congratulations! I am overjoyed. I wish you well. I am at your service. Wish me well and let me know what you are doing and what is afoot."[1] On the other hand we have Suetonius' account of the funeral in the Forum.

> "The throng of bystanders heaped dry branches on the pyre, benches, judges' seats, and whatever else would serve as an offering. . . . Veterans of the legions threw into the flames the arms with which they had accoutred themselves for the funeral. Many women, too, threw in the jewels which they wore and the amulets and robes of their children. At the height of the public grief a multitude of foreigners went about lamenting, each after the manner of his nation—above all, the Jews, who night after night flocked to the place of cremation."[2]

Cicero's delight was premature. Cæsar had been the main moderating influence in his own party. With his death the demand of the people and the legions for vengeance became irresistible. The traditional story, immortalized by Shakespeare, of a pliable mob lashed to fury by a designing Antony is unhistorical. Cicero's correspondence, our main contemporary authority, makes no allusion to the alleged inflammatory speech. We hear of it for the first time in his *Philippics*, composed nearly a year later; and Cicero the orator, unless corroborated, is not a safe witness. Antony was a tough soldier, useful on the battlefield, but without, so far as can be traced, an idea in his head except those normal to his kind. Cæsar's assassination found him quite unprepared for desperate courses. At the funeral, according to the credible

[1] *Letters to his Friends*, VI, 15. [2] *Julius*, LXXXIV.

account preserved by Suetonius, he ordered a herald to read out the honours voted to Cæsar by the senate, but himself said very little. He was undoubtedly inclined to accept the accomplished fact and conciliate the assassins. Far from inciting the popular riots which followed the funeral, he repressed them as consul to the best of his ability, hurling the ringleaders from the Tarpeian rock and crucifying slaves who participated. Only after the lapse of a month, when it was plain that the people, and above all the soldiers, were implacable, that they had unofficially deified Cæsar and expected vengeance for his murder, that they were only waiting for a leader, and that if Antony did not lead them they would find someone else, did Antony begin to cast himself for the part of Cæsar's successor. And by then someone else was on the scene.

Cæsar's grand-nephew, Octavian, the future Augustus, was by nature no more a revolutionary than Antony. He came of a rich family at Velitræ (Velletri) in Latium. His father, Gaius Octavius, had in 63 B.C. wiped out a remnant of the revolutionary armies of Spartacus and Catiline in southern Italy. The rôle of revolutionary leader was forced on his son by circumstances not of his seeking. Cæsar had made him his principal heir and adopted him. Family loyalty, of which this youth of eighteen was not devoid, would prompt him to avenge his uncle and benefactor. As Antony, who was in authority, made no move and repelled his advances, Octavian turned to the legions. Months of manœuvring followed—Antony and Octavian each trying to win the soldiers; Cicero, an old fool to the end, mistaking his man and trying to use Octavian to prop up the doomed republic against Antony; and the soldiers not caring who led them, so long as they were led to victory, vengeance, and booty. In the end the veterans in 43 forced Antony and Octavian to compose their feud and march on Rome. This time there were no half-measures. The men who had sowed the wind reaped the whirlwind. Antony, Octavian, and Lepidus, created by a popular vote " triumvirs for the reconstitution of the State," executed out of hand two thousand three hundred of the Roman upper class—Cicero among the first—

and confiscated their property. In the graphic words of Ferrero:

> " Those who had spoiled the world were now despoiled; a retired muleteer held the consulship, an outward and visible sign of the political triumph of the poor over the rich; while the vast fortunes amassed within the circuit walls of Rome and drawn from the ruin of many a shattered civilization were abandoned to a horde drunk with the lust of plunder." [1]

In 42 a popular vote officially deified the dead Cæsar, and Nemesis overtook Cassius and Brutus on the field of Philippi. Let Suetonius sum up the matter in his own words:

> " Hardly any of Cæsar's assassins survived him for more than three years, or died a natural death. They were all condemned, and they perished in various ways —some by shipwreck, some in battle; some took their own lives with the self-same dagger with which they had impiously slain Cæsar." [2]

With the end of Cicero's letters we lose, after twenty-five years in his company, an unrivalled contemporary commentator on events. Of the sequel we have no continuous first-hand account, though many extracts are embodied in works of later times. The important contemporary inscription known as the *Monumentum Ancyranum* (because the best preserved copy is at Ankara in Turkey), in which Augustus records his own life-work, though authoritative, is of necessity partial and no more than a summary. The poems of Virgil and Horace throw some light on the events of the time, at least as reflected in the opinion of their set. For fuller information we are dependent in the main on Plutarch, Suetonius, Appian, and Dio.

The Roman nobility had been liquidated; and the legions

---

[1] *The Greatness and Decline of Rome*, vol. III, chap. xi. The " retired muleteer " was Ventidius Bassus, one of Cæsar's *parvenu* officers and a zealous avenger of his death.

[2] *Julius*, LXXXIX.

had entered into its inheritance. But neither Antony nor Octavian was at heart a revolutionary. It had been necessary to avenge Cæsar and to reward the legionaries, on whom their power depended, with land, slaves, and other property confiscated from the wealthy. That done, it was necessary to consolidate the new order. It was to the interest of each triumvir, if he could, while retaining the support of the soldiery, to forestall his colleagues in assuming the rôle of "saviour of society." Thus Antony in 41, through his brother Lucius, tried to sabotage the distribution of land in Italy, and so discredit Octavian with the veterans, while himself gaining credit with the owners of property. But the veterans rallied to Octavian, the landowners' revolt fizzled out, and Antony had to disavow his agents. The triumvirs were temporarily reconciled by a common danger. Sextus Pompeius, the son of Pompey, had seized Sicily and was threatening Italy with a fleet and army manned largely with slaves recruited by a promise of freedom. In 36 Octavian defeated Sextus and proved himself a pillar of society by returning thirty thousand slaves to their owners. Thenceforward the cards were in his hands. All Italy rallied to the former revolutionary who had so convincingly proved his devotion to law and order. Significantly, it was just then that Octavian was for the first time invested with the "tribunician authority" which made him constitutionally sacrosanct. No reward could be too great for the saviour of slave society. While Antony, fatally entangled with Cleopatra, addressed abusive letters to him from Alexandria, Octavian, brilliantly aided by Agrippa, consolidated his popularity in Italy by public works and doles, and successfully represented himself as the defender of Roman institutions against Oriental despotism. Nevertheless he was not allowed to forget to whom he owed his power. In the very year of Actium and in the very hour of victory he had to cope with a mutiny of soldiers demanding discharge and gratuities. He was able to meet them only when he had annexed Egypt, enriched himself and Rome with the accumulated treasure of the Ptolemies, and returned to Italy more indisputably master of the world than Sulla, Pompey, or even Julius had been before him.

The part played in these events by Cleopatra has given rise to a famous speculation. How far would the course of history have been materially different if her personal charms, her intellectual endowments, or both had been less remarkable than they were? How far, in short, are human affairs determined by mere accident? The question betrays a curious misapprehension of the situation. Cleopatra—an extraordinary woman—in an age when Oriental thrones were toppling before the power of Rome, tried to save her own by fascinating first one Roman general and then another. If thrones could be saved in that kind of way, no doubt she would have succeeded. Let us suppose that she had been less irresistible. Antony in that case might not have fallen in love with her, might have avoided the blunders which alienated Italy, and might have retained enough support in the West to outmatch Octavian. In that event Antony, not Octavian, would have annexed Egypt and founded the first imperial dynasty. But even if he had done so, the government set up in the Roman Empire would not have been very different from that established by his rival. The principate, or military dictatorship functioning under republican forms, which lasted from Augustus to Diocletian was a product not of the personality of its founder, but of the conditions of the problem. It was impossible that the Roman ruling class should continue to dominate the Mediterranean world through an army recruited no longer to any considerable extent in Rome, but over the length and breadth of Italy, and attached far more closely to its officers than to the senate and magistrates of the republic. Political power had to conform to reality, not to a fiction. In the absence of any representative system, this meant vesting political power in the commander of the army. The dictatorship of Julius, the triumvirate of Antony, Octavian, and Lepidus, and the principate of Augustus were so many recognitions of this simple fact. But in order that the new machinery might work with a minimum of disturbance to the social order, republican appearances had to be kept up, magistrates elected in due form, and the iron hand of dictatorship concealed as far as possible in a velvet glove. As to this, there was no real difference between Antony and Octavian. The idea that Antony, if victorious, would have treated republican forms with less ceremony than Octavian is not borne out by the evidence. Even at the height of his infatuation with Cleopatra he never styled himself king, but always triumvir or *imperator*. The rivalry of the two men was personal, not political. Each from time to time might try to outbid the other for the support of the people, the senate, or the legions; each from time to time might try to discredit the other by demagogy; but each, in the event of success, must inevitably have made the same kind of settlement. How little lasting difference was made by Actium is shown by the fact that three-quarters of a century later Rome was ruled by the emperor Claudius—a grandson of Antony and a grand-nephew of Augustus. After a full century neither triumvir had any descendants left. The dynastic issue was ephemeral. But the principate, the product of the revolution, survived.

One further fact is worth noting about the Roman revolution. In appearance it replaced free institutions by a dictatorship. Hence the legend which the eloquence of Cicero, reinforced by second-hand authorities like Plutarch, was able to impose on Europe from the revival of learning until recent times. The free Roman republic, in which the people were sovereign, and magistrates and generals their obedient servants, became an ideal which all reformers and all revolutionists aspired to realize in the modern world. Actually, even if we ignore the slavery on which it was based, the republic could not, except in the thinnest theoretical sense, be called a democracy. In the partnership of the "senate and people of Rome" the senate, a close corporation of wealthy ex-magistrates, was always predominant. It was in permanent session and in control of day-to-day administration, foreign affairs and finance; and its members as a matter of course used the opportunities of office to feather their nests. The popular assembly, though theoretically sovereign and with direct powers of legislation, was difficult to convene, and increasingly so as citizenship was extended first to the Latin cities and then by degrees to the whole of Italy. Only the most wealthy and leisured class of Italian could travel to Rome to vote. In the last age of the republic there was no force, with the single exception of the legions, capable of opposing the irresponsible power of the senate and ending its intolerable misgovernment of Italy and the provinces. The revolution carried out by Cæsar, Antony, and Octavian (largely, as we have seen, in spite of themselves) was doubtless illegal, violent, and sanguinary. It doubtless destroyed free institutions, if the unlimited freedom of the senatorial nobility to obstruct necessary reforms by political chicanery can be dignified by that phrase. But at least it put an end to the unlimited plunder of the Mediterranean world by the plutocracy of a single city-state. It opened a career to the free Italians who had till then fought the battles of Roman imperialism without any proportionate share in its winnings, and it thereby paved the way for a yet wider extension of citizenship under the later empire. The fault of the Roman revolution lay not in what it did, but in what it did not do. Slavery remained the basis of the social fabric. Three-fourths of the population of the Roman world were still the chattels of the other fourth. In that fact lay the canker which, notwithstanding the best-devised imperial administration, was to eat away the heart of the Roman Empire and to bring about its decline and fall.

CHAPTER IX

THE EAST GOES WEST

THE history of the early Roman emperors is indelibly coloured by the sombre pen of Tacitus. This greatest of Roman historians was born early in the reign of Nero, entered public life under Vespasian, and held high office under Domitian, Nerva, and Trajan. He wrote his *Histories* early in the last-named emperor's reign and the *Annals* later. Although he was for the most part not contemporary with the events related in the *Annals*, we know that he used contemporary sources. Some of them he names—among them the *Acta Diurna*, the lost memoirs of the empress Agrippina, and the lost history of the elder Pliny. The credit we attach to Tacitus will depend to a large extent on our estimate of his sources; but his incisive style and passionate conviction place him head and shoulders above any other Latin historian.

Apart from inscriptions and coins, our other evidence is poor in quality. The one extant contemporary historian of the early empire, Velleius Paterculus, wrote under Tiberius. He is as partial to the emperors as Tacitus is hostile, and a far inferior writer. The Jew Josephus, who wrote a little before Tacitus, though an invaluable authority on the small corner of the empire with which he is concerned, has little to say on the main current of events. Suetonius, a junior contemporary of Tacitus and author of the *Lives of the Cæsars*, was secretary to the emperor Hadrian, and as such must have had access to much inside information on earlier reigns, but is a credulous gossip quite incapable of putting his information to critical use, and observes next to no chronology. Our remaining authority, Dio, wrote his history a century after Tacitus and Suetonius, when the empire was in full decline and heading for disruption. Like Suetonius, he held official posts and had access to important material, but he was superstitious and uncritical, and his work is poor stuff. Unfortunately we are dependent on Suetonius and Dio for periods in the early empire not covered by Tacitus, including the whole reign of Augustus.

Suetonius and Dio tell us that, after the defeat of Antony, Octavian (as he then still was) thought of restoring the republic. There is no reason to doubt that, if the thing had been possible, he would have done it. As we have seen, Octavian was not at heart a revolutionary. The rôle had been thrust on him by the army in spite of himself. As soon as he safely could, he had shown himself a friend of property and order. Once Antony was out of the way, his tired and often sickly rival would have been pleased enough, no doubt, to take a rest and let the republic run itself. But that was the very last thing desired by the frightened property-owners whom he had saved from social revolution. The logic of the situation required that the commander of the army should rule; and so long as he ruled with due regard to their interests and dignity, the senate were content to have it so. So were the people, if they could be sure of their daily bread; and the soldiers, if they could be sure of gratuities and land. The conquest of Egypt, with its treasure and its cornfields, had put Octavian in the happy position of being able to please everybody. Senate and people, soldiers and civilians held out their hands in one rapacious cringe, and were not disappointed. The unlimited powers heaped on him, the sacred title of Augustus voted him by the senate, and the adulatory language of Virgil and Horace were the natural reward of the man who had ended the Roman revolution and glutted Italy with the loot of Egypt.

The essentially conservative policy of Augustus showed itself in the establishment of a high property qualification for the senate, in the expulsion of two hundred *parvenus* who had entered it during the revolution, in the discontinuance of the publication of its proceedings, in the stiffening of military discipline,[1] in the limits set to the manumission of slaves,

[1] Once the civil wars were over, Augustus never addressed his men as " comrades " and forbade the use of this familiarity by others. It was no longer the army of the revolution, but of the State.

in the exclusion of freedmen from enlistment in the army, and in legislation for the revival of religion and the enforcement of a stern sexual morality. Such legislation was both unpopular and futile. Its main outcome was two major scandals in the imperial family, when Augustus, caught in his own net, had to banish first his daughter Julia, then ten years later his granddaughter, of the same name, for adultery. A minor result was the banishment of the poet Ovid, the light-hearted singer of illicit love, who was implicated somehow in this imperial *cause célèbre*.

It was not so easy to dodge the logic of events. In taking over the East, Augustus had assumed, whether he liked it or not, the functions of the god-king. At Rome he lived with studied simplicity, avoiding any semblance of regal or dictatorial power, voting and canvassing at elections, giving evidence in court and submitting to cross-examination like an ordinary citizen. But in the East he was a Pharaoh, an Alexander, a king of kings and lord of lords. He could not, even if he wished, stop the provinces from erecting temples in his honour. From the East the cult soon spread to the West. Augustus could only insist that such temples should be dedicated jointly to Rome and himself, and refuse to sanction their erection in Italy. Even there and at Rome itself the *plebs*, half Oriental in composition owing to the continued importation and manumission of slaves, extended to Augustus in his lifetime the unofficial deification which they had bestowed on Julius immediately after his death. To them Augustus was the heir and avenger of Julius. He had smashed the power of the senate, he had given Rome corn from Egypt and brave shows, he had kept peace at home, and withal he had mixed with them as a plain citizen. Therefore they forgave him much.

The *Annals* of Tacitus open with the death of Augustus in A.D. 14 at the age of seventy-five. From his first page Tacitus gives us the impression of a man with great literary, but little critical, power, boiling over with a violent and long-repressed indignation. Not till recently, he says in effect— not till the time of Nerva and Trajan, in which his historical works were written—has it been possible to tell the truth about the empire. Now, " without bitterness or partiality," [1] Tacitus will tell it. A dreadful thing has happened to Rome. For material benefits, for peace, for cheap food, for administrative efficiency, she has bartered away her freedom. The essential mischief was done under Augustus. By the time he died full of years and honours, " how few were left who had seen the republic!" [2] The results of the mischief are to be read in a sickening story of tyranny at the top, sycophancy below, and universal degeneracy which Tacitus unfolds in detail until the *Annals* break off in the middle of Nero's reign of terror.

Tacitus is undoubtedly right in his contention that the Roman Empire was a degenerate society. What we miss is any attempt, such as Thucydides would have made, to treat that degeneracy scientifically. Roman society under the late republic and empire, like Greek society after the Persian wars, illustrates in anticipation Abraham Lincoln's dictum that a State " cannot endure permanently half slave and half free." In the Roman world the proportion was not even half and half, but something more like three slaves to one freeman. In such a society it was impossible that any institution from the family to the State, from daily work to daily recreation, should not be tainted. We see the effect in the economic decline of Italy : what dignity was there in labour when hordes of slaves were being imported to do all that was necessary? We see it in the extinction of public spirit : who cared for forms of government when the main business of the State was the repression of the majority for the sake of the minority? We see it in the lubricity of poets and satirists : what kind of refinement could be expected when every man of property had an establishment of human chattels among whom to gratify his itch for varied sexual experience? Finally we see it in the rapidly growing profusion and popularity of gladiatorial shows. The fact that, while ten thousand gladiators fought during the whole reign of Augustus, an equal number are said to have perished in four months of Trajan's reign speaks more eloquently of Roman degeneracy than anything recorded by Tacitus or Suetonius.

[1] Tacitus, *Annals*, I, 1.   [2] Ibid., 3.

Instead of seeking for causes, Tacitus seeks for scapegoats, and finds them in individual emperors. Of these not one escapes the lash, but Tiberius is the whipping-boy in chief. The portrait of this emperor by Tacitus is such that we have only to read it critically, carefully distinguishing fact from comment, to see that something is wrong. Tacitus plays a game of "heads I win, tails you lose." If Tiberius recalls a general, it is from jealousy; if he prolongs his command, it is because he is too lazy to make a change or because he grudges promotion to others. If he refuses to relieve an impoverished senator, he is pitiless; if he relieves sufferers from a disastrous fire, it is to "turn the calamity to his own glory."[1] Tacitus rings the changes on this kind of innuendo indefinitely. Few reputations could stand up to such a barrage. His final summary of the character of Tiberius has only to be read to be disbelieved by anyone not hypnotized by the prestige of a classic author. Under Augustus, that is until the age of fifty-four, Tiberius, we are told, enjoyed an excellent reputation. After succeeding to the empire, for nine years he craftily assumed virtues which he did not possess. For another six years "he was a compound of good and evil." In his seventieth year he became cruel and debauched, but "veiled his debaucheries" in deference to his wicked minister Sejanus. At last, at the ripe age of seventy-one, after executing Sejanus, Tiberius indulged his vicious inclinations without fear or shame.[2]

This is a psychological chimera. No such monster of delayed iniquity ever wore human shape. Light is thrown on the matter by the fact that one of Tacitus' authorities, and probably his main authority for what went on in the palace, was Agrippina, grand-niece of Tiberius and mother of Nero. There could hardly be a worse witness. A woman who sold herself to her uncle Claudius for the sake of power and then poisoned him for the sake of more power would not stick at lying to further a family feud. Tacitus seems to have copied her quite uncritically. It cannot be an accident that the character of Tiberius touches bottom about the time when Agrippina was first of an age to take notes.

[1] Tacitus, *Annals*, VI, 45.   [2] Ibid., VI, 51.

With this preamble, and using Tacitus and Suetonius with discrimination, let us look at the facts. Tiberius Claudius Nero was sprung on both sides from one of the oldest and proudest families in Rome. His father, who bore the same name, had proposed in the senate to reward the assassins of Julius Cæsar and had taken part in the landowners' revolt of 41 B.C., but had later rallied to Octavian as saviour of society. In 38, when his son was three years old, the elder Tiberius divorced his young wife Livia that she might marry the triumvir. That this transaction was voluntary on the part of all concerned is proved by the fact that the discarded husband was present at the wedding and on his death-bed made Octavian guardian to his children. Tiberius, therefore, though brought up under the eye of Augustus, belonged by tradition to that class which accepted the principate only as a regrettable necessity in the interests of property and order. By inclination he seems to have been an intellectual aristocrat averse from public life and from the rivalries and intrigues of the imperial court. Under Augustus he commanded with distinction in the army and pushed the Roman frontier to the Danube. But it is evident that he did not wish for the succession. He did his best to avoid it by burying himself at Rhodes for seven years, to the disappointment of Livia and the deep displeasure of Augustus. Only in A.D. 4, when the death of the emperor's two grandsons (not by Livia, but by an earlier marriage) had left Tiberius the only possible candidate, and when further evasion was a moral impossibility, did he allow himself to be adopted by Augustus and associated with him in the government. It is clear from the letters of Augustus (quoted by Suetonius) that the two men were now wholly reconciled, and that the ageing and failing emperor relied implicitly on his younger colleague. The reluctant acceptance of the empire by Tiberius at the hands of the senate ten years later, though represented by Tacitus and Suetonius as hypocritical, was entirely in keeping with his earlier career.

It is plain from the narratives of both Tacitus and Suetonius that Tiberius as far as possible deferred to the senate as the supreme constitutional authority. It was his misfortune that

that body of sycophantic, grasping plutocrats was wholly incapable of its task and unworthy of his confidence. He did his best for them. He paid them the compliment of entrusting to them the annual election of magistrates, till then vested in the popular assembly. He encouraged freedom of debate, on one occasion going so far (if we are to believe Suetonius) as ironically to beg a senator's pardon for opposing him. He relieved pecuniarily embarrassed senators with a liberality which we should call demoralizing, but which they seem to have thought less than their deserts. Both Tacitus and Suetonius record his hatred of flattery and of adulatory forms of address. Tacitus characteristically treats this as a restriction on free speech!

Far from encouraging frivolous prosecutions, Tiberius, as long as he resided in Rome, set his face against them. Tacitus tells us how, when a man was charged with treason because he had included a statue of Augustus in an auction, Tiberius stopped the case, saying: " Wrongs done to the gods are the gods' concern ";[1] and how in another instance he vetoed proceedings against a man who had melted down a statue of himself for domestic use. An often-quoted case is that of Cremutius Cordus, the historian, who was brought to trial before the senate for having praised Brutus and Cassius, the assassins of Julius Cæsar. It is as if a historian of the present day were to glorify the Phœnix Park murderers of 1882.[2] We are told that Tiberius listened to the case with " an angry frown " (whether at the behaviour of Cordus or at the waste of public time is not stated) and that Cordus went home and ended his own life. It is difficult to see how Tiberius was responsible for that. These prosecutions were initiated and tried, not by him, but by those very senators who were the first to squeal when they themselves were laid by the heels. Well might Tiberius exclaim in disgust as he left

[1] Tacitus, *Annals*, I, 73.
[2] The parallel is nearly exact. The lapse of time between the assassination of Cæsar and the prosecution of Cordus was the same as between the Phœnix Park murders and the present day (1950). In each case the murder was political, and the murderers thought themselves patriots. In each case the act was not only a crime, but a blunder. Only Brutus and Cassius were rich aristocrats, and the Phœnix Park murderers men of the people.

the senate-house: "How ready they are for slavery!"[1]
We are driven to regret that Julius or Augustus had not
stamped that miserable body out of existence.

Among other charges laid by Tacitus against Tiberius are
that on the occasion of a disastrous flood he refused to consult
the Sibylline books and preferred to consider practical means
of confining the Tiber to its banks; that he recalled his nephew,
Germanicus, from a costly attempt to conquer Germany;
that he preferred diplomacy to war; and that he was indifferent to the expansion of the empire. Such reproaches may
be left to speak for themselves.

The real limitations of Tiberius appear in a matter on which
for once emperor and historian are in perfect accord. We
have already noticed the hostility with which the Roman
ruling class viewed the infiltration of alien religions into Italy.
In the age following the conquests of Alexander, the cult of
Isis, the Egyptian corn-goddess, had spread over the Greek-
speaking world, and by the time of Sulla had reached Rome.
The ritual and myth (already familiar to the Mediterranean
world in other versions) of the dolorous goddess annually
bewailing her slain lover and comforted by his joyful resurrection had a warmer and more intimate appeal to the toiling
masses than the official cults of their conquerors and exploiters.
For that very reason the conservative Roman senate combated
it, and again and again in the last years of the republic suppressed the worship of Isis in the capital. After Actium the
cult fell into further disfavour through its association with
Egypt and Cleopatra. Nor was Isis the only foreign deity to
affront the authorities. Since the time of Pompey the Jews
had been subject to the Roman Empire, and a considerable
Jewish population, mostly slaves and freedmen, had found
its way to Italy. At first Judæa had been allowed to continue
as a client-state under the Herodian dynasty; but in A.D. 6
Augustus had subjected it to direct Roman rule and to imperial taxation. This step was to involve Rome in a more
prolonged and bitter struggle than any other of her Oriental
annexations. Not only did Palestine become a simmering
hotbed of revolt, but every synagogue in the Mediterranean

[1] Tacitus, *Annals*, III, 65.

world became a potential centre of subversive propaganda. In A.D. 19 Tiberius and the senate found pretexts to strike at both cults.[1]   Four thousand freedmen of military age, either Jews or Isis-worshippers, were pressed for service against brigands in Sardinia—"a cheap sacrifice," says Tacitus, "should they die from the pestilential climate." [2]   Other adherents of the two forbidden cults were ordered to recant by a stated day or to quit Italy.

Tiberius in this was not actuated by religious bigotry. The man who said, "Wrongs done to the gods are the gods' concern," and refused to open the Sibylline books, obviously did not care a straw whether people worshipped one god or another.   Apart from a weakness for astrology he seems to have been indifferent to religion.   But the clash between Rome and Judaism was far more than a theological quarrel. It was a struggle between two ways of life; and Rome knew it.   Cæsar, the revolutionary, had patronized the Jews; Augustus and Tiberius, the conservatives, held them in contempt.   On the one hand was a civilization based on gradations of rank and wealth, seeing in mass slavery the natural and necessary foundation of any culture worth having, and in slaves chattels without legal rights, to be bought or sold, employed as prostitutes or gladiators, thrown to the fishes or crucified if their owners saw fit.   That was Roman order, unmodified as yet by the palliatives which later emperors were to introduce.   On the other hand was a community (according to its own legends, of servile origin) which indeed owned slaves, but whose law contained noteworthy provisions in their favour—denied, for example, to masters the power of life and death, enforced a weekly day of rest, allowed cohabitation with female captives only on condition of manumission and marriage ("she shall be thy wife . . . thou shalt not deal with her as a slave" [3]), and forbade the return of runaways to their owners.   How far these and similar provisions were at any time enforced by the priestly aristocracy

---

[1] We know of the pretexts only from Josephus, *Antiquities*, XVIII, 3, 4-5. This passage immediately follows a notorious interpolation on the subject of Jesus Christ, and has probably itself been tampered with.

[2] *Annals*, II, 85.   [3] Deut. xxi, 13-14.

of Jerusalem may be doubtful. But to thousands upon thousands of Jews, whether resident in Palestine or scattered over the Mediterranean, they were divine commands, read publicly in the synagogues and driven home by the often-reiterated reminder: " Thou shalt remember that thou wast a bondman in the land of Egypt, and the Lord thy God redeemed thee: therefore I command thee this thing today."[1] Many thousands of proselytes must have been won to Judaism by these proclamations of social justice in the law and the prophets. The mere existence of Judaism was offensive to Rome. A proselytizing Judaism was more than offensive: it was menacing. A Judaism which not only proselytized, but announced the imminent advent of a kingdom of God wherein the promises of the law and the prophets should be fulfilled, was a challenge to the Roman Empire sufficient to provoke its rulers to sharp action.

Failing honest and efficient administration by the senate, Tiberius had to seek it where he could. This accounts for the rise to power of Sejanus, the commander of the prætorian guard, and for the tragedy of the later part of the reign. Sejanus, a Tuscan, was a typical member of the rich Italian middle class on which Augustus and Tiberius drew to supply the deficiencies of the effete Roman nobility. Tacitus is so unwilling to admit the plain fact that he is reduced to ascribing the rise of Sejanus to " heaven's wrath against Rome."[2] He allows that he was competent, energetic, and for many years personally loyal to Tiberius. He probably prompted (if prompting was necessary) the harsh measures against the Jews. It was certainly through his influence that Pontius Pilate ("inflexible, merciless, obstinate" the client-prince Agrippa called him) was made procurator of Judæa.

Unfortunately the loyalty of Sejanus was based on an expectation of eventually stepping into the shoes of Tiberius. The problem of succession is one which all dictatorships have to solve. The principate founded by Augustus was not in theory a hereditary monarchy. There was no constitutional reason why Tiberius, if he had wished Sejanus to succeed him, should not have adopted him and associated him in the government

---

[1] Deut. v, 15; xv, 15; xvi, 12; xxiv, 18, 22.   [2] *Annals*, IV, 1.

as he himself had been adopted and associated with Augustus. But Tiberius did not want this. He had a son, a grandson, and grand-nephews (children of his dead nephew, the popular Germanicus), and a natural weakness for his own family. Sejanus therefore embarked on crooked courses. He secretly poisoned the emperor's son Drusus (a young lout chiefly interested in gladiatorial shows, whom nobody seems to have liked), carefully sowed suspicion between Tiberius and his family, and in A.D. 26 persuaded the old man to retire to Capreæ (Capri), leaving Sejanus practically in control of affairs. Tiberius was sixty-seven, he had never wanted the empire, and now he was sick to death of Rome, of business, and of the fawning senate which did its best to make good government impossible. The story that he withdrew to Capri to hide his vices (probably put into circulation by the vitriolic pen of Agrippina, and reproduced by both Tacitus and Suetonius) is refuted, so far as it can be refuted, by the admission of Suetonius that he enjoyed excellent health almost to the day of his death. Tacitus tells us that he was attended in his retirement by a coterie of learned men, mostly Greeks. They do not sound like boon companions. No doubt he preferred their conversation to debates in the senate.

In any case the effects of his withdrawal were wholly lamentable. Sejanus, having got him out of the way, used his authority to ruin the family of Germanicus and any who might bar his own path to empire. The history of the years 29-31 is missing from Tacitus, and has to be gathered from other sources. From Suetonius and Dio we know that in 31 Tiberius awoke to the situation, appointed a new commander of the prætorian guard, and denounced Sejanus to the senate. The senators put to death with wolf-like alacrity the hated minister who had been promoted over their heads, and followed this up with a bloody vendetta against his family and friends. Tiberius never returned to Rome. The treachery of Sejanus seems to have wrecked his nerves. At any rate from that time he rarely interposed, as in better days he had often done, between suspects and their sentence. He died in 37, a most unhappy old man, broken by a burden which he had not sought, betrayed by his friend, alienated from his family, and detested by his people. He was not deified : indeed, the military had to protect his body from a raging mob bent on consigning " Tiberius to the Tiber."[1]

The snobbish preoccupation of Tacitus with misfortunes in high life is apt to blind his readers to the fact that all this time the Roman Empire, or at least its free subjects, enjoyed as good a government as a basically vicious social order allowed. Under the principate, for the first time in Roman history, a governor who feathered his nest irregularly might be sure at the very least of exile to a Greek island and could not hope to escape by bribery, as delinquent governors had often done under the republic. Tacitus himself at the outset of his *Annals* admits that the provinces were better protected under the emperors than under the republic from the rapacity of officials. Yet he illegitimately swells the list of Tiberius' victims by including among them many men who were convicted of extortion and very properly punished. Under senatorial rule the Roman upper class had become used to treating the provinces as fair game ; and the habit was hard to break. Though Roman rule at its best was harsh to the lower ranks of society, even the iron repression of a Pilate was better than the unregulated rapacity of a Verres.

For ten years following the death of Tiberius there is a gap in the *Annals* which we have to bridge with the help of Suetonius and Dio. In addition, we have useful contemporary sidelights in the works of the two Jews, Philo and Josephus. The grand-nephew and immediate successor of Tiberius, Gaius Caligula, was by universal consent insane—and about as bad an advertisement of the hereditary principle as could be wished. He was the first emperor who attained power without any preliminary training in responsible posts, and the first who not only allowed divine honours to be paid to him, but claimed and enforced them, even at Rome, in his lifetime. That the principate could survive nearly four years of this madman is proof positive that no other form of government was then possible. As it was, after his assassination the senate seriously meditated the restoration of the republic. Such a folly, which could have led only to a new civil war

[1] Suetonius, *Tiberius*, LXXV.

and a new usurpation, was prevented by the prætorian guard, who, supported by the populace, acclaimed Claudius, the brother of Germanicus, as emperor and forced him on the reluctant senate.

Claudius, like Tiberius, has been badly treated by history. Suetonius depicts him as feeble in mind and body, an ungainly pedant, a universal butt, and utterly unfit to rule. Tacitus shows him helpless in the hands of worthless wives and unscrupulous freedmen and, if not himself a tyrant, yet a passive instrument of tyranny in others. Actually he was anything but a fool. He seems to have been of the type now known as the " dreamy professor," and for that reason to have been deliberately passed over by his great-uncle Augustus and his uncle Tiberius, who could not imagine the sickly, stammering, absent-minded scholar to be suitable for any public employment. Nevertheless, when in his fiftieth year the empire was thrust upon him, he proved himself their worthy successor. Following their line, he set himself in general against expansion, causing military martinets like Corbulo to lament the good old days of empire-building. His only considerable departure from this policy was his expedition to Britain, which resulted (A.D. 43—nearly a century after Cæsar's abortive invasion) in the annexation of the south and east of the island and in the plantation of a colony of discharged soldiers at Camulodunum (Colchester). He was the first emperor to mitigate in some degree the savagery of Roman slavery by forbidding the brutal practice of marooning sick and worn-out slaves on an island in the Tiber to save the expense of treatment. He enacted that slaves so misused should be freed, and that masters who killed their slaves to save treatment should be guilty of murder. In Gaul he suppressed the barbarous rites of the Druids, and in 48 (in the teeth of much senatorial opposition) extended full Roman citizenship, with the right to hold public office and enter the senate, to certain of the nobles of that country.

Thus by progressive extension of citizen rights the Roman Empire became less and less Roman, and the seed was sown of the Romance culture of later ages. The most effective agent, however, in the Latinization of the West was not the

literate noble, but the simple legionary. Encamped along the
Rhine and Danube frontier, or settled on discharge in colonies
dotted over the frontier provinces, he conducted his daily
business not in the literary Latin of Cicero or Tacitus, but in
a Latin differing at least as much from what we call " classical "
as the English of a village " pub " differs from that of a *Times*
leader. We get some idea of this idiom from inscriptions
(notably those unearthed at Pompeii) and from sketches of
low life in comic or satirical writers from Plautus to Petronius.
Interaction between this vernacular Latin, with its clipped or
slurred syllables, dropped aspirates, and simplified grammar,
and the speech of the surrounding Iberians, Celts, or other
natives was to produce in the course of many centuries the
national languages and literatures of a new Europe.

Such developments, however, lay beyond the horizon of
even the most far-sighted administrators of the first century.
They were concerned with the conservation of society as
they had inherited it. Gross oppression might be punished,
and the worst abuses corrected; but none doubted that the
mission of Rome (even if the name " Roman " were extended
to include free Italians and high-born provincials) was to
impose her dominion and way of life on her natural slaves.
Since the death of Tiberius, the Jews, whom he had banished
from Italy, had infiltrated back into the capital and, under
Claudius, carried their disaffection to the empire to the point
of rioting. Claudius replied by reimposing his uncle's ban.
" Since the Jews constantly made disturbances at the instigation of Chrestus," says Suetonius, " he expelled them from
Rome."[1] Whatever may have been the case before, by the
date when Suetonius wrote (about 120) the name " Chrestus "
or " Christus " had come to denote the founder of a new,
illicit, and dangerous movement of Jewish origin; and
there can be no doubt that in this curt sentence Suetonius
identifies the rioters with the Christians. The bearing of his
statement on the problem of Christian origins will be considered later.

Like many men of the " dreamy professor " type, Claudius
was unfortunate in his relations with women. He had been

[1] Suetonius, *Claudius*, XXV.

twice unhappily married before becoming emperor. His third wife, Messalina, over thirty years his junior, made her name the byword which it has ever since remained. In 48 she overstepped the limit by plotting with her latest lover against the life and throne of her elderly and absent-minded husband. At this the emperor's secretary, the Greek freedman Narcissus, decided to save his master from himself, and by revealing the truth procured the execution of Messalina and her paramour. But Claudius seems to have been able to live neither with women nor without them. Hardly was he rid of Messalina when he allowed himself to be ensnared into marriage with his widowed niece, the unspeakable Agrippina. In 50 her twelve-year-old son was adopted by Claudius and given the name of Nero. In 54, having no further use for Claudius (who had begun to see through her), she despatched him to join the gods and secured the empire for her son.

Nero, like Caligula, is a pathological case. He had some good natural qualities : his passion for the arts was not as wholly base as Roman prejudice liked to pretend. In Seneca he had a good tutor and adviser, and in Burrus, an old soldier who had served Tiberius and Claudius, a trusty commander of the prætorian guard. In the early years of the reign Seneca's influence was manifest. Nero refused the title of " father of his country " and other flatteries heaped on him by the servile senate; professed devotion to the constitutional traditions of Augustus; replied to a vote of thanks by saying, " Wait till I have deserved it "; limited gladiatorial shows; remitted oppressive taxation; and set a precedent by publishing a budget. But the principate had not been built to stand the strain of government by a youth in his teens, and—we may add in charity to Nero—youths in their teens are not built to stand the strain of being Roman emperors. Irresponsible power turned his brain, as it had turned Caligula's. Agrippina had imagined that by elevating her son she would become mistress of the empire. Desperately attempting to assert her authority, she was pushed aside and finally in 59 murdered. It is almost as difficult to be sorry for her as to approve of matricide. Clytæmnestra had engendered Orestes.

Tacitus is in his element in his description of the murder, which took place in his own childhood and of which there were many contemporary accounts. The story of the collapsible boat and its failure to work, of Agrippina's escape, of Nero's terrified consultation with Seneca and Burrus (no less embarrassing to them), and of the doomed woman's cry— "Smite the womb that bore him!"—is among the grimmest and most graphic pieces of writing in historical literature.

But purple passages on tragedies in high life, in which Tacitus excels, must not blind us to more important sides of imperial history. That the Roman Empire survived the rule of a maniac like Nero was due to the fact that under preceding emperors, and especially under Claudius, it had evolved a very efficient governmental machine. The senate having proved itself incapable of government (or indeed of doing anything except fawn on the strong and stamp on the weak), the emperors recruited their administrators from the middle ranks of society. Claudius showed his enterprise and earned the special obloquy of the diehards by throwing open the public service to men who had risen from slavery. This employment of freedmen had its good as well as its bad side. It meant that, for the first time in the history of the empire, administration was in the hands of men who knew what hard work was and how the social fabric was maintained. It did not guarantee their honesty or their humanity. The slave who won his freedom in ancient Rome might owe his manumission to industry and special talent, or to toadying and dirty dealing. He might fill creditably any post to which he was promoted, or he might be a walking disaster. Ancient historians, belonging themselves to the slave-owning class, naturally concentrate on the bad cases. Actually there is no evidence that freedmen made worse administrators on the average than the senatorial nobility who had plundered the provinces under the republic. We hear much from Tacitus and Suetonius of the peculations and oppressions of Narcissus and Pallas, the Greek secretary and treasurer of Claudius, and of Felix, the brother of Pallas, who as procurator of Judæa "exercised the powers of a king in the spirit of a slave."[1]

[1] Tacitus, *Histories*, V, 9.

Yet, on the showing of Tacitus, Narcissus served Claudius faithfully in the matter of Messalina, tried to dissuade him from marrying Agrippina, and after the murder of his master paid for his loyalty with his life. We learn from Suetonius that Vespasian, afterwards emperor, owed his first command to Narcissus. For Pallas and Felix there is very little to be said. But the bulk of the civil service must have been reliable, or the empire would have collapsed.

Promotions of this sort were naturally unpleasing to the senate; and under Nero we find that body making vicious efforts to tighten the chains of slavery. A debate recorded by Tacitus in the year 56 shows the fear with which the upper class regarded the servile mass on which their wealth and ease depended. A motion that offending freedmen should be reduced to slavery at the discretion of their former owners found wide support in the senate, but was opposed on grounds of expediency. Freedmen, it was stated, made up the majority of the city populace, the public services, and the police. Even some senators had freedmen for fathers.[1] Any attempt to brand freedmen as a class apart would only draw attention to their numbers. Nero, doubtless on the advice of Seneca, ruled that their offences should be dealt with by ordinary law.

But the senate did not let the question sleep. An old law provided that if a master were murdered by a slave all his household slaves should be executed. In 57 the senate extended this penalty to those manumitted under the will of the murdered man. In 61, on the murder of Secundus, the city prefect, the law was put into force. Tacitus shows the direction of his own sympathies by reporting at length the speech of a senator in favour of the execution of the law, while merely noting the fact that there was a minority against it. On this occasion the city populace, in agreeable contrast to their rulers, showed that even constant familiarity with gladiatorial shows had not quenched all their decent instincts. They were not so far removed from slavery themselves. They turned out with stones and firebrands to rescue the victims from execution. Nero thereupon lined the route

[1] Nero, however, debarred such men from office. Suetonius, *Nero*, XV.

with soldiers; and four hundred slaves, the great majority admittedly innocent, suffered the penalty of the law. The senate in fact outdid Nero in brutality; for a proposal that the freedmen of Secundus should be punished by transportation was stopped by the imperial veto.

In 62 Burrus died a (perhaps) natural death, and Seneca, whose influence had long been waning, retired into private life. Nero was thenceforth swayed by the Sicilian Tigellinus, the new commander of the prætorian guard, and by his own maniacal temperament. Some of the enormities laid to his charge by Tacitus and Suetonius we should now dismiss as venial. We could even wish that the performances as actor, musician, and vocalist, put by Suetonius in the forefront of his crimes, had been more numerous and his gladiatorial shows fewer. Nor can we much censure Nero's design, if he ever entertained it, of abolishing the senate and governing entirely through the civil service. The senate was in no sense a representative assembly and had never been a check on misgovernment. There could be no more scathing verdict on a governing body than that of Tacitus on the abject senate of Nero's day. "As often as the emperor directed banishments or executions, so often was there a thanksgiving to the gods, and what formerly commemorated some prosperous event was then a token of public disaster." [1] And Tacitus is a senatorial partisan.

We cannot pass as lightly over the murder of Nero's divorced wife Octavia, or over the great fire of 64. Tacitus leaves it in doubt whether this latter was accidental or deliberate. Suetonius categorically states that Nero ordered it; and such was the popular belief at the time. If true, it would be proof positive of Nero's lunacy, to which many other indications point. Some of the details given by Suetonius can be dismissed as gossip. It cannot be true, for example, that Nero sang of the sack of Troy as he watched the fire; for we know from Tacitus that he was away at Antium (Anzio) when it began, and did not return until the flames approached and destroyed his own palace. Tacitus mentions this musical entertainment as a " rumour," but places it on

[1] *Annals*, XIV, 64.

a " private stage "—presumably at Antium, not at Rome.[1]
Even if the charge of incendiarism is false, the fact that Nero
could be credited with burning Rome is a measure of the
unpopularity which he had accumulated in ten years. His
accession had been welcomed with enthusiasm. The murder
of Agrippina, though reprehensible, had been covered by the
authority of Seneca and Burrus, and had left most people
indifferent; for she was an evil woman. The execution of
the slaves of Secundus had roused the populace; but it was
legal, and the odium had been shared with the senate. The
divorce and murder of Octavia had shocked public opinion;
still it was a tragedy of the imperial family with which the
people were but distantly concerned. The fire demon-
strated, as nothing else had done, that the irresponsible lunacy
of the head of the State could endanger not only senators and
relations of the emperor, but the hearths and homes of ordinary
citizens.

Its main interest to the historian lies in its connection with
the first recorded imperial persecution of Christianity. The
account in Tacitus has been questioned, and is rejected almost
as a matter of course by most of those who uphold the " myth "
theory of Christian origins. But a vast majority of Latin
scholars accept the Tacitean passage; there is nothing in-
credible in it; and it is borne out by Suetonius, who briefly,
after his wont, enumerates the punishment of the Christians,
" a class of men given to a new and mischievous superstition,"
among Nero's *good* actions.[2] Tacitus is more informative.
To divert suspicion from himself, he says, Nero punished as
incendiaries " a class hated for their abominations, called
Christians by the populace." They were the followers of
one Christus, executed by Pilate in the reign of Tiberius.
Repressed for the moment, the " mischievous superstition "
later spread from Judæa to Rome, " where all things hideous
and shameful from every part of the world find their centre
and become popular. Accordingly an arrest was first made
of avowed Christians;[3] then upon their information an

---

[1] *Annals*, XV, 39.   [2] *Nero*, XVI.
[3] The Latin *qui fatebantur* may mean either " avowed Christians " or
" avowed incendiaries."

immense multitude was convicted, not so much of the crime
of firing the city as of hatred against mankind." [1] They
were thrown to dogs, crucified, or burnt alive. Yet, it seems,
Nero defeated his own object; for the populace (the same
populace who had pitied the slaves of Secundus) pitied the
Christians too as the victims of his cruelty.

There is no difficulty about this. The "immense multitude," which some find a stumbling-block, may have been
less than a thousand. Such a number of convicted incendiaries would seem startling, and therefore "immense,"
compared with the mere handful of Catilinarians put to
death 126 years before. As a Roman moving in good
society and repeatedly holding public office in the last quarter
of the century, Tacitus had ample opportunities of finding
out what had occurred when he himself was a small boy.
He writes as we should expect him to write. The Christians
are a mischievous sect founded by a condemned malefactor.
They are part of that noxious stream of Oriental religions
which has been infiltrating into Rome for many generations
past. Even if they did not fire Rome, they are enemies of
mankind. What a pity, then (he reflects), that their exemplary punishment should have moved people to compassion
just because it was inflicted by Nero!

A Christian forger, we may be sure, would not have written
like this. He would not, as Tacitus does, have imputed
"abominations" or "hatred against mankind" to the
infant Church. He would not, as Tacitus does, have made
those first arrested give their brothers away. The hostile
and contemptuous attitude to Christianity stamps the passage
as authentic, and at the same time explains why no Christian
writer refers to it until after the final victory of the new
religion. It would have been an awkward passage to quote
to a pagan public. Only those so wedded to the pure myth
theory that they must condemn any apparently early testimony to the historicity of Jesus as *ipso facto* spurious will
hesitate to accept the account as Tacitean.

Whether he ordered it or not, the fire of 64 was the beginning of the end of Nero. It finally alienated the Roman

[1] *Annals*, XV, 44.

populace, who persisted in believing him the author of the calamity; and it exhausted Italy and the provinces, which were compelled to contribute in money and material to the restoration of the capital and the erection of Nero's new palace. Roman exasperation showed itself in the so-called Pisonian conspiracy of 65, which had ramifications among all classes and in the armed forces, and failed only through the inability of one of the senators in the plot to keep his own counsel. The most striking feature of this mismanaged affair is the poltroonery with which these rich Romans, when arrested, denounced one another, and the bravery with which humbler folk faced torture and death in the same cause. Even Tacitus, who rarely has a good word for anyone of servile origin, is moved to admiration by the freedwoman Epicharis, who " had never before had a thought of anything noble " (one wonders how Tacitus knew that) but who strangled herself rather than betray under torture " strangers whom she hardly knew." [1] The soldiers, too, made good ends, one centurion telling Nero to his face that death was the best service he could have rendered to one so infamous. The detection of the conspiracy was followed by a reign of terror in which Seneca and many others perished.

From 66 on the *Annals* are missing. Suetonius relates the end of the story: Nero's triumphal progress through Greece, which his mad brain believed " the only country with an ear for music and worthy of his artistic efforts "; [2] the revolt of the western provinces, Gaul and Spain, against his misgovernment; his desertion by the prætorian guard; and the last, sordid scene in his freedman's villa in the suburbs of Rome, when the fallen emperor tremblingly anticipated the sentence of his own servile senate by cutting his throat.

So, in 68, ended the line of Augustus. The *Histories* of Tacitus, an earlier work than the *Annals*, deal in detail with the disastrous " year of four emperors " (Galba, Otho, Vitellius, Vespasian) which followed the death of Nero. In their original form the *Histories* extended to the death of Domitian in 96; but the fragment which survives tantalizingly breaks off just before the fall of Jerusalem in 70. The disappearance

[1] *Annals*, XV, 51, 57.   [2] *Nero*, XXII.

of the greater part of this history of his own times, covering as it did the youth and prime of Tacitus himself, is one of the major losses of literature. We are driven to wonder whether this mutilation of the text of Tacitus, both at certain points of the *Annals* and by the excision of most of the *Histories*, may be deliberate censorship designed to conceal facts compromising to Christianity. For the story of the destruction of Jerusalem (from the point of view of world history the most important event of the period) we are dependent on the *Jewish War* of Josephus—a participator in the tragedy which he records, but a self-confessed double-dealer, sickeningly self-righteous, and not to be trusted an inch where his own conduct is involved. Suetonius deals in very summary fashion with the same events, and is our only contemporary authority for the years from the end of the Jewish War to the death of Domitian. Unfortunately, his later lives are far poorer in detail than his earlier and tail off at the end into little more than disconnected notes.

Both Josephus and Suetonius mention among the causes of the Jewish revolt what the former calls "an ambiguous oracle," and the latter "an old and established belief spread over all the Orient," that Judæa at that time would give a ruler to the world.[1] Josephus, as a Romanized Jew concerned to conciliate his patrons, naturally minimizes the extent of this Messianic ferment. Suetonius has no such motive for concealing the truth. The plain fact is that the disaffection of the Oriental masses to their Western conquerors (a disaffection dating from the successors of Alexander and not confined to Jews, though finding a focus and a rallying-point in Jewish prophetic and apocalyptic literature) came to a head in the first century of our era. The subjection of Judæa to Roman rule and taxation, the agitation which led to the expulsion of Jews from Italy by Tiberius and Claudius, and the beginnings of the Christian movement (to which we shall return later) were so many milestones to the upheaval in which Judaism dashed itself to pieces against Roman imperialism.

At the same time it would be wrong not to connect the

[1] Josephus, *Jewish War*, VI, 5, 4; Suetonius, *Vespasian*, IV.

upheaval with the general debility of the empire in the last years of Nero. That emperor's insane extravagance, and in particular the sums laid out in rebuilding Rome after the fire of 64, had drained the provinces dry and led to universal discontent. Furthermore, a deep-seated weakness, more fatal than the idiosyncrasy of any emperor, was becoming manifest. The steel framework of the empire, the Italian soldiery that had built it, was disappearing. With the extinction of the free peasantry in spite of all efforts to recreate it, recruiting had dried up. The legions were now manned by Gauls, Germans, Illyrians, Thracians, Syrians—men whose loyalty was not to Rome nor to Italy, but to the commander who paid them best.

The spark which kindled the Jewish revolt in 66 was the seizure of money from the Temple treasury by the procurator Florus and his savage repression of popular protests. The economic causes underlying the revolt are evident from the fact that one of the first acts of the Zealots was to burn all records of debt—"the nerves of the city," says the rich Josephus [1]—and that both the rival ringleaders, John of Gischala and Simon Bargiora, recruited their followers from runaway slaves.

But though the Jews were the first people to take up arms and the most desperate in their resistance to Rome, the uprising in the western provinces which ended Nero's reign shows that similar causes were at work elsewhere. Vindex, who first raised the standard of revolt in Gaul, was a Romanized provincial, and probably had in view not only the overthrow of Nero, but the recovery of Gallic independence. That at any rate was the view taken by the legions of the Rhine, who promptly crushed him and offered the empire to their own commander. For a year after Nero's death the Roman Empire was on the brink of disruption—the Jews in arms in the East; the lower Rhine and part of Gaul following suit in the West; the legions, east and west, and the prætorians at Rome all fighting for their own hand. Disruption was averted because the subversive movements had no mutual cohesion. The western peoples, little as they might like

[1] *Jewish War*, II, 17, 6.

imperial rule, had not yet evolved any kind of national unity to put in its place. In 69 the legions of the East and the Danube provinces rallied to Flavius Vespasianus, the commander in Judæa, for want of any reputable competitor, and imposed him by superior force on the distracted West. Rome, the titular mistress of the world, was sacked by an army mainly composed of Illyrians and Orientals. The senate hastened to ratify the accomplished fact. The shadowy "empire of the Gauls" melted away in a day. When it came to a choice between the *pax Romana* and an independence which they had not the faintest idea how to organize, the Gallic nobles chose peace.

The Jews, who alone of the revolted peoples fought for an idea, were now isolated. Still they held out—"the slaves, the scum, the spurious and abortive offspring of our nation," says Josephus with the rancour of a renegade.[1] Not until Titus, the son of Vespasian, had crucified thousands of Jews round the walls of Jerusalem *pour encourager les autres*; not until the Temple had been fired and thousands more had perished in its flames; not until the last of the Zealots, besieged in the stronghold of Masada, had killed their wives and children and then one another rather than fall into the hands of Rome, was the Jewish War over. Jews throughout the empire were thenceforth required to pay to the temple of Jupiter Capitolinus the tax formerly paid to the temple at Jerusalem. So ended the desperate attempt to set up the kingdom of heaven by force.

Vespasian was the first emperor of Rome who was not a Roman by extraction. He came of a middle-class family of Reate (Rieti) in the Sabine uplands, and had no hereditary ties with the senatorial plutocracy, which was still theoretically the governing body of the Roman State. A professional soldier, owing his elevation to a largely Oriental army, he was far less inclined than Augustus, Tiberius, or Claudius to stand on constitutional ceremony, and frankly regarded himself as a dynastic monarch. "Either my sons will succeed me," he told the senate, "or no one."[2] Josephus, following what was no doubt the fashion among the richer Jews who had

---

[1] *Jewish War*, V, 10, 5.   [2] Suetonius, *Vespasian*, XXV.

embraced the Roman cause, affects to see in Vespasian's accession a fulfilment of Messianic prophecy; and Rome was content that such Jews as he should think so. The ten years' reign of Vespasian was mainly occupied in rescuing the finances of the empire from the ruin to which Nero had brought them. He seems to have done this with method and success.

Titus survived his father only two years. It was under Domitian, Vespasian's second son, that the full force of the new absolutism was felt. Domitian seems to have been a weak man over-conscious of his middle-class origin, for which he tried to compensate by an exaggerated parade of power ending in odious tyranny. Suetonius tells us that he was badly educated and read nothing except the memoirs and other papers of Tiberius—a clear case of a *parvenu* trying to model himself on a born aristocrat. From Tiberius he learnt to administer ordinary justice well and to keep his provincial governors in strict order. But he did what Tiberius had never done : he assumed divine honours in his lifetime and had himself styled " our Lord and God " in official documents. He supported this pretence to divinity by lavish gladiatorial and other shows, and by fussy and tyrannous meddling in morals and religion, even going so far as to revive the ferocious old practice (which had fallen into disuse) of burying alive a Vestal virgin convicted of unchastity. His hand lay heavy on the Jews, who were subjected to a rigorous inquisition to prevent evasion of the tax payable to the temple of Jupiter. Suetonius says that he himself saw an old man of ninety stripped in a crowded court to see if he was circumcised. Moreover, the Jews were forbidden to make proselytes on pain of death or confiscation of property.

These proceedings seem to have occasioned the first organized persecution of Christians as such—as distinct from the adventitious charge of incendiarism on which they had suffered under Nero. Domitian's Jew-baiting revealed the fact that there were many who, in the words of Suetonius, " lived as Jews without acknowledging themselves as such." [1] Secret adhesion to a community which had lately been in rebellion against Rome was obviously even more dangerous

[1] *Domitian*, XII.

than open adhesion. There was a simple way in which supposed crypto-Jews, as we should call them, could clear themselves: by burning incense to the gods of Rome or to the emperor's statue they could prove themselves good subjects and leave the court without a stain on their character. The word went forth that that was to be the test. Most of those who suffered, whether as Jews or as Christians, were of small account; but it must have caused a sensation in Rome when early in 96 the emperor's first cousin, Flavius Clemens, lately consul, was executed and his wife, Domitilla, banished on a charge of "atheism and Jewish practices."[1] There is no doubt that both were Christians. The oldest of the catacombs lay in Domitilla's grounds. Another catacomb contains the epitaph of an Acilius Glabrio, possibly identical with or related to an ex-consul of that name put to death in 95 for "plotting revolution."[2] Eight months after the death of Clemens, Domitian was assassinated in his palace by a band of conspirators headed by Stephanus, the steward of Domitilla. We have no evidence that Stephanus was a Christian. But his employer was; and only by presupposing the pacifism of all early Christians can we exclude a connection between the two events.

For nearly two centuries from the death of Domitian, i.e. until the final decline of the Roman Empire, no contemporary histories are extant, and contemporary records of any sort, apart from inscriptions and coins, are very deficient. Our best witness for the immediately ensuing years is the younger Pliny. He was the nephew of the great historian and natural philosopher who perished in 79 in the eruption of Vesuvius, and a friend of Tacitus and Suetonius. A wealthy man owning no fewer than six country houses, Pliny held many official posts under Domitian and Trajan, and has left us a voluminous correspondence extending from the end of Domitian's reign to his own governorship of Bithynia and Pontus in 111–113. We also have a lengthy and fulsome

---

[1] Suetonius does not give the charge against Clemens, merely mentioning his "contemptible laziness." Dio, writing a century later, specifies the offence.

[2] *Domitian*, X.

speech (the *Panegyric*) in which he returns thanks to Trajan for nominating him consul in the year 100. To supplement Pliny we have only the late history of Dio; and this, for the period now reached, survives only in extracts made centuries later still.

On the death of Domitian the empire was conferred by acclamation on Nerva, an elderly senator who had successfully survived the terrors of Nero and Domitian. He reversed his predecessor's policy, recalling all exiles and quashing all pending prosecutions, and initiated a useful programme of reform. But it soon became evident that no emperor, however worthy, could reign without the support of the legions. To this end in 97 he adopted and associated in his government Trajan, the commander of the army of the Rhine; and when Nerva died after reigning only sixteen months, Trajan succeeded him without opposition.

Trajan was the first emperor who was not even Italian by birth. His father was a common legionary stationed in Spain who by good service rose from the ranks to be a consul and provincial governor. We read in Pliny's *Panegyric* of Trajan's unassuming manners; of his conciliation of the senate, soldiers, and people; of the good discipline which he nevertheless kept in the army; and of the reform programme which he took over from Nerva and carried on—in particular, of the establishment of State maintenance and education of the children of poor but ·free families in Italy. This was part of a last and, as it proved, forlorn attempt to re-create a free Italian peasantry and promote recruiting for the legions. For Trajan was first and last a soldier. If he conciliated the senate, it was because the senate was no longer the obstacle it had once been to the good government of the empire. From the reign of Vespasian onward the old Roman nobility, the plague of the early emperors, had been swamped by wealthy families of Italian or provincial origin, to whom Brutus and Cassius were names in a history book and not ancestors to be feverishly admired or feverishly repudiated. In fact wealthy provincials everywhere in the West were being rapidly Romanized. Tacitus in his *Life of Agricola* records the growing taste of British chiefs for Roman ban-

quets, Roman baths, and Roman architecture, adding in his
sour way: "This, in their innocence, they call civilization,
when really it is part of their slavery." [1]

Under Trajan the Roman Empire reached its peak of
external power and splendour. The conquest of Dacia in
106 (commemorated on his column at Rome) and its plantation with Latin-speaking colonists left a permanent mark
on the map of Europe. Even today, after seventeen centuries
of Teutonic, Turanian, and Slav conquest and racial admixture,
that people of the lower Danube still speak a Romance language and call themselves *Ruman*. The colossal gladiatorial
shows given at Trajan's triumph, with the slaughter of ten
thousand men and eleven thousand beasts, show that if he had
the qualities, he had also decidedly the limitations of a Roman
general.

Most important of the historical records of Trajan's reign
is his correspondence with Pliny during the latter's governorship of Bithynia and Pontus. Pliny was sent out to remedy
the considerable disorder into which those provinces had
fallen under previous senatorial governors. One example of
that disorder was subversive religious propaganda, which
had gone to such a length in the two provinces that temples
were almost deserted and sacrificial animals found very few
purchasers. Pliny's first action, taken under Trajan's direction, was to ban under penalties any sort of guild or association
(*collegium*): even a fire-brigade was forbidden lest it should
turn into a political club. Under this edict a large number
of Christians were arrested. This time there is no question of
Jews. The proceedings at the end of Domitian's reign had
made plain to the authorities the difference between the two.
But Domitian's measures were an unsafe precedent. After
inducing many to worship the gods, burn incense before the
emperor's statue, and revile Christ, and executing a certain
number of recalcitrants, Pliny grew uneasy and wrote to
Trajan for instructions. Investigations on the spot, he submits, have failed to establish any criminal act on the part of
the Christians of Bithynia except that they pay divine honours
to Christ. In this they are guilty of a " perverse and extrava-

[1] *Agricola*, 21.

gant superstition "[1] which alone, thinks Pliny, ought to be
punished. Trajan's reply approves Pliny's action. Christians are not to be hunted out; no action is to be taken on
anonymous information; but if Christians are charged, they
are to be punished unless they deny Christianity and prove
their denial by worshipping the gods of Rome. The correspondence makes it clear that Christians were punished not
for their opinions, nor for the crimes imputed to them by
common report (which Pliny does not believe), but as bad
citizens, and that their bad citizenship consisted in proclaiming
Christ to be more worthy of worship than the head of the
State or the gods of the State. On the whole this tells in
favour of the historicity of Jesus. The worship of a strange
god would not in itself have troubled the authorities. They
had long learnt to tolerate strange gods. They no longer
proscribed, as they had once done, the cult of Bacchus or of
Isis. But the cult of an executed rebel was another thing.
Trajan was prepared to ignore it in holes and corners, but was
not prepared to allow it in the light of day.

Trajan's prosperous reign ended in disaster. In 113 he
became involved in war with Parthia, and by 116 had carried
the Roman eagles to the Persian Gulf. The Jews, doubtless
in collusion with the other Oriental enemies of Rome, rose
in his rear and avenged the destruction of Jerusalem on the
Greek populations of Cyprus and Cyrene. Trajan had to
retreat, and in 117, before the Jewish revolt was stamped out,
he died—probably more than ever convinced that the venera-
tion of Jewish Messiahs, dead or alive, was a danger to the
State.

From the last years of Trajan onward our only contemporary evidence is that of inscriptions and coins. Hadrian,
his cousin and successor, wrote an autobiography which we
would give much to possess and which served as material for
later historians. But the earliest extant literary evidence
consists of extracts from the later books of Dio, and the next
earliest is the *Augustan History*, an uncritical and superficial
set of lives of the later emperors compiled in the third and
fourth centuries by writers of whom we know nothing. So

[1] Pliny, *Letters*, X, 97.

devoid of any literary or scientific merit are the ancient
authorities that most readers will prefer to approach the
period through the masterly compilation of Gibbon or the
more up-to-date scholarship of Bury and other moderns.

Hadrian abandoned Trajan's eastern conquests as untenable,
and devoted the rest of his reign to the internal reform of
the empire. He is remarkable for his humane legislation on
behalf of slaves. The period of imperial expansion was now
over. The slave-owning class could no longer rely on the
armies for a continual supply of cheap human chattels. It
was therefore necessary on grounds of economy as well as
humanity to protect the labour force of the empire from
wanton wastage. Hadrian deprived owners of the power of
life and death, extended to slaves the protection of the courts,
and prohibited their sale for gladiatorial purposes or for
prostitution. He also began the work of reducing the un-
wieldy mass of Roman law to a codified system. The tragedy
is that these enlightened reforms came too late. The Roman
Empire was dying from the centre outwards. Italy and
Sicily had long since been ruined by mass slavery. The only
living parts of the body politic were the frontier provinces,
and they were knit together by no common bond except
a negative interest in peace—while peace could last. Hadrian
himself, probably with the best of intentions, provoked a
new Jewish revolt by his prohibition of circumcision and his
erection of a temple to Jupiter on the site of the demolished
temple of Jerusalem. From 132 to 135 Palestine was deluged
in blood in this last, desperate clash between the Gentile and
Jewish ways of life. It ended in the uprooting of the Jews
from their homeland for eighteen hundred years.

The reformist policy of Hadrian was continued by his two
successors, Antoninus (138–161) and Marcus Aurelius (161–
180). Gibbon ascribes the paucity of materials for the history
of this era to its relative exemption from " the crimes, follies,
and misfortunes of mankind."[1] A more likely reason is
that the Roman world had ceased to produce historians able
and willing to deal with contemporary events. Appian and
Arrian, both of whom belong to the Antonine age, chose to

[1] *Decline and Fall of the Roman Empire*, chap. III.

write of the past rather than their own times. Indeed, it is characteristic of the age that nearly all its writers lived in and on the past. Ptolemy of Alexandria in his mathematical, astronomical, and geographical work summarized and arranged the discoveries of his predecessors, particularly of Hipparchus, but added nothing useful of his own. Pausanias, an Asiatic Greek and a plodding and commonplace antiquarian, wrote a guide-book to the Greece of his day which has proved a gold-mine to modern anthropologists. Lucian of Samosata is a brilliant exception to the flat mediocrity of his contemporaries. The Voltaire of his age, he lashes with impartial wit gods and philosophers, the paganism which had degenerated into a hypocritical racket and the Christian fanaticism which aspired to supersede it. Galen, another Asiatic Greek, made important contributions to medicine. All these writers, it will be noted, came from the eastern half of the empire. The only two extant Latin authors of the time, Fronto and Apuleius, came from Roman Africa. They show their obsession with the past by trying to revive a pre-classical form of Latin—which is much as if a present-day English author were to write in the idioms of Shakespeare and the Authorized Version of the Bible. Rome and Italy are unrepresented, unless we include Fronto's pupil, Marcus Aurelius; and he, though Roman by birth, was Spanish by extraction. Worn out by public and private cares, facing enemies external and internal, the Stoic emperor governed without hope an empire without a future. The other authors of the time are rhetoricians or grammarians who spend their ingenuity on commentaries on dead masterpieces or in composing imaginary speeches, letters, and table-talk on dead or trivial subjects. It is the literature of an age which has forgotten all the arts except that of elegantly saying nothing.

The wonder is not that the empire declined and fell, but that it stood as long as it did. By the time of Marcus the structure was beginning to give way under the weight of its own defences. The barbarians were still held at bay, but only by enlisting other barbarians against them. After twelve years (180–192) of misgovernment by his maniac son Commodus (another bad advertisement of the hereditary principle), rival armies again fought over the dying empire. Finally Septimius Severus, an African by birth who spoke Latin with a Punic accent, defeated his competitors and imposed an African dynasty on the Roman world. Hannibal was avenged. Africans were to be succeeded in due course by Syrians, Thracians, Arabs, and Illyrians, but never again, except for fleeting moments, by a Roman.

While conquered provinces turned the tables on their conquerors, a religion of the conquered, in the teeth of persecution which, though savage at times and places, was never sustained or universal, continued to undermine the religion of the State. Its advocates might be fanatics, but at least they had something to say. In 197, the year which saw the final victory of Severus, his countryman Tertullian [1] addressed a manifesto to the imperial authorities on behalf of the Christians in language vibrating with defiance.

> " We are but of yesterday, and we have filled everything you have—cities, islands, forts, towns, exchanges, yes! and camps, tribes, town councils, palace, senate, forum. All we have left to you is the temples! . . . Go to it! my good magistrates. . . . Torture us, rack us, condemn us, crush us. . . . The blood of Christians is seed. . . . We are condemned by you, we are acquitted by God." [2]

Severus did not think so. He prohibited conversion to Judaism or Christianity under heavy penalties. The day of the Christians was not yet. But the exhaustion of Italy, the impoverishment of the old Roman nobility, the humiliation of the senate, and the transfer of power to provincial armies and provincial generals were pointers to the eventual victory of the Church.

[1] Perhaps even his distant kinsman. Tertullian too was a Septimius.
[2] Tertullian, *Apology*, XXXVII, 4; L, 12, 13, 16.

CHAPTER X

SACRED HISTORY

BUT what was this Church, this assembly or association (*ekklesia*) of apparently insignificant people, which in the first century began to disturb the peace of the Roman Empire, in the second began to be regarded as a standing nuisance, in the third became a serious rival to the imperial government, and in the fourth forced it to come to terms?

History has not yet answered the question. Indeed, it may be said that professional historians have not yet even begun to ask it. The lines of historical research are adapted to an educational system which assumes as its foundation the truth of dogmatic religion. In conformity with that assumption, ancient history is divided into two departments and its teaching entrusted to two different faculties of experts. The historian proper deals with " secular " history (known in the curriculum simply as " history "), that is with events in which natural causes are presupposed and which he accordingly interprets by ordinary canons of probability. The theologian deals with " sacred " history (known in the curriculum as " scripture " or " divinity "), that is with events in which, divine intervention being presupposed, ordinary canons of probability may at need be set aside. The historian, being a busy man and as a rule uninterested in theology, usually treats Judaism and Christianity as facts which it is beyond his province to explain. Even Gibbon, it will be remembered, in his fifteenth chapter abandons to the theologian " the pleasing task of describing Religion as she descended from Heaven, arrayed in her native purity," and reserves to the historian the " more melancholy duty " of discovering " the inevitable mixture of error and corruption, which she contracted in a long residence upon earth, among a weak and degenerate race of beings." Much more do the professional historians of today keep off the forbidden grass. The theologian, who as a rule is not a historian, is thus able to pursue his "pleasing task" undisturbed except by free-lances whom, since they hold no academic posts and have limited leisure for research, he can plausibly ignore as un-qualified poachers on his domain.

The result is that, side by side with the secular history of antiquity reproduced in essence in the last few chapters, we learn in our youth a sacred history based on the books of the Old and New Testaments. Naturally there are points of contact between the two. Sacred history would not even be plausible if there were not. But the two are qualitatively different. While the events of secular history (allowing for differences in the economic, social, political, and cultural environment) are of an order identical with that of events in the world of today and are connected with them by a con-tinuous process, sacred history, on the other hand, is presented to us as a divine dispensation attested by a series of miraculous events different in kind from anything which we should accept if recorded by a secular narrator of the past or present, or by a sacred historian of any other religion. Most of those who believe or think that they believe in the miracles of the Bible, or at any rate of the New Testament, would dismiss as unbalanced anyone who told them that anything of the kind (say a virgin birth, a resurrection, or an ascension) had occurred in the next street. Miracles do not happen now— even if they formerly did. Secular history goes on; sacred history stopped when the canon of the New Testament was closed. The Catholic Church sees the difficulty, and provides for the benefit of the faithful a continuation of sacred history in the lives of the saints and in such miraculous happenings as those at Loreto, Naples, and Lourdes.[1] But these are

---

[1] According to a story dating from the late Middle Ages, the house of the Holy Family at Nazareth was carried by angels (in three hops) to Loreto in Italy, where it is still on show. The blood of Januarius, patron saint of Naples, is preserved in the cathedral and publicly liquefies twice a year. The organized pilgrimages and "cures" at Lourdes are highly lucrative to the Church, the hotels, and the railways.

strictly for the benefit of the faithful. They occur and recur only among ignorant peasants or before highly suggestible Catholic crowds.

The problem before the historian is to fit what can be known of Jewish and Christian origins into the secular history of antiquity. The theologian finds this perfectly simple. At a remote date, perhaps contemporary with the eighteenth dynasty in Egypt (fifteenth or fourteenth century B.C.), the Creator of the universe revealed himself to some nomad tribes held in serfdom by the Pharaohs. Miraculously delivered from Egyptian bondage, Israel took possession of Palestine and established there a cult and commonwealth purer than any previously known to history. Their descendants, however, degenerated and, in spite of prophetic warnings, became no better than the idolatrous peoples around them. They consequently lost their independence and were deported to Assyria and Babylonia. Under the Persian Empire a righteous remnant were re-established at Jerusalem; and inspired prophets foretold that in the fullness of time the world order would be overthrown and all nations be converted to the Jewish way of life and live in peace under a heaven-sent ruler. So far Jewish and Christian tradition agrees. Christian theology adds that under the Roman Empire the final divine revelation took place; that God became man in the person of Jesus Christ, the predicted Messiah; that the Jews, in spite of the evidence of miracles wrought before their very eyes, blindly rejected him and gave him up to be crucified by the procurator, Pontius Pilate; and that Christ, risen from the dead, founded a Church to proclaim his kingdom to all nations and to inherit the privileges forfeited by the unbelieving Jews.

The historian, unless he is content to leave his work half done, is bound to demand as stringent evidence for these statements as for any others purporting to relate to historical facts. One difference between secular and sacred history at once leaps to the eye. We derive our knowledge of secular history from authors of whom we know in nearly every case the names and dates, and in many cases even the life-stories— Herodotus of Halicarnassus, Thucydides of Athens, Polybius of Megalopolis, Livy of Padua, Plutarch of Chæronea, Appian of Alexandria, Arrian of Nicomedia, and so forth. Some of them were wholly or partly contemporary with the events they relate; others, though they lived centuries later, at least had access to contemporary authorities, some of whom they name, and, if they make mistakes, can be checked by the evidence of other historians or of inscriptions and coins. But when we turn to sacred history we are confronted for the most part with anonymous writings, the dates of which have to be inferred from such external and internal evidence as is available. Even those writings which contain evidence of authorship are often demonstrably composite or spurious. Moreover these anonymous, pseudonymous, or at best precariously authenticated works are nearly all written with a purpose; and that purpose is not impartial history, but partisan propaganda, from which edifying fiction is naturally not excluded. To put the propaganda of a cult on the same level as critical history is contrary to every canon of scientific inquiry. None of us would dream of doing it if we had not been taught in youth to think that in matters of religion belief is a duty and unbelief a crime.

A critical study of Judaism and Christianity starts with certain known data. In the sunset of Asiatic civilization—when Babylonia and Egypt have fallen a prey to Persia, herself soon to fall a prey to Greece—a Jewish community with a peculiar religion, a peculiar code of law, and a peculiar prophetic literature is found established around Jerusalem. In the sunset of Græco-Roman civilization—when Rome, after reaching the peak of her imperial expansion, hovers on the brink of her decline and fall—a Christian community, which has made the Jewish religion and literature its own, though with vital differences of interpretation, is found troubling the peace of Græco-Roman society. We have no right to assume without proof that these people were the recipients of a divine revelation. But we have equally no right to assume without proof that they were knaves or fools. They were people basically like ourselves, but without our command over nature, our knowledge of the world we live in, our distrust of the marvellous, or our means of checking and verifying what we hear or read. We have to explain the data by causes known to have operated in ancient society.

The sacred history common to Judaism and Christianity is contained in the books of the Old Testament. These fall traditionally into three divisions. The first five books, the Pentateuch or " law of Moses," are accepted not only by Jews and Christians, but by the Samaritan community, of which a tiny remnant survives in Palestine today. As the Jewish and Samaritan communities broke away from each other in the fourth or fifth century B.C. and had no further mutual dealings, the Pentateuch must have existed then. But it cannot in its present form be much older than that. For the Pentateuch prescribes a rigorous monotheism, and limits the priestly office, and with it the right to offer sacrifice, to the descendants of Aaron. This is in accordance with the practice of Judaism from that time, but not with old Israelitish practice as portrayed in the books of Judges, Samuel, and Kings, where idolatry is the rule rather than the exception and where laymen offer sacrifice and, in notable instances, even human sacrifice without a word of reprobation. The Pentateuch, therefore, in its present form is later than the old kingdoms of Israel and Judah; and although it embodies strata much older than the date of its compilation, there is no reason to suppose that any part is anything like contemporary with the events which it purports to relate.

It is therefore not surprising that Egyptian monuments should have failed to confirm the traditional bondage of Israel in the land of Egypt. The first mention of Israel is on a monument of about 1200 B.C. recording the conquest by Pharaoh Merenptah (nineteenth dynasty) of that and other tribes in Palestine—an event not mentioned in the Bible. We cannot dogmatically deny that there was ever an Egyptian oppression. Under the eighteenth dynasty Palestine and Syria had been part of a great Egyptian Empire, and Egypt had been filled with plunder, tribute, and slaves, among whom no doubt were many Semitic tribesmen. But the detailed history of that age cannot be reconstructed from writings compiled with a religious purpose a thousand years later.

Outside the Old Testament we do not hear of Israel again

until the ninth and eighth centuries B.C., when Assyria pushes westward, imposes tribute on the petty kingdoms of Syria and Palestine, and finally, after a revolt, deports twenty-seven thousand Israelites and replaces them by colonists from other parts of her empire. There is no evidence that Israel or Judah at this time worshipped one God, or that their religion differed materially from those of other petty peoples in that part of the world.

It is, however, in these and the following centuries—the period when Assyrian armies were wasting, slaying, and raking in plunder and tribute, until Assyria tottered to her fall under the onset of Scythian savages from the north, and the Medes and Babylonians partitioned her empire between them, and Persia in turn mopped up Media and Babylonia—that we must date the origin of Judaism. Western Asia must have been a scene of appalling misery. Man found it too much. His gods—the personifications of his social group, made in his own image—had let him down. Prophets, free-lance soothsayers opposed to the official priesthoods, began to inveigh against the established cults, to denounce usury, oppression, bribery, and forced labour, to organize, and to put forth literature. Prophets were not peculiar to Palestine; but conditions in Palestine favoured their multiplication. Palestine was the last country in Western Asia to be devoured by Assyria. While petty kingdoms to the north were being slowly annexed, Israel and Judah enjoyed a temporary respite of which the prophets made full use. Moreover, although Palestine was constantly fought over by great military empires, yet, until Rome appeared on the scene, none of them held it securely, and few of them held it long. This insecurity of tenure was favourable to movements of revolt. The hope of deliverance from oppression lived on and flickered up again and again in Palestine long after it had been extinguished elsewhere.

The prophetic writings—the second of the three traditional divisions of the Jewish Bible—are the oldest revolutionary literature that has come down to us. Unfortunately they have come down much interpolated and corrupted—so much so that some parts are almost unintelligible. After all, what can we expect? These writings were the production of an opposition party and, to a large extent, of what we should now call an underground movement. They passed from hand to hand and were interpolated according to taste from generation to generation. Naturally the original writings became overlaid with later matter, and passages, topical when they were written, were reduced to gibberish by copyists ignorant of their meaning. Add that in many cases the meaning must have been deliberately veiled to elude the attentions of the authorities; and the obscurity of much of the prophetic literature will not surprise us. Yet, when all is said and done, one fact stands out. So far as it is intelligible, the message of the prophets is one of revolt against wealth and privilege, particularly of the official priesthoods. There are few franker pieces of anti-clericalism in all literature than the outbursts of Amos and Isaiah against feasts and solemn assemblies, burnt offerings and meal offerings, new moons and sabbaths. But, scientific Rationalism being as yet unknown, the opponents of established cults had to speak in the name of some god. In claiming to speak in the name of Jah or Jahveh, the ancestral god of Israel, the prophets appealed from an evil present to an idealized past of desert simplicity, when there had been no sacrifices, no temple, no forced labour, and no usury. That ideal past was a mirage : the nomadic ancestors of Israel had been savages, and Jah a bloodstained idol. But by turning him into the champion of the poor against their oppressors the prophets built better than they knew.

As official cults and priesthoods were more and more discredited by the disasters of the time, the priests of Jerusalem were forced in self-defence to adopt the reform programme and to incorporate it in the law-book now called Deuteronomy. There is to be no God but one and no place of worship but one; other sanctuaries are to be destroyed; usury is forbidden; there is to be a periodic cancellation of debts; the peasant and the slave are protected; military service is voluntary. Soon afterwards the destruction of the Jewish kingdom by Nebuchadnezzar cleared the path for the new Judaism. The whole history of Israel was rewritten by the prophetic party to fit their thesis : we have the result of their labours in the books of Judges, Samuel, and Kings, the compilers of which condemn *ex post facto* the idolatry they are obliged to record. When in due course the temple was rebuilt and Jerusalem re-fortified under the Persian Empire, the new community was a theocracy, " the people of a book "—the newly compiled Pentateuch, in which the early folk-lore of Israel is deftly dovetailed into Deuteronomy and the later Priestly Code, and the whole passed off as the thousand-year-old law of Moses from which the nation had sinfully deviated during the intervening centuries. The protection granted by the Persian Empire to the new theocratic community at Jerusalem is probably to be explained by the weak situation of Persia after her failure to conquer Greece, and by the vital necessity of placing the approaches to Egypt in the hands of a loyal vassal.

But the priestly aristocracy had yielded to the reformers only under duress. Throughout the period of the second temple there were struggles between the hierarchy of Jerusalem (after the conquests of Alexander increasingly permeated by Hellenism) and those Jews, the lineal successors of the prophetic party, to whom Judaism was not just a local cult but a movement to be propagated among the nations until it had revolutionized the world. We catch the echoes of this propagandist Judaism in the later prophetic writings (Deutero-Isaiah, Haggai, Zechariah), in many of the Psalms, and above all in the book of Daniel and in other apocalyptic works not included in the Bible. The struggle emerges into the light of history in the attempt of Antiochus IV to suppress Judaism and in the successful Maccabean resistance. In apocalyptic literature popular Judaism vents its hatred of the robber empires which one after another devour mankind, and its aspirations for a millennial reign of righteousness on earth. By the second century B.C., therefore, Jewish sacred writings fell into three categories—the law, recognized by all Jews and even by Samaritans; the prophets; and books not included in either class and not yet at that date reduced to a cut-and-dried canon.

So far our conclusions would be endorsed by most Biblical scholars not tied hand and foot to Fundamentalism. It is otherwise when we approach the origins of Christianity. For here we are dealing with a revolution of the past whose true history has never been written, and whose ostensible history is an officially propagated myth deemed by its defenders to be essential to the existence of civilization itself— even as the worship of the gods and deified emperors was deemed in its day to be essential to the existence of *pax Romana*. But humanity is a hardy plant. As the gods and deified emperors departed, and ancient civilization with them, leaving men and women just as determined as before to go on living, so perhaps is the Christian myth, and with it much of what doubtfully passes as civilization, destined to depart and to leave us wondering why we ever deemed these frail products of time to be eternal.

After the Maccabean victory pious Jews (*Hasidim*, later Pharisees) may have believed for a moment that the "Ancient of Days" had established a kingdom of the "son of man" which in due course would destroy the beast-empires around it and inaugurate universal justice.[1] They were soon undeceived. The later Hasmonæan rulers, especially Alexander Jannæus (103–76 B.C.), to whom the priestly aristocracy (Sadducees) had now rallied, crushed popular opposition by massacre and crucifixion. The civil war between Alexander's two sons led in 63 to the intervention of Pompey and to the conquest of Judæa by Rome. The Jewish people still cherished the prophetic dream of a kingdom of God on earth, but they began to despair of its realization by human agency. Some still hoped for an earthly leader, an anointed king or Messiah, who would put down princes from their thrones and exalt them of low degree. Others looked for redemption by supernatural agency—by some hero of the past (say Joshua) who would come again to deliver his people, or by some Son of Man from the clouds. We have examples of these dreams in the apocalyptic book of Enoch, and in a commentary on the prophet Habakkuk discovered in 1947 with other scrolls in a cave near the Dead Sea. In this scroll

---

[1] Dan. vii, 9–14. "Son of man" in this context means simply "man" as opposed to "beast". The phrase has not yet the Messianic sense which it takes on in later apocalyptic.

the writer refers to the persecution of the sect to which he belonged (conjectured to have been the Essenes, a sort of Pharisee "left wing") and to the torture and execution of its leader, the "master of justice," by a high priest who from other data must be identical with Aristobulus II, one of the sons of Alexander Jannæus. The capture of Jerusalem by Pompey is a judgment on this crime. Further judgment is in store: the executed leader will return, put to confusion the reigning high priest (Hyrcanus II, brother of Aristobulus), and judge Israel and all nations. Only those who believe in the "master of justice" will be saved. This important discovery proves that the idea of a Messiah triumphant over suffering and death was already current a century before the rise of Christianity.[1]

Messianic expectations were not confined to Palestine. In the centuries since Alexander the Great, Jewish colonies had sprung up in all the chief Mediterranean cities—Alexandria, Antioch, Cyrene, Ephesus, Corinth, Rome itself. Some of these Jews of the *diaspora* were prosperous, especially at Alexandria, where they were favoured by the Ptolemies. But most were in humble walks of life—slaves, freedmen, petty traders. They spoke Greek as the common language of Mediterranean civilization, they used the Greek version of the scriptures, and they tried to convert their neighbours to the Jewish dream of the kingdom of God on earth. Their neighbours were inclined to listen. Most of them, too, were slaves or freedmen. They, too, felt the world to be evil and were seeking compensation in dreams. Many found in the various "mystery" cults—those of Dionysus, Attis, Isis, Mithra—something to take the place of the communal life from which they had been uprooted. But Judaism promised them something in this world. Thousands were converted—carrying with them into Judaism scraps of myth from the mystery-cults they abandoned. We have already seen the alarm occasioned to the Roman government by these conversions and the sharp action taken against them by Tiberius and later emperors.

[1] See the article, "New Light on Habakkuk," in *The Times*, May 30, 1950.

But it was not only the Romans who had cause for alarm. Well-to-do Jews of the stamp of Philo of Alexandria, with a Greek education and a stake in the world, had reason to fear this Messianic ferment among the masses. They tried to conciliate the Greek world; to restate Judaism in terms of Greek philosophy; to identify Jahveh with the Absolute of the metaphysicians, and the word by which he created heaven and earth with the Stoic *logos*, the reason immanent in nature and in man; and to interpret the rest of the Jewish Bible in the same allegorical fashion. To these ingenious escapists or " Gnostics " propaganda about the kingdom of God on earth and about a Messiah who would execute vengeance on the rich and great was very disturbing. It could only lead to a head-on collision between the Jewish community and Rome —a collision in which Rome might not draw nice distinctions between Jew and Jew.

We are now in a position to weigh the available documentary evidence on the subject of Christian origins. That evidence is contained in the books of the New Testament, supplemented by other early Christian writings and by such pagan testimony as is available.

Any critical student of early Christian documents must be struck by their contradictory character. Not only do they contradict one another on plain matters of fact, but the doctrine propagated is different in different documents. The Pauline Epistles, for example, which, in so far as they are genuine, are the oldest Christian writings we possess, are good evidence of the kind of propaganda conducted by some Greek-speaking missionaries in the second half of the first century. They have next to nothing to say of the life, and nothing of the teaching of the traditional founder of Christianity. They are concerned first and foremost with a divine figure called Jesus Christ, said to have been crucified by " the rulers of this world " [1] and to have risen from the dead in order that believers in him may rise from death to eternal life. We have here a saviour-god of a type familiar in the mystery-cults: in fact Paul himself calls his doctrine a " mys-

---

[1] I Cor. ii, 8. The Greek *archontes tou aiônos toutou* is Gnostic and means demons, not men.

tery" and his converts "initiates" (*teleioi*).[1] Paul represents himself (or is represented by his impersonators) as having received his doctrine from no human source, but from Christ himself by revelation. For the most part the Epistles refer to Christ in terms appropriate only to a god—the projection and personification of the society which worships him. "We, who are many, are one body in Christ."[2] "Ye are the body of Christ, and severally members thereof."[3] Only very rarely has the Pauline Christ the attributes of a man, "born of the seed of David according to the flesh,"[4] with human "brethren" known to Paul.[5]

Theology overcomes the contradiction by proclaiming that Christ was true God and true man. But the extreme paucity of these Pauline references to a human Jesus is easier to explain if we regard them as later interpolations in documents which originally related only to the saviour-god of a mystery-cult. By no possibility can the Epistles have been written to propagate the teaching of a human founder. They do not record or even cite it.

If we turn from the Pauline Epistles to a document of a very different tendency, the Johannine Apocalypse, written in Asia Minor under Domitian, we still find scarcely any trace of a human Jesus. The Christ of the Apocalypse is "the first and the last," "the beginning of the creation of God."[6] By a mysterious death, suffered apparently "from the foundation of the world,"[7] he has purchased an earthly kingdom for "men of every tribe, and tongue, and people, and nation"[8] —a kingdom to be erected on the smoking ruins of the persecuting power of Rome. Only once is the Lord said to have been crucified in an earthly city; and that may be an interpolation.[9] In the case of the Apocalypse we must make some allowance for figurative and poetical language. Still, such facts as the above have been legitimately used

---

[1] I Cor. ii, 6–7. *Teleioi* is translated in our Bibles "perfect"—the Revised Version adding a footnote "full-grown." But the word is borrowed from the mystery-cults.

[2] Rom. xii, 5.   [3] I Cor. xii, 27.   [4] Rom. i, 3.

[5] I Cor. ix, 5; Gal. i, 19.   [6] Rev. i, 17; iii, 14.

[7] Rev. xiii, 8.   [8] Rev. v, 9–10.   [9] Rev. xi, 8.

to support the theory that Jesus is wholly a mythical figure.

But the myth theory is an over-simplification. When we turn to the Synoptic Gospels we are confronted with documents which are clearly composite. In their present form they are not very much earlier than the middle of the second century, but they are compiled from material some of which is demonstrably generations older. A comparison of Matthew, Mark, and Luke shows that they are based on a common source or sources (sometimes appearing in almost identical language in all three, sometimes only in two) which internal evidence proves to be not far removed in date from the destruction of the temple in A.D. 70. In one such source Jesus is made to predict that event in so many words ("there shall not be left here one stone upon another, which shall not be thrown down"[1]) and to add a more detailed prophecy of the horrors leading up to it. The catastrophe will be followed (Matthew says "immediately," Mark "in those days," Luke implies an interval) by the coming of the Son of Man "in power and great glory." In all three, "this generation shall not pass away, until all be accomplished."[2] Such a prophecy cannot have originated much after the events of 70. Cognate passages elsewhere in the Synoptics, such as the woes again and again denounced on Jerusalem, suggest that the nucleus of the Gospel story took shape under the immediate impact of the horrors of that time.

Now it is remarkable that in the Gospel strata used by two or three Synoptics, and by that criterion relatively early, Jesus is not only not God, but manifestly a man with human limitations and weaknesses. At the outset he is depicted as tempted by the devil—an experience conceivable in a man, but not in a God who cannot sin. At the end he cries that God has forsaken him. Supposing these stories to be invented,

[1] Matt. xxiv, 2; Mark xiii, 2; Luke xxi, 6.
[2] Matt. xxiv, 29–34; Mark xiii, 24–30; Luke xxi, 24–32. The theory, vented by some orthodox commentators and by some not so orthodox, that the prophecy of the advent of the Son of Man was *fulfilled* by the fall of Jerusalem (with its attendant horrors of cannibalism and massacre) is so grotesque that to state it is to refute it.

at least their inventors cannot have supposed him to be God.[1] The impression left by these early strata is of a human prophet, with human parents, brothers, and sisters, proclaiming that the kingdom of God is at hand and promising earthly rewards (houses, land, and human comradeship) to his followers.[2] Since such stories were circulating round about A.D. 70, and since they point to a human and not improbable prophet, it is not irrational to conclude that such a prophet existed.

It does not follow that everything that is set down in these early strata is true. Between the procuratorship of Pilate and the date when the material took shape a whole generation elapsed—ample time for a miraculous legend to grow up. Moreover, the possibility cannot be excluded that in that legend we have a conglomerate of stories told at different times of different men—an Essene leader executed by Aristobulus before 63 B.C.; a Nazarene crucified by Pilate nearly a century later; perhaps even Jesus ben-Hanan, a fanatic who for years before the fall of the city went about crying, " Woe, woe to Jerusalem ! " who persisted in spite of cruel beatings, and who was killed during the siege by a stone from a Roman catapult.[3]   He, however, made no Messianic claim. We are so accustomed to employing " Christ " or " Messiah " as a proper name that we tend to forget that it was originally the generic term for an anointed king, and that there were during this period many claimants to that title, many of whom came to violent ends.   The point is that, whatever the origin of these stories, they were told originally of a man or men, and not of a God.

We have, then, in early Christian literature, putting aside secondary discrepancies, two primary and contradictory traditions—one (represented by the Pauline writings) of a saviour-god who is crucified by demons and who by rising from death confers eternal life on his worshippers; and one

---

[1] The stories of the temptation and the " cry of dereliction " are taught to us in childhood simultaneously with the dogma of the deity of Jesus. We give them verbal assent. But does anyone give more than *verbal* assent to the propositions that God incarnate was really tempted to sin, and really forsaken by—himself?

[2] Matt. xix, 29; Mark x, 29-30.   [3] Josephus, *Jewish War*, VI, 5, 3.

(discernible in the Synoptic Gospels) of a human prophet put to death for preaching the kingdom of God on earth. The conflicting traditions persist throughout the early centuries. Because the fusion of opposites which we call "orthodoxy" eventually won the day, we must not suppose that it was dominant from the first. In the *Teaching of the Twelve Apostles*, a manual of instruction compiled, it seems, in Syria about the end of the first or the beginning of the second century, we have an invaluable picture of a type of church as yet unaffected by Pauline influences. The *Teaching* reproduces part of the so-called Sermon on the Mount (but not from our existing Gospels) and gives the Lord's Prayer in the form we know. Otherwise it displays no knowledge of the New Testament. It prescribes a form of eucharist, but says nothing about the bread and wine representing in any way the body and blood of the Lord. Jesus is not God, but the "servant" of God. The organization of the Church is democratic and rather like that of a modern trade union branch: it has its elected officials ("bishops" and "deacons") and its visiting speakers ("apostles" and "prophets"). In dealing with these latter, the *Teaching* lays down rules designed to keep "Christ-mongers" at arm's length: for example, visitors are to be allowed subsistence, but are not to be paid in money. Evidently the churches, like other struggling organizations, suffered from men who tried to live on them. The *Teaching* ends by predicting a last and worst persecution, after which the Lord will come on the clouds of heaven and set up the kingdom of God. In the *Shepherd* of Hermas, a Christian allegory written at Rome about 140–150, we get a similar point of view. Jesus is a trusty servant of God in whom his Holy Spirit dwelt, and who for "labouring much and enduring many toils" and "walking honourably in holiness and purity" is promoted to be the Son of God and deputed to reveal God's commandments to his fellow-servants.[1] Justin, writing at Rome about the same time, though himself believing in the deity of Jesus, admits that there are Christians who consider him "a man and the son of men; with whom I do not agree, nor could

---

[1] Hermas, Parable V.

I do so even if the greater number of my co-religionists were to say the same." [1]   Right on into the third and even the fourth century there were Christian teachers, especially in the East (Theodotus, Artemon, Paul of Samosata, Archelaus, Aphraates), who maintained that Jesus was a mere man, though supernaturally favoured by God, and who claimed, moreover, that this had been the teaching of the first apostles and of the majority of Christians in the first two centuries.

How came it that these two diametrically opposed views persisted side by side in the Christian churches until a formula of reconciliation was imposed by the Council of Nicæa? Neither can be explained by the other or reduced to the other. The deification of a man Jesus in such terms as are used in the Pauline Epistles, and the identification of a god Jesus with a Jew executed as a rebel by Pilate in the reign of Tiberius, are equally inexplicable except on one hypothesis.   That is that Christianity had not one, but at least two and very probably more origins, and that by force of circumstances two or more initially independent movements fused into one.

Let us try to reconstruct the story to the best of our ability. In the last century B.C. disillusionment with the Hasmonæan régime and final loss of independence led to revolutionary movements in Palestine which were in fact a revival of the prophetic movement of centuries before, and which found articulate expression in the Messianic hope.   From time to time actual outbreaks occurred and were put down by the later Hasmonæans, by the Herodian dynasty, and by Rome with ruthless ferocity.   Thousands of rebels ended their lives on the cross.   Still the movement continued.   The theme of an executed Messiah triumphant over death already figured in revolutionary propaganda before the Christian era.   This propaganda spread from Palestine to the *diaspora* in the Mediterranean cities, and by the first century of our era had provoked Rome to strong measures against Jews in Italy.   The Jews whom Claudius expelled from Rome for making " disturbances at the instigation of Chrestus " [2] may not have been Christians in our sense of the word, but they were certainly Messianists—though whether the Messiah

---

[1] Justin, *Dialogue with Trypho*, 48.   [2] Suetonius, *Claudius*, XXV.

they followed had appeared elsewhere in the empire or there in their midst, in the Roman ghetto, is impossible to say on the meagre evidence of Suetonius.[1]

It was vital to well-to-do Jews and Jewish sympathizers in the *diaspora* to counter this popular Messianic propaganda and prevent the head-on collision with Rome which it threatened to bring about. But it could not be countered by mere negation. To be effective, counter-propaganda must be framed in terms which the masses could understand. This could be done by adopting the Messianist slogans and interpreting them in a mystical and therefore harmless sense. The kingdom of God? Yes, but a kingdom not of this world. To be inaugurated by the Messiah, the new Joshua, *Christos Iesous*? Yes, but by no earthly warrior : by the Son of God, the conqueror of death and hell. Vengeance on the rich and great? No, salvation for all, Jew or Greek, bond or free, who believed and were united to the Son of God in baptism.

That is the actual propaganda which from the first century of our era was carried on in the Mediterranean cities by a number of Greek-speaking Jews or half-Jews, of whom Paul and his associates are the best-known examples. " We were buried with him through baptism into death, that as Christ was raised from the dead through the glory of the Father, so we also might walk in newness of life." [2] " We, who are many, are one body in Christ, and severally members one of another." [3] To the slaves and freedmen who came to the synagogues of the *diaspora* looking for release from an evil society this sounded (and was meant to sound) like the preaching of a new mystery-cult. There is nothing here about the kingdom of God on earth or a Son of Man who will put down princes from their thrones and exalt them of low degree. The name " Christ " is indeed used; but the anointed king of popular apocalyptic has disappeared, and is replaced by the dying and risen saviour-god of an age-old myth. The

---

[1] Eisler's guess that this Messiah was Simon Magus, posing as Jesus risen from the dead, may be mentioned—as a guess. *The Messiah Jesus and John the Baptist*, p. 581.

[2] Rom. vi, 4.   [3] Rom. xii, 5.

substitution was facilitated by the fact that the Messiah had already in the last century B.C. begun to take on some of the attributes of a saviour-god.

Travelling through the Mediterranean, Pauline propaganda before long encountered a movement of a very different kind and origin. Agitators from Palestine claimed that the Messiah had appeared there in the flesh—no theological creation like that of the Pauline missionaries, but an actual man, accredited by miracles of healing such as everyone expected a Messiah to perform. He had been chosen by God to set up his kingdom; and though the Romans had caught and crucified him, was it not written that the Messiah should suffer? He would soon return and gather his elect into a kingdom of peace and plenty on earth, in which all who dare risk a Roman cross and join him would share. Of some such nature was the propaganda of those Christians (*Christiani* on the analogy of *Cæsariani*—not worshippers of a *god*, but followers of a *leader*) who spread from Judæa to Rome and in 64 enabled Nero to fasten on them, with some plausibility, the charge of firing the city. It was one and only one example of the Messianic ferment which led in 66–70 to the revolutionary war ending in the destruction of Jerusalem and its temple.

After that catastrophe it became more than ever necessary for Pauline mystics to dissociate the Christ-cult from revolutionary Judaism and, so far as they could, to carry the *diaspora* with them. The angry clash between the two propagandas echoes and re-echoes in Pauline (or pseudo-Pauline) attacks on those who preach " another Jesus, whom we did not preach," [1] and in counter-attacks on " them which call themselves apostles and they are not." [2] For the purposes of their polemic the Pauline party took the inflammatory literature circulated by the Messianists about their crucified leader and (as the pagan critic Celsus was to point out) " revised it three or four times, nay, many times, and refashioned the story so as to provide themselves with replies to objectors." [3] The process of revision is to be seen in the Synoptic Gospels, in which the original story of a human,

[1] 2 Cor. xi, 4.　　[2] Rev. ii, 2.　　[3] Origen, *Against Celsus*, II, 27.

but divinely endowed Jewish prophet has been progressively
worked over and made to conform to Pauline theology.
In the Fourth Gospel the process is complete : Jesus is God
from the beginning, and has only an outer show of manhood,
such as an Egyptian might have attributed to Osiris or a
Greek to Dionysus.

Such literary devices, however, would have been fruitless
but for the co-operation of hard economic facts. Messianic
propaganda appealed mainly to the oppressed classes—
slaves, freedmen, and the poor in general. Gnostic and
Pauline propaganda, on the other hand, had its roots chiefly
among the well-to-do—prosperous master-craftsmen like
Paul himself, who takes credit (or is given credit by his impersonators) for not being " a burden on any man," [1] but,
on the contrary, " ministering to them that were with him." [2]
The Messianists, with their material appeal, had the makings
of a mass movement, but little money. The Pauline mystics
had money, but little mass appeal. Nevertheless, money
talks. By throwing their money into the scale, the Pauline
party gradually got control of most of the Christian churches
and drew the sting of the Messianic movement. The clergy,
originally elected officials of the local church, gradually
came to be regarded as irremovable and as holding their
office from God. The accounts in the Acts and the Pauline
Epistles of collections taken in Gentile churches for the " poor
among the saints that are at Jerusalem " [3] may be partly historical. They undoubtedly suggest to realistic readers the
process by which in the course of a century or so Paulinism
with its mystical theology became orthodoxy, while first-
century Messianism with its millennial dreams became an
eccentricity and finally a heresy. Excommunication or expulsion from the Church was not merely a spiritual, but a
material weapon. It meant exclusion from the benefits
disbursed by the Church, and particularly from the communal meal or *agape*, and was a powerful weapon by which
the leadership could keep the rank and file in order.

The same economic factor helps to solve another riddle.
Many of us must have wondered why early Christianity in-

[1] 2 Cor. xi, 9.   [2] Acts xx, 34.   [3] Rom. xv, 26.

spired such violent antipathy in educated Greeks and Romans
—why Pliny (after torturing two unfortunate female slaves)
condemns it as an "absurd and extravagant superstition,"[1]
Tacitus as "deserving extreme and exemplary punishment,"[2]
Suetonius as "new and mischievous,"[3] Marcus Aurelius as
"mere obstinacy,"[4] Celsus as a "secret conspiracy against
the law"[5]—when almost all the Christian writings which
have come down to us in the New Testament and the Fathers
enjoin submission to the powers that be except in the one
matter of idolatry. Surely idol-worship was not of vital
moment to philosophers and men of culture! Our uncritical
ancestors were content to explain this antipathy by saying
that pagans were wicked people who took a cruel pleasure in
tormenting Christians. But Pliny, until he came across the
Christians, was a kindly and refined gentleman. Tacitus was
a passionate moralist, sensitive enough to suffering when the
sufferers were of his own class. Marcus was a humanitarian
Stoic, though his humanity may not have been noticeable
in the amphitheatre at Lyons. Celsus was a highly intelligent,
well-informed, and broad-minded philosopher. The para-
dox disappears if we reflect that the early Christian literature
we possess is, in the nature of the case, mainly the work of
the better-off and better-educated Christians. We cannot be
sure that Paul's exhortations to passive obedience or Justin's
professions of loyalty represented the sentiments of the rank
and file. In fact we can be pretty sure that they did not;
for Paul (or whoever wrote in his name) would hardly have
felt it necessary to threaten in such strong terms those who
resisted the power of Rome unless resistance had been in
the air.

It is significant that the one contributor to the New
Testament who writes not only colloquial, but ungrammatical
Greek—the author of the Apocalypse—calls Rome a harlot
drunk with blood and her empire a beast from the abyss, and
threatens both with fire and brimstone, which, we suspect,
he would not have minded administering personally. From

[1] Pliny, *Letters*, X, 97.　　[2] Tacitus, *Annals*, XV, 44.
[3] Suetonius, *Nero*, XVI.　　[4] Marcus Aurelius, *Meditations*, XI, 3.
[5] Origen, *Against Celsus*, I, 1.

the Apocalypse we can learn more of the mind of the slaves and freedmen who composed the majority of the early Christian community than from the more carefully edited Gospels and Epistles. Whatever apologists might say, behind the refusal of the rank-and-file Christian to burn incense to the emperor's statue lay no mere monotheistic scruple, but a deep hatred of the "kingdom of the beast." Whatever Gnostics might say, the Christ whom the rank-and-file Christian died for rather than revile was no other-worldly mystery-god, but a crucified rebel, or perhaps a composite figure made up of many crucified rebels, whom he expected to come on the clouds of heaven to feed the birds of the air with the flesh of the kings of the earth and their armies.

Thus, from a fusion between rich Gnostics and poor Messianists, was born the Catholic Church. The dogma eventually formulated of the union of perfect God and perfect man in one Christ reflects in terms of theology the union of the two movements in one Christian society. By the second half of the second century the fusion was as complete as it could ever hope to be. The Catholic Church, with her bishops by now well in control of their followers, sloughing off heresies to the right and left, dexterously appropriating the Jewish Bible, and appending to it her four Gospels and a canon (still somewhat in dispute) of apostolic literature,[1] offered Christianity to the Roman Empire as a new opium for the people.

[1] The Muratori Canon at the end of the second century ignores the Epistle to the Hebrews, those of James and Peter, and 3 John. Even as late as Eusebius (early fourth century) some still rejected James, 2 Peter, 2 and 3 John, Jude, and Revelation. Eusebius, *Ecclesiastical History*, III, 25.

CHAPTER XI

END OF A WORLD

B
Y this time the Roman Empire was far on in decay. With the cessation of imperial expansion in the second century the supply of cheap slave labour dried up, and mass slavery became uneconomical. The exhausted soil was tilled more and more by serfs (*coloni*), who, in return for security on their smallholdings, paid the landowner in kind, in personal labour, or in both. Some of them were slaves manumitted on that condition, others free peasants reduced to it by distress. The owners in their turn were taxed more and more heavily to support the legions. These, as we have seen, were no longer Roman or even Italian, but raised from the provincial populations among whom they served, and more concerned to enrich themselves than to defend the empire as a whole. These provincial armies were becoming less and less reliable; for under Marcus Aurelius and his successors it became increasingly necessary to fill the gaps in their strength with Germans from over the frontier, who were settled on the land on condition of military service. The ancient world was beginning to dissolve into feudalism.

In such a situation there could no longer be any objection to an Oriental religion as such. The Roman upper class, the traditional upholders of the State religion, were in the last stages of impotence and impoverishment. Even the Italians were powerless under the military heel. The legions were carrying Oriental cults, such as that of Mithra, into every corner of the empire. The only question about Christianity was whether it was treasonable or not. Were the loyal protestations of its apologists to be taken seriously, or had the empire still to fear a subversive Messianism? Severus, as we saw, prohibited both Jewish and Christian propaganda. But there was no universal or sustained persecution. The trend of the time was towards toleration even of the queerest religions. In 211 Severus made way for his mad son Caracalla; and in 218, after another scuffle among the legions, the Oriental troops showed their contempt for everything Roman by elevating to the empire the effeminate priest of a Syrian fertility-god, Elagabalus. By thus insulting the senate and people of the imperial city they unwittingly helped to pave the way for Christianity. Many must have felt that if Rome could stand Elagabalus she could stand anything.

Alexander Severus (222–235), the young cousin and supplanter of Elagabalus, was the first emperor to consider the official recognition of Christianity. He seems to have meditated something in the nature of a concurrent endowment of paganism, Judaism, and Christianity: at any rate, he is said to have had busts of Abraham, Orpheus, Apollonius of Tyana, and Christ in his private chapel and to have proposed to build a church at the public expense, but to have been dissuaded by the pagan priests. Whether the bishops would have accepted this compromise and whether they would have carried their followers with them, we shall never know; but as Eusebius tells us that Alexander's household was filled with " believers," it is probable that he discussed the project with them. In any case he was not given a chance to try it. The defences of the empire were rocking under barbarian attacks. Persia, under her new and vigorous Sassanid monarchy, took the offensive in the east; and German tribes crossed the Rhine in the west. In 235 the western legions murdered the Syrian Alexander and proclaimed as emperor the Thracian Maximin, a rough peasant who had risen from the ranks to high command in the army. In the ensuing purge of Alexander's supporters a number of the clergy lost their lives; and Church historians accordingly reckon Maximin as a persecutor. But the executions were obviously political: on the showing even of Eusebius they were confined to " the leaders of the churches " and did not extend to the rank and file.[1] In the years of struggle which followed

---

[1] Eusebius, *Ecclesiastical History*, VI, 28. By an inexplicable slip Gibbon ascribes to Maximin a " promiscuous massacre " of " a great number of Christians of every rank." *Decline and Fall*, XVI.

between rival pretenders to the purple the lot of the Christians was no more miserable than that of other subjects of the empire.

Power was again within the reach of the Church in 244, when Philip the Arab incited the Oriental troops to murder the young emperor Gordian III and put him on the throne. Philip, if we may credit Eusebius, was a Christian; but for intelligible reasons the Church has never been anxious to claim him. In any case, he went down in 249 before the Illyrian Decius, who initiated the first systematic and general persecution which the Church had endured in its whole history. It must be remembered that at this time the Roman world faced an appalling crisis. Armies kept together by no common loyalty, and maintained only by crushing taxation, had to hold the frontiers against barbarians whose victory could hardly increase the misery to which the empire was already reduced by its defenders. Such an organization as the Church could fill one of two rôles: it could be the rival or the ally of the hard-pressed imperial power. Decius saw in it a rival, and resolved to crush it. He was not given time to do so, for within two years he fell fighting the Goths in the marshes of the lower Danube. After that the Roman world relapsed into military anarchy, during which the Goths ravaged Asia Minor and the Balkans, the Franks swept through Gaul, and the emperor Valerian (who had resumed Decius' policy of persecution) fell alive into the hands of the Persians. The empire literally went to pieces. Independent emperors were proclaimed in Gaul, Syria, Egypt, and the Danube provinces to defend countries which could no longer be defended from Rome. It looked as if the end had come. In that confusion no one any longer persecuted the Christians. To a competitor for empire they might be dangerous enemies or useful allies. In fact, during the weakness of the empire in the third century, Christianity emerged as a formidable mass movement, particularly in the eastern provinces. The conversion of Armenia, a small but important buffer-State between Rome and Persia, belongs to this time and was a notable step forward.

For the story of the final victory of the Church we are

almost entirely dependent on Christian sources. Extant
pagan writers of the time, such as the compilers of the *Augustan
History*, say next to nothing about Christianity. The last
pagan historian of any merit, Ammianus Marcellinus, wrote
after its triumph. It is remarkable, to say the least, that the
whole of his work down to and including the reign of Constantine is lost. It looks as if pagan histories of the period
had been weeded out on the principle of the survival of the
least fit, and as if Christian censors had taken care to transmit
to us only the more puerile, the more meagre, and the more
innocuous of their opponents. We are left with the *Ecclesiastical History* of Eusebius as our chief contemporary authority
on the momentous revolution which ends the history of the
ancient world.

Eusebius was born somewhere in the eastern provinces,
probably of Christian parents, about 260. In his youth he
witnessed the restoration of imperial unity by Aurelian and
the reorganization of the empire under Diocletian. In his
middle years he came unscathed (physically, if not spiritually)
through the last and worst persecution of Christianity. Later
he became bishop of Cæsarea in Palestine, a courtier and
panegyrist of the emperor Constantine, and the father of
Church history. In dealing with the earlier history of Christianity, Eusebius is the prisoner of his own orthodoxy and
valuable chiefly for his quotations from older authors now
lost. But on his own times he is an important authority,
though naturally partial and not always scrupulous; and his
evidence, when not self-contradictory or refuted by other
sources, deserves due attention. In addition to Eusebius, we
have a contemporary tract *On the Deaths of Persecutors*, doubtfully ascribed to Lactantius—a violent party pamphlet on the
unsupported authority of which it would be rash to accept
any statement whatever.

The restoration of the empire after its disruption in the
third century was the work of Illyrian emperors, mostly of
obscure origin, who had risen from the ranks in hard fighting
and owed their elevation to the acclamation of frontier
armies. They were men without roots in Rome or the Roman
past. Such was Claudius II (268–270), who drove the Goths

back over the Danube and earned the title " Gothicus." Such was Aurelian (270–275), who reconquered Egypt, Syria, and Gaul, and assumed the proud title of " restorer of the world." Such was Probus (276–282), who had uphill work to secure the gains of Aurelian and was murdered by his own soldiers for his pains.[1] Such, finally, was Diocletian, who in 284, when rival armies were again about to rend the empire in pieces, made himself master of the Roman world and prepared the way for Constantine.

The empire restored by Aurelian and Diocletian was very different from that of Augustus or Trajan, or even from the moribund fabric which had gone to pieces a generation before. Only by straining language could it now be called Roman. Its rulers were not Roman; its armies were not Roman; and under Diocletian Rome ceased even to be the capital city. All that remained was a ramshackle and cosmopolitan collection of provinces, armies, and populations precariously riveted together by military force and by a simulated loyalty to a dead past. The shaky foundations of his work were evident to Aurelian himself. He, first of all the emperors, found it necessary to fortify Rome itself against barbarian attack. Italy was no longer secure: the *pax Romana* was a thing of the past. Dacia was abandoned to the Goths. And infiltrating into provinces, armies, and populations was a rival power, also not Roman, also cosmopolitan, openly spurning the past, proclaiming a new loyalty, and with its face to the future. Those two powers had now to come to terms or fight a duel to the death.

The nature of the issue was illustrated by a significant incident in the reign of Aurelian. During the years of disruption the Arab chief of Palmyra, Odainath or Odænathus, had made himself master of the eastern provinces and waged war on Persia, ostensibly in the Roman interest, but really as an independent ruler. After his death his widow, Bath-Zabbai or (in Greek) Zenobia, dropped all pretence of allegiance to Rome and openly set up an Arab empire of the

---

[1] Gibbon's vigorous style betrays him into a much quoted exaggeration. " A thousand swords were plunged at once into the bosom of the unfortunate Probus." *Decline and Fall*, XII.

east. The Semitic empire was to have a Semitic religion. To this end Zenobia showed favour to Jewish rabbis in her dominions and took into her counsels the bishop of Antioch, Paul of Samosata. This was not as inconsistent as it might seem; for Paul was a Christian with a difference. Contrary to the now preponderant opinion in the Church, but agreeably to that of more eastern Christians than is usually admitted, he denied the divinity of Christ and (if we may believe his enemies) tried to stop the singing of hymns " to Christ as to a god " which had been in use in the Greek churches from the time of Pliny. Did Zenobia—a woman of unusual parts—hope to bring about with his help a concordat between the Jews and the Oriental Christians, and to sweep the East with a simplified monotheism which would have forestalled the achievement of Islam nearly four centuries later? It is an interesting speculation. Whatever her plans were, she reckoned without Aurelian. In 272 he marched east, destroyed her army, and took her prisoner, and in 273 sacked Palmyra. The orthodox bishops seized the occasion to invoke the secular arm against Paul. Aurelian ruled that the property of the church of Antioch should be transferred to a candidate recognized by the bishops of Rome and Italy. Thus did pagan power-politics sow the seed of papal pretensions to be!

The incident suggests that Aurelian was at least considering the use of the Church as an instrument of government. If so, he quickly abandoned the idea. He found a more immediately handy instrument in the cult of Mithra, the old Iranian sun-god, which under the Roman Empire had been carried by traders and legionaries to the limits of the West. In its passage from its native Persia, Mithraism had picked up from Babylonian and other sources a wealth of ritual and myth which had many points of contact with Christianity: Mithra was the mediator between God and man, communicating his grace through sacraments which ensured everlasting life. The cult was especially strong in the military stations along the Rhine and Danube; and Aurelian, himself a soldier from the Danube, decided to make the " unconquered sun " the patron deity of the empire. From an imperial point of view Mithraism had the advantage over Christianity that sun-worship was already a long-established cult, and that no one could say that Mithra had been crucified as a rebel against Rome. It had the disadvantage of being an exclusively mas-culine religion; for no women were admitted to its mysteries. The temple of the "unconquered sun" was dedicated at Rome in 274 on December 25, the birthday of the god. No one as yet associated the date with any rival deity.

According to Eusebius, Aurelian was about to follow up his establishment of Mithraism with an edict against Chris-tianity when he was assassinated. His immediate successors were too busy defending the frontiers to pursue the matter; and the final combat was deferred until the last years of Dio-cletian.

Diocletian, like Aurelian, was an Illyrian soldier of humble origin who had fought his way up from the ranks. His first act was to accept the fact, hammered home by a generation of anarchy, that the empire could no longer be defended or ruled from a single centre. Disruption was once more on the march. In Gaul the peasants, driven to desperation by their economic burdens, had risen in one of those outbreaks which were to recur through the Middle Ages and right on until 1789. Instead of waiting for independent emperors to be proclaimed in his despite, Diocletian took the initiative by handing over the West to his countryman and comrade Maximian, reserving the East for himself. The eastern capital was Nicomedia (Ismid) in Asia Minor. The western was no longer Rome, but Milan. Maximian had hardly put down the revolutionary peasants (*Bagaudæ*) in Gaul when he was faced with revolt in Britain, where a Gallic officer named Carausius proclaimed himself emperor of the island. From 286 to 293 Diocletian and Maximian accepted the accomplished fact. Then they decided to meet the challenge by a new subdivision of the empire. Diocletian's son-in-law, the Thracian Galerius, was given the Danube provinces, while another Illyrian, Constantius, was given Gaul and Spain and entrusted with the recovery of Britain. This reconquest was effected in 296. For the next few years the four emperors co-operated amicably and defended the various frontiers with

success.   But the price paid was a multiplication of the cost
of administration, and a grim economic crisis which in 301
Diocletian tried to meet by fixing (for the first time in the
history of the empire) a maximum price for commodities and
a maximum rate for wages and salaries.   Inscribed fragments
of this edict have been found at various places in Asia Minor,
Egypt, and Greece.   It seems to have operated only in
Diocletian's part of the empire.

Not till 303 did Diocletian turn his attention to the religious
question.   We must remember what the situation was.
Only by desperate measures could the empire now be held
together.   Compulsion was the order of the day.   In a
society without any common interest men had to be compelled
to co-operate, compelled to carry on the necessary work of
the world, and compelled to serve a government not noticeably worth serving for its own sake.   Compulsion in the
matter of religious observance naturally followed.   The men
who had to cope with the situation were not philosophic
Greeks or Romans.   We are no longer dealing with Julius
Cæsar or even with Marcus Aurelius, but with self-educated
or uneducated Balkan peasant-soldiers who understand the
strong arm and nothing else; who look to the "immortal
gods" for the peace and prosperity which they themselves
have failed to achieve; and who call on their subjects, under
pains and penalties, to co-operate in the ritual by which the
gods are swayed.   A further factor which may have hardened
the rulers of the empire against Christianity was the recent
conversion of the people and royal house of Armenia.   Till
then the Christians had been merely an objectionable sect
within the empire: now they were a "fifth column" connected with a foreign State.

If we may believe Christian writers (the only ancient
authorities we have), the prime mover in the persecution was
Galerius. He took the initiative by cashiering Christians in
his army, and then persuaded Diocletian to issue an edict
ordering the demolition of churches, the burning of copies
of the scriptures, and the exclusion of Christians from public
office and of Christian slaves from any hope of freedom.
Reading between the lines of Eusebius, we can see that the

Christians were by no means as passive under persecution as
is usually supposed. The edict, as soon as it was posted at
Nicomedia, was torn down by a Christian, who was instantly
seized and put to death.[1] Soon afterwards the palace of
Diocletian was fired. Eusebius repudiates the suspicion of
Christian complicity; but his repudiation will convince only
those who assume without proof the pacifism of all early
Christians. The immediate result was a reign of terror in
Nicomedia. Eusebius mentions, without giving details,
armed revolts in Melitene on the upper Euphrates and in
Syria. Nothing further is known of these risings; but the
places were close to the Armenian frontier. We cannot
exclude the possibility that Christians, supported from Armenia, were involved. Diocletian at any rate took it for
granted, and immediately followed up his first edict with
others ordering the arrest of all clergy and compelling them,
on pain of torture and death, to sacrifice to the gods. Against
the general body of Christians the dormant laws of the empire
were revived and enforced. There can be no doubt about
the savagery of this persecution. Even if we ignore the
cruelties which Eusebius reports at second hand, we cannot
reject those which he relates as an eyewitness. He himself
in Palestine, Phœnicia, and Egypt saw Christians flogged,
thrown to the beasts, beheaded, burnt alive, until " the execu-
tioners themselves grew utterly weary and took it in turns to
succeed one another." [2] Diocletian was not a monster, nor
even Galerius. They were able and hard-working soldiers
defending an all but indefensible empire in time of crisis, and
they believed themselves to be fighting a dangerous and
treacherous fifth column. We, who have seen civilized and
conscientious statesmen order the obliteration of cities and
the massacre of men, women, and children by high explosives

---

[1] This martyr has without a particle of evidence been identified with
George, the patron saint of England. Eusebius does not give any name.

[2] Eusebius, *Ecclesiastical History*, VIII, 9. Eusebius (VIII, 7) relates that
at Tyre, when he was present, the beasts miraculously refused to attack
the martyrs, who had consequently to be beheaded. The story, though
" written up," may be in substance true. Crypto-Christians in the
menagerie department doubtless fed the animals on the sly.

and atomic bombs, are in a better position than our Victorian
fathers to understand Diocletian.   One of the lessons learnt
from history is that, as Hegel says, tragedy is not the conflict
between right and wrong, but the conflict between right and
right.

Eusebius, though not the most candid of historians, is honest
enough to admit that " countless " clergy, not being of the
stuff of which martyrs were made, " proved weak at the first
assault " and recanted.[1]   This natural weakness only sets off
the heroism of others.   Incidentally, Eusebius mentions
without any censure Christians of Antioch who threw themselves from house-tops to avoid arrest, and a lady of that city
who drowned herself and her two daughters to escape outrage
by soldiers.   Evidently Eusebius and other Christians of that
day held more rational views about suicide than their medieval
and modern successors.   Too many of us were brought up
to regard the early Christians as people of legendary and in-
human virtue who spent their lives in turning the other cheek
to the smiter and ended as passive victims in the arena.   Those
thousands of recanting clergy, that fire in the emperor's
palace, those obscure revolts on the Armenian frontier, and
those suicides at Antioch remind us that they were, after all,
people not unlike ourselves; and who is not grateful for the
reminder?

One flaw in the policy of persecution was obvious from the
first.   It could succeed only if all four emperors kept step.
Now Constantius, who governed Gaul, Spain, and Britain,
was not in agreement with his colleagues and refused to execute their edicts.   Consequently any Christian who could
afford the journey had only to escape to the western provinces
to be perfectly safe.   That was enough to doom the whole
policy to futility from the start.

In 305 Diocletian abdicated at Nicomedia. He was fifty-nine,
ill and worn out; perhaps also he felt himself a beaten man.
Eusebius says that his intellect was deranged.   This is untrue
and unfair; but a historian who had seen what Eusebius had
seen in Palestine and Egypt could hardly be expected to be

---

[1] Eusebius, *Ecclesiastical History*, VIII, 3.   Eusebius was accused later in
life of having purchased his own freedom by apostasy.

fair to Diocletian. Simultaneously, by prearrangement, Maximian abdicated at Milan. Constantius succeeded him in the West; and Galerius stepped into the shoes of his father-in-law in the East. Next year Constantius died at York. At once it became apparent how precarious had been the respite from anarchy. The British legions immediately acclaimed as emperor Constantine, the young son of Constantius; the prætorian guard at Rome, not to be outdone, put up Maxentius, the son of Maximian; Maximian himself re-emerged to take a hand in the game; and the empire was soon torn between no fewer than six rival dynasts, none of whom trusted the others and any of whom (unless too deeply compromised as a persecutor) might at any moment steal a march on the rest by a deal with the Church. Meanwhile the war preparations of the rival emperors exhausted the provinces and brought trade to a standstill.

Constantine had the advantage of a clean sheet in the matter of persecution. For six years he exercised his troops on the Rhine and played off his competitors one against another, knowing that he had a ready-made fifth column in their rears if he chose to mobilize it. At first he allied himself with old Maximian, and became his son-in-law. But in 310 they fell out, and Maximian was handed over by his own men to Constantine and either executed or made to commit suicide. In 311 Galerius, seeing himself beaten, called off the persecution, and soon afterwards died. We need not believe Eusebius' story of his death-bed repentance. The old soldier never became a Christian. His edict of toleration expresses neither remorse nor regret; it merely recognizes that the force against him is stronger than he had supposed. He had hoped that the Christians would abandon their folly and return to the religion of their ancestors; but as, in spite of his measures, they will not, and any religion is better than none, they may please themselves, always provided that there is no sedition, and that as good subjects they remember the emperor in their prayers. Better have such obstinate fellows with you than against you!

The competitors for empire were now reduced to four: Constantine in the western provinces; Maxentius in Italy and Africa; Licinius, an old officer of Galerius, in the Danubian and Balkan provinces; and Maximinus Daia, a nephew of Galerius, in the East. In 312 Constantine with an army of Gauls and Germans invaded Italy. Maxentius was odious to both pagans and Christians owing to his incapacity and misgovernment, and therefore easy game. Constantine fell on him outside the gates of Rome, drove him into the Tiber, and drowned him. The famous story of Constantine's conversion to Christianity on the eve of the battle by a miraculous vision of the cross in the noonday sky does not occur in Eusebius' *Ecclesiastical History*, but in his *Life of Constantine*, published after the emperor's death. It can be dismissed as a pious fiction. Constantine was a complete opportunist. After his victory he met Licinius at Milan and with him issued an edict of toleration, but did not break with the old religion. He still recognized the pagan priesthoods; as *pontifex maximus* he was their supreme head; and pagan symbols still appeared on his coins.

The next rival to be destroyed was Maximin in the East. With Licinius and Constantine allied against him, his dominions more Christianized than any other part of the empire, and Armenia in his rear, he was a lost man. Striking wildly at his enemies without and within, he renewed the persecution of the Christians, and in 313 threw himself at Licinius, only to meet with crushing defeat and to die, possibly by poison, a few months later. There was only Licinius left to dispute the empire with Constantine. He was old and altogether unequal to the situation; in fact, he must have been an exceptionally stupid man not to have seen through the designs of Constantine from the first. In 321, after a few years of open war or uneasy peace, this last of the pagan peasant-emperors set about purging his court and his army of Christians, demolishing churches, and arresting bishops. In 324 Constantine made war on him, defeated him, made him prisoner, and put him to death. The last book of Eusebius' history is a prolonged war-whoop over the victory of his master and patron, won, he assures us, by the special grace of the Lord of Hosts,

" who smote great kings, and slew mighty kings; for his mercy endureth for ever." [1]

Meanwhile Constantine had begun to find that the establishment of Christianity was not so simple as it looked. The opportunism (to put it mildly) of many bishops and clergy during the years of persecution had earned them the contempt of the more fanatical rank and file. Especially was this so in the African provinces, where acute social misery, due to the concentration of land in the hands of a few great owners, tended to accentuate the subversive and revolutionary side of the new religion. The rift came in 311 over the election of a new bishop of Carthage. The successful candidate, Cæcilian, was denounced by his opponents as having handed over copies of the scriptures to be burnt during the persecution. In 312 he appealed to Constantine, the new master of the West, who, after convening a council of western bishops, gave in 316 a final ruling in his favour. Constantine was prepared to establish and endow Christianity: he was not prepared to disqualify men from office in the Church for compliance with the persecuting edicts of his predecessors. The defeated party were treated as rebels and deprived of the benefits of toleration which Constantine extended to their opponents. So began a struggle between those Christians who accepted establishment on Constantine's terms and those —known as Donatists, from Donatus the rival bishop of Carthage—who did not. The bitter and protracted nature of the schism shows that far more was at issue than a disputed election. The Donatists, spiritual heirs of the fierce Tertullian, met force with force, rallied to their side fugitive slaves, distressed peasants, and other revolutionary elements, and contributed materially to the final downfall of the Roman Empire in Africa.

The Donatist schism turned on matters of discipline and on the relations of Church and State. A more complex problem awaited Constantine when in 324 he became master of the East. As we have seen, the early Christians were never unanimous as to the nature of the Christ from whom they took their name. To many he was a man chosen by God,

---

[1] Ps. cxxxvi, 17–18; cited in *Ecclesiastical History*, X, 4.

raised from the dead, and destined to reign on earth in the Messianic kingdom, but nevertheless a man and not God. This was the prevalent opinion in those eastern churches which might be expected to preserve with most fidelity the traditions of primitive Christianity—those of Palestine, Syria, Commagene, and Armenia. To others, whose faith owed more to Greek philosophy and Gnostic speculation than to historical tradition, Jesus Christ was the Creator of heaven and earth, who for us men and for our salvation became incarnate, suffered, and rose again, but had never for a moment been other than the eternal God. This was the prevalent opinion in the Greek and Latin churches. No sooner had the victory of Constantine given Christianity peace from persecution than the doctrinal rift threatened to shiver it to pieces.

Arius, the Alexandrian presbyter whose preaching brought the trouble to a head, was by no means an extremist. He tried to mediate between the low views of Christ's divinity prevalent in the Syrian churches and the high views held at Alexandria. He admitted that Christ was divine, and even that he was the only-begotten Son of God, but not that he was eternal. A Son, if words have any meaning, cannot be one with his Father. Sonship implies origin in time and subordination in dignity. Many passages in the New Testament could be quoted in support of Arius: after all, the New Testament is a conglomerate of incompatibles. To converts fresh from paganism, and therefore familiar with the idea of superior and inferior deities, Arius would seem to be talking plain common sense. But he raised a hornets' nest at Alexandria, where to the rank and file of Christians he seemed to be preaching two gods and selling the pass to the pagans with whom they had only recently been at death-grips.

To Constantine the point at issue was not important, or even intelligible, but it was vital that his new instrument of government, the Church, should not be rent in pieces over such questions as this. In 325, therefore, he convened a general council of bishops at Nicæa and commissioned them to hammer out an orthodox formula. As the council was held in the heart of the Greek world, the majority of the bishops present were Greeks. It is noteworthy that the bishop of Rome was represented only by two presbyters. By an overwhelming majority, but probably more for the sake of peace than from reasoned conviction, the bishops voted that the Son of God was one in essence with his Father, and anathematized any who said that there had been a time when he had not existed. Constantine ratified the decision, banished Arius and the recalcitrant bishops, and ordered the works of the heretic to be surrendered and burnt on pain of death.

Thus within a few years of the edict of Milan the policy of toleration lay in ruins. The chief significance of the Council of Nicæa lies in the admission by the Church, for the first time in its history, of the right of the State to enforce dogma by persecution. The particular dogmas enforced might vary. Within a few years Constantine had changed his mind, recalled Arius and the banished bishops, and sent the fiery Athanasius into exile in their place. But whatever dogmatic form it might assume, Christianity had become an instrument of government, and under Christian emperors dissenters from orthodoxy, whatever orthodoxy for the moment might be, could expect no more consideration than Christians had had from pagans in the past. Indeed, heretics were soon to find that it was better to be tried by a pagan governor than by an orthodox Christian.

Hardly less significant is the concentration of episcopal attention on the interpretation of Pauline or Johannine theology to the exclusion of the social application of Gospel teaching. The bishops put millennial dreams into cold storage and sold their flocks for pelf and place. The plunder of the civil population to pamper the army, which had been systematically practised by the later pagan emperors, continued unabated under their Christian successors. To stop the wretched peasantry from running away from their holdings and leaving the land waste, Constantine in 332 bound them and their posterity to the soil under penalties, thus making them serfs in law, as they had long been in fact. A population so downtrodden had nothing to lose by barbarian conquest; and since the imperial armies were increasingly manned and even commanded by Germans, the end could not long be delayed.

The reign of Constantine, in fact, marks more definitely than any other era the end of the ancient world. The transfer of the seat of empire to Constantinople in 330 was symbolic in more senses than one. It was an outward and visible repudiation of that Roman past which for more than a century had been less and less regarded by the military adventurers who held sway. With the economic ruin of Italy and the transfer of power to the provincial armies, Rome had long ceased to be the real mistress of the world. The history of the third century had shown that the strategic centre of the empire was in the Balkans. If government from a single centre was still possible at all, that centre could not be Rome, but had to be some city in the Balkan area. Of all those so situated none was so well placed for defence as the city on the Bosphorus. Further, experience had shown that government could not be carried on without the goodwill of the Church. It was better therefore that the city selected should be unencumbered by pagan cults and priesthoods. The fact that Byzantium was a strategic prize had exposed it to repeated sieges and captures during the time of imperial disintegration. By the time Constantine took it over, the old city was wellnigh a ruin, and he could do what he liked with the site. In so far as it is possible to associate so great a revolution with a date, we may say that by rebuilding Byzantium as Constantinople and excluding from it all worship but that of orthodox Christianity, he wrote *finis* to classical antiquity and inaugurated the Middle Ages.

Constantine failed to reunite the empire for more than a few years. That was now past anyone's power. On his death in 337 his sons divided their inheritance with the sword. Ammianus Marcellinus, the last pagan historian of importance, in the extant part of his work tells the sorry story of the ensuing generation: the Roman world as misgoverned by Christian rulers as it had ever been by pagans—the prey of ruffianly emperors, rapacious officials, and hardly more rapacious barbarians; Christians persecuting Christians more savagely than any wild beasts; Julian's idealistic, but forlorn attempt to galvanize a dead paganism into life; Franks, Goths, and other Germans taking service with the emperors and finally pouring in *en masse* to complete the dismemberment of an already stinking corpse.

Swinburne in one of his best-known poems has pictured the feelings of a pagan after the victory of Christianity at Rome :

O lips that the live blood faints in, the leavings of racks and rods!
O ghastly glories of saints, dead limbs of gibbeted Gods!
Though all men abase them before you in spirit, and all knees bend,
I kneel not neither adore you, but standing, look to the end . . .
Though the feet of thine high priests tread where thy lords and our fore-
   fathers trod,
Though these that were Gods are dead, and thou being dead art a God,
Though before thee the throned Cytherean be fallen, and hidden her head,
Yet thy kingdom shall pass, Galilean, thy dead shall go down to thee
   dead.[1]

To which the short and simple answer is that, if you build your domination on racks and rods, their leavings will take revenge on you. That is what Rome had done. For centuries her legions had swept the Mediterranean world for slaves to minister to her wants; for centuries she had kept her slaves down by fear of the scourge and the cross; and now she was forced to bend the knee to a scourged and crucified God. There is no need to judge Rome by her worst sons. It is enough to judge her by her best. It is the cultured Pliny who returns thanks to Trajan for his lavish gladiatorial shows —" no nerveless and relaxing spectacle, nor one to soften and break men's spirits, but an incentive to face honourable wounds and to think lightly of death." [2] It is the eloquent Symmachus, the diehard defender of paganism in the last years of the fourth century, who regrets that a band of Saxon gladiators whom he purchased for the arena should have strangled one another rather than be butchered to make a Roman holiday. It is a little too much to ask us to regret the downfall of such a civilization as that. The case against the Christian Church is not that it destroyed pagan civili-

[1] Swinburne, *Hymn to Proserpine*.   [2] Pliny, *Panegyric*, 33.

zation, but that it perpetuated so many of its worst features. And when the end forecast by Swinburne comes and the kingdom of the Galilean passes, it will not be by a revival of dead paganism, but by the agency of an atheistic humanism as hostile to the established and endowed churches of today as was Christianity, in its vigorous youth, to the cults of the ancient world and of *divus Cæsar*.

CHAPTER XII

MEDIEVAL HISTORY

THE term "Middle Ages" was coined by writers of the Renaissance to denote the period of approximately a thousand years between the decline of ancient civilization and the revival of learning in their own day. This use of the term has been much criticized by modern historians. It has been pointed out that the thousand years in question were by no means a blank in human achievement; that if the first half of the period was truly a Dark Age, an age of civic decay and rustic stagnation, of political dismemberment and brutal anarchy, nevertheless in the second half trade revived, a robust city life took shape, the nations of modern Europe were born, the critical spirit was alive, and the artistic and literary expansion, for which the Renaissance wrongly claimed the whole credit, was visibly in preparation. All this is true, yet the term "Middle Ages" is not inapt. The end of the Græco-Roman world marks an epoch. The ancient social organization based on the city-state had broken down. There was a general loss of nerve. Men felt the world to be evil, and sought compensation in the myth of another world which, they believed, would soon supersede it in a miraculous catastrophe. And though the catastrophe never arrived, and in default of it men and women went on living and made do with the imperfect world about them, and in due course evolved a new civilization and braced themselves to make it worth while, yet it was a full thousand years before the new civilization became strong enough and self-conscious enough to revolt decisively against the vested interests which had fed and grown fat on the poverty, insecurity, and illiteracy of the centuries between.

Turning from an ancient historian to a medieval chronicler is like turning from a man with some stake in the world and some pride in his heritage (even if the stake is selfish and the pride narrow) to a child who knows nothing except what pleases him, what hurts him, what frightens him, and what his elders tell him. Such writers as Bede in the earlier Middle Ages, or Malmesbury, Paris, and their compeers in the later, give us graphic descriptions of the violence of their times and (monks though they are) caustic exposures of the corruption of the Church to which they belong. They are to that extent invaluable. But of critical history none of them has a glimmering conception. None attains even to the hesitant scepticism of a Herodotus, far less to the scientific precision of a Thucydides. None has the least idea of what is really happening to the world beneath the showy melodrama of battle, murder, and sudden death. To all alike what really matters is the prosperity of the Church, and in particular of the monastic foundation to which the writer belongs.

Hence medieval chronicles, though indispensable to the student, do not carry him far unless supplemented by sources which go a little deeper into the economic, social, and political history of the period. Of these there is a veritable wealth. So far as England alone is concerned, the reader who finds life too short for first-hand research among pipe rolls, charters, statutes, and other national and local records will find a mine of information in such works as Vinogradoff's *Growth of the Manor*, Chadwick's *Origin of the English Nation*, Seebohm's *Tribal Custom in Anglo-Saxon Law*, Stubbs' *Select Charters and Other Illustrations of English Constitutional History*, Maitland's *Domesday Book and Beyond*, Cunningham's *Growth of English Industry and Commerce*, Ashley's *Introduction to English Economic History and Theory*, J. R. Green's *Short History of the English People*, and Alice Stopford Green's *Town Life in the Fifteenth Century*. By the time he has absorbed this amount he will probably conclude that one country's history is as much as he can tackle and, for the general medieval background, will be content to rely on books of reference. For this reason we shall be concerned mainly with English history. But it will be a pity if, having begun Gibbon, the student does not continue him to the finish and follow him up with some such work as Lecky's *History of European Morals from Augustus to Charlemagne* or Coulton's *Five Centuries of Religion* before returning to our island.

From the works named we get the general impression of a smashed civilization in which the majority are of necessity serfs to the strong arm. The Church has entered into partnership with the feudal lords as joint exploiter of the tillers of the soil. For five or six centuries after the fall of Rome— that is, until the migrations are over and the last Vikings have carved out their duchies or their kingdoms and settled down —there is no real recovery. What keeps life going is the village economy—the peasants with their waste land common and undivided, and their arable land allotted by customary rules of turn and turn about under the open-field system. Slavery still existed; but gang-slavery had disappeared with the decline of the Roman Empire. The northern conquerors never practised it : even in the time of Tacitus the slave in Germany " has control of his own house and home. The master imposes a fixed charge of grain, cattle, or clothing, as he would on a tenant." [1]   Such slavery was to all intents and purposes the same as serfdom, and no worse than the condition to which formerly free peasants were everywhere gradually reduced in the unsettled times of the later Roman Empire. This accounts for the fact that the Latin word for slave, *servus*, gave rise to the French and English *serf*, while a new word, *slave*, had to be coined when in the eighth century numbers of Slav captives were sold to German feudal lords and reduced to a more rigorous bondage than that suffered by native peasants. The Latin word *villa*, meaning a country house or seat, came to denote a feudal lord's establishment of more or less servile tenantry, and *villanus*, " villein," the individual villager. The distinction between villein and serf was theoretical rather than practical. Domesday Book still tries to draw it; but by the thirteenth century it is forgotten. In the course of time, with the revival of trade and urban life, from the downtrodden *villa* emerged the thriving *ville*—the chartered town or city of the later Middle Ages. But the chartered town was an anomaly in medieval life, an exception

[1] Tacitus, *Germania*, 25.

to the rule, though an exception which was to grow until it broke up the system.

The mark of the later Middle Ages is the ever-increasing importance of this new class, the burghers or bourgeoisie. They are originally people of the *burgh* or stronghold—traders who gather in a place fortified by a king or lord, and therefore safe, to exchange their wares, because they would be robbed anywhere else. Then, as the tastes of the upper class grow more expensive, a whole community of traders and artisans springs up round a castle or abbey to supply those tastes. Then these communities by cash payments to the lord or the king win freedom from feudal control and become *communes* or corporate towns, each with its self-governing merchant guild and guildhall. Corporate towns admit runaway villeins from the surrounding countryside, beard abbots and bishops to their faces, and finally so grow in size, wealth, and importance that their representatives are summoned to the royal counsels as a third estate of the realm—the rivals and future supplanters of the feudal lords spiritual and temporal.

With this background in mind, let us now turn to the chroniclers. And first let us note this about them: until the last century or two of the Middle Ages they are one and all churchmen; for though it would be inexact to say that no one else could read or write, nevertheless in those unsettled times ecclesiastical foundations were the only seats of learning, and no one else had the leisure and equipment to write any sort of history. Of the men on whom we depend for our medieval annals, Gildas, Bede, Alcuin, Asser, Malmesbury, Newburgh, Coggeshall, Paris, Knighton, Froissart, Walsingham, Capgrave (to name no others out of a great number) are all ecclesiastics, and mostly monks. Not until the fourteenth century in Italy or the fifteenth in England do we find laymen writing chronicles. The whole history of the Middle Ages, except the very end of the story, is told by Catholic clerics. This is an important point; for it is the fashion to accuse critical historians of the Middle Ages of anti-Catholic muck-raking. The best answer to the charge is to let the monkish chroniclers speak for themselves.

Gildas, the oldest British historian, need not detain us long.

We do not know when or where he was born or died: the only lives of him date from the eleventh and twelfth centuries and are worthless. He himself tells us that the year of his birth was that in which the Britons fought the Saxons at "Mount Badon"; but as that event is variously dated between 497 and 520, the statement does not help us much. It has nevertheless a certain negative value; for later medieval romance numbered this battle among the victories of Arthur, and the total silence of Gildas, the only contemporary British writer, goes far to relegate that Celtic hero to the realm of myth. Gildas was evidently an ecclesiastic: his book on *The Destruction of Britain* professes to be written from "zeal for God's house and for his holy law," and consists chiefly of invective against the vices of contemporary British chiefs, between whom and the Saxon invaders there seems little to choose. Britain had naturally been one of the first provinces abandoned by Rome as the empire tottered to its fall. Its outlying position rendered it indefensible when Germans were already overrunning Gaul. Nor need we doubt the statement of Gildas that British rulers called in the Saxons to defend them against the Picts and Scots. That would be all of a piece with imperial policy in the days of decline. Gildas' general capacity as a historian may be judged from his statement that Christianity was introduced into Britain in the reign of Tiberius—an event unnoticed by any earlier writer. His lamentable account of his own time, of cities laid desolate by foreign and civil war, is credible enough. Indeed, a conclusive proof, if no other existed, of the ruin of Britain in the sixth century is that it produced only one writer, and that writer Gildas.

With our next historian, Bede, we pass from the wreckage of Britain to the beginnings of England. But at this point English history cannot be understood without some reference to its continental background.

The fall of the Roman Empire had led to the rise to power of the Roman Church. This does not mean merely that the removal of the seat of empire to Constantinople gave the bishop of Rome an opportunity to make claims which he would not otherwise have been able to make. An effective Germanic domination of Italy would have denied him that opportunity. But in the sixth century the Goths were not strong enough to hold Italy; and Constantinople, though able to turn them out at the price of twenty years' terrific slaughter and devastation, had not the strength to hold the country it had "liberated." The Roman Church stepped into the vacuum. Endowed by the gifts and bequests of the faithful over many centuries with ample resources in land and serfs in Italy and elsewhere, the bishop of Rome was in a better position than the emperor to see to the government and defence of the city; and Constantinople was content to leave the task to him. So originated the temporal power of the Papacy.

In 590 the popular abbot Gregory was elected Pope—the first monk to be so elected. Monk though he was, and saint though he is said to have been, he was undeniably a master of power-politics, and never hesitated to make friends of the unrighteous if it served his purpose. He was an ardent flatterer of the Frankish queen Brunhilda, whose main merits were that she was a convert from Arianism and a protectress of the Church. Worse still, " in two letters full of passages from Scripture, and replete with fulsome and blasphemous flattery,"[1] he calls on heaven and earth to rejoice at the accession of the usurping emperor Phocas, for no better reason than that his murdered predecessor, Maurice, had forbidden serving soldiers to become monks and had supported the claims of the see of Constantinople against Rome. We need not, therefore, suppose that Gregory's decision to send a mission to England was due to disinterested zeal for the souls of the English. The story told by Bede of Gregory's interest in English slave-boys at Rome and of his feeble punning on the name of their country and king almost stamps itself as apocryphal. It was Gregory's policy and that of his successors to build up as wide as possible a spiritual dominion in the West in order to render themselves temporally independent and to make the Papacy what eventually it became, " the ghost of the deceased Roman Empire, sitting crowned upon the grave thereof."[2]

---

[1] Lecky, *History of European Morals*, chap. IV.   Cf. Gibbon, *Decline and Fall*, chap. XLVI.
[2] Hobbes, *Leviathan*.

We learn from Bede of the masterly opportunism enjoined by Gregory on his missionaries. Pagan temples are not to be destroyed, but are to be converted into churches, idols being replaced by relics of martyrs, and pagan festivals by Christian " church ales" at which the faithful eat and drink to the glory of God. This is in keeping with ecclesiastical practice in every converted country. From the first days of the victory of the Church in the fourth century relics had been credited with miraculous powers similar to those previously attached to pagan images. From this it was a short step to their fraudulent manufacture. Before the fourth century was out the Christian world was full of pieces of the " true cross." The thing became a racket which nothing could stop. No church was validly consecrated unless a relic was placed in the altar. Not only so, but before the end of the sixth century images, too, were venerated. Gregory forbade a Gallic bishop to destroy them, since (said he) they were useful " for instructing the minds of the ignorant." [1] Educated pagans had defended idolatry on similar lines. The Christianity propagated by Gregory was in fact a baptized paganism. So long as pagans were baptized and became his spiritual subjects he seems to have been content that they should remain in essentials pagan.

Bede, a Church historian of unusual candour, makes it clear that this was in fact the case. Pious writers, who never tire of repeating the edifying story of Gregory and the English slaves, slur over the actual process of the conversion of England. This, as with other barbarian peoples, meant in the first place the conversion of the kings. Once a king was baptized his people followed his example. Bishoprics and monasteries were founded and endowed with land; and in return the Church became the loyal ally of the secular arm. The time-honoured picture of saintly men of evangelical poverty preaching the gospel of peace to the rude barbarians and subduing them by moral influence alone is not borne out by the facts. Conversion was by no means always by peaceful persuasion. On the contrary, as early as 640, less than fifty years from the landing of Augustine, we read that Ercon-

[1] Gregory I, *Letters*, viii, 2, III; ix, 4, II.

berht, king of Kent, " first of the kings of the English ordered
by his princely authority that idols should be forsaken and
destroyed in his whole kingdom, and also that the Lenten
fast should be kept. And that none might lightly despise
these commands, he imposed worthy and sufficient punishment on transgressors." [1] In 686, when Bede was a boy in
his teens, Ceadwalla of Wessex completed the conversion of
England by a brutal massacre of the inhabitants of the Isle
of Wight, the last stronghold of paganism. It is not surprising that Christianity imposed in this fashion was only
skin-deep. Penda, the last pagan king of Mercia, is said to
have tolerated Christian missions in his kingdom, but to
have despised Christian converts for their pagan way of life.
The story of ecclesiastical corruption begins, not in the times
immediately preceding the Reformation, but at the very
outset of medieval history. Bede, writing in 734 to Egbert,
archbishop of York, complains that there are many villages
which have not seen a bishop or a Christian teacher of any
kind for years on end, but are nevertheless forced to pay dues
to a bishop, and that countless monasteries are anything but
monastic in their manner of living.

After Bede, our next authority is Alcuin of York. He was
born in 735, the year of Bede's death, entered the Church,
and in 780 was invited to the court of Charles the Great,
who loaded him with favour and preferment. The rest of
Alcuin's life, except for two visits to his own country, was
spent at the Frankish court or in Frankish abbeys. He was
employed by Charles to procure the condemnation of the
Adoptionist heresy, which, under the influence of the Spanish
Moslems, had revived the old and probably primitive belief
that Jesus was a mere man by birth, but Son of God by adop-
tion. As Renan acutely observes, Islam derived an essential
part of its strength from the adhesion of Christian sectaries
persecuted by authority.[2] To Catholic rulers heresy was a
" fifth column."

Although Alcuin wrote no chronicle, he left a voluminous
correspondence with Charles, Offa of Mercia, and his own

[1] Bede, *Ecclesiastical History*, III, 8.
[2] Renan, *Marc-Aurèle*, chap. XXXIII.

fellow-ecclesiastics, mainly dating from the last decade of the eighth century. These letters throw a light very similar to that of Bede on the social conditions of the time, and in particular on the state of the Church. By this time the Viking raids on western Christendom, the second great wave of Teutonic migration, had begun. Abbeys with their accumulated wealth were a special temptation to marauders; and Alcuin's letters tell a double tale of internal corruption and external attack. Writing to Offa, he speaks of "holy places wasted by the heathen, altars defiled by perjury, monasteries profaned by adultery, a land befouled with the blood of lords and princes." In a later letter he complains that "throughout the churches of Christ teachers of truth have perished; well-nigh all follow the vanities of the world and have in hatred the discipline of their rule; and their men of war follow after covetousness more than justice."[1] This is the evidence, not of a disgruntled heretic, but of the most learned and orthodox churchman of his day.

It is unintelligible to many moderns that medieval rulers should have taken so much trouble to enforce orthodoxy in belief and so little to enforce, or even practise, tolerable standards of conduct. Charles the Great, for example, forced the Saxons of North Germany to accept Christianity on pain of extermination, convened two successive synods to condemn Adoptionism, and induced the Pope to add the *filioque* to the Nicene Creed.[2] Yet Charles had two wives and a veritable harem of concubines, to say nothing of illegitimate sons. Had he lived ten generations earlier and worshipped Woden and Thor, his private life would doubtless have been much the same, but he would not have been so particular in theology. A barbarian chief of the fourth or fifth century might have put to death tribesmen who refused to worship Woden, but he would not have bothered his head whether Woden had always been a god or had begun as a man and worked his way up. Things like this lead impatient Ration-

[1] Alcuin, *Letters*, XLVIII and LXXIV.
[2] That is, to decree that the Holy Ghost proceeds from the Father *and the Son.*

alists to conclude that Christianity contributed nothing to civilization except a greater propensity to intolerance.

This is to misunderstand the historical situation. The later Roman emperors and their barbarian successors adopted Christianity, not on its spiritual merits, but for its secular utility. Charles the Great was trying (as it proved, with only ephemeral success) to build an empire out of the wreckage of the West. The mob of feudatories over whom he ruled—Franks, Gauls, Burgundians, Lombards, Italians, Bavarians, Saxons—had no common nationality and no common language. The only unifying force was the Church. By veiling the primitive beliefs of her converts with a thin veneer of Christianity, by dazzling them with priestcraft and bemusing them with miraculous relics and images, the Church had stepped into the shoes of paganism. With that force Charles had to keep on good terms : hence his orthodox zeal. The condemnation of Adoptionism served to distinguish the God of Christendom, whose body the faithful ate at the altar every Sunday, from any mere prophet whom even a Moslem might honour. The addition of the *filioque* to the Creed served to distinguish the West, which owed spiritual obedience to Rome and temporal obedience to Charles, from the Greek and alien East. On both points piety spelt political convenience.

The chief authority for English history from the eighth to the twelfth century is the *Anglo-Saxon Chronicle*—or rather chronicles; for the work which passes under that name is a collection of monkish annals by different hands, ranging in date from the time of Alfred to the accession of Henry II, and having nothing in common but the fact that they are in Anglo-Saxon. Events prior to the reign of Alfred are dismissed for the most part in brief notes based either on the Bible, on Roman history, on the works of Gildas and Bede, or simply on tradition. Only on grand occasions, as in relating the foundation of his own abbey, does a monkish author let himself go. But from the time of Alfred the chronicles " come alive." We feel that we are reading no longer a bored monk's transcription of the doings of dead cut-throats, but a contemporary's appreciation of a probably still living king. From the dreary scenes of Viking devastation there begin to emerge, as it were, the rudimentary organs of the England we know.

> " The same year also King Alfred fortified the city of London; and the whole nation turned to him, except that part of it which was held captive by the Danes. He then committed the city to the care of Alderman Ethered, to hold it under him." [1]

We read in the tenth century of the fortification of many such places—Hertford, Stafford, Warwick, Nottingham, Manchester, and many others: chartered towns of the age to come. The establishment of these petty strongholds in the warfare between English and Danes was pregnant with a future undreamt of by the kings who ordered it or the monks who recorded it.

After the union of England into a single kingdom by Athelstan in 926 the chronicles tail off into brief notes, broken only by the virile ballad of the battle of Brunanburgh (surely not of monkish origin) and other old poems, until we come to the troubled reign of Ethelred II, when a contemporary hand again writes a connected history. A miserable tale of rapine and extortion leads up to the Danish conquest by Cnut. The wretched condition of England at this time, during which the people had to pay Danegeld to an invading army as well as their ordinary taxes, seems to have led to popular risings of which record is lost. At any rate, the chronicler mentions in 1017, and again in 1020, the outlawry of a certain " Edwy, king of the churls," of whom we should like to know more.

And so we come to the Norman Conquest, which cannot be understood without knowing a little of the Normans. The Scandinavian sea-rovers who called themselves Vikings were called by their enemies in western Europe Northmen or, in monkish Latin, *Normanni*. After Alfred had secured Wessex against them they turned their attentions to the ramshackle Frankish Empire. This was easy game. The

[1] *Anglo-Saxon Chronicle*, 886. " Alderman " here means a king's officer and not a civic dignitary.

Carolingians (descendants of Charles the Great) were no more able to hold it together than their predecessors, the later Roman emperors, had been able to hold theirs in their day. The Northmen sailed up the Meuse, Scheldt, Somme, and Seine, ravaging at will, until in 911 the feeble West Frankish (or as we may now say, French) king, Charles the Simple, ceded the lower Seine and the adjacent coast to their chief, Rollo, on condition that he did him homage and accepted Christianity. To the sea-rovers the one condition probably meant as little as the other.

Settled in France as feudal lords among a peasant population which had known no freedom for a thousand years, the Normans adopted the language of their neighbours—the clipped, slurred, adulterated Latin which was by now evolving into something like French—and assumed with gusto the rôle of *grands seigneurs*. Hilaire Belloc rhapsodizes picturesquely about "some odd transitory phenomenon of cross-breeding" which "produced the only body of men who all were lords and who in their collective action showed continually nothing but genius."[1] The Normans were all lords, for the simple reason that they had taken a slice of France and shared it out among them. Cross-breeding and genius had as much to do with it as with a Chicago gunman. Like many who take over a system ready-made, the Normans were quicker to work out a theory of feudalism than those who had arrived at it experimentally through centuries of struggle. In particular they were quick to note the key position held in feudal Europe by the Papacy, and the profit to be derived by making themselves its hired bravoes and bullies. By the end of the tenth century Normandy was too small to hold them. Peasants were in revolt against lords who skinned them to the bone. Cloaking their ancient trade of piracy under a show of piety, the Normans in the eleventh century began to sally and carve out kingdoms for themselves north, south, east, and west.

At first they went south. No northern adventurer could resist the lure of the sunshine. In 1018 they were fighting the Moors in Spain. Later, having established themselves in

[1] Belloc, *Hills and the Sea.*

Apulia and proved in 1053, by taking Pope Leo IX prisoner, that they were not men to be trifled with, Norman freebooters under Robert Guiscard struck a bargain with him, bartered their temporal aid for his spiritual support, and as feudatories of the Holy See soon made themselves masters of southern Italy and Sicily, and the faithful henchmen of the Papacy in its quarrel with the empire. That set the precedent for Norman proceedings for the next hundred years.

England was not so rich a prey as Italy, but it was nearer at hand. The way in which the story of the Norman Conquest is taught to us at school is a national disgrace. The close alliance of the Normans with the Papacy, which made the whole thing as much a piece of papal power-politics as of Norman filibustering, is carefully suppressed. Instead we are told a silly tale of Harold's shipwreck in Normandy, of his swearing an oath to William on relics which were not shown him till he had sworn, and of his perjury thereupon being a pretext for William's expedition. The story is told only by Norman writers who, as Freeman points out, " all contradict one another." [1] It would be a poor compliment to William to suppose him so puerile as to expect any man to keep an oath extorted by a trick.

What the Conquest really did was to nip in the bud an English attempt, premature by some centuries, to slip the yoke of Rome. The story can be pieced together from the Anglo-Saxon and Norman chronicles. The pious Edward, more monk than king (and therefore a favourite with the monkish chroniclers), had tried to strengthen the connection with Rome by appointing Norman bishops to English sees. The result was a national movement in which Earl Godwin and his sons were in the position of popular leaders. They were certainly not disinterested : Saxon and Norman chroniclers agree that Godwin had appropriated abbey property. But the movement had a popular basis. It is significant that now, for the first time in English history, we read of townsmen playing an independent rôle. The national movement begins with an affray between the retinue of a French count and the

[1] Freeman, *Short History of the Norman Conquest*, chap. V.

men of Dover, in which the town has the best of it.   Godwin, ordered to chastise the townsmen, refuses, and is outlawed with his sons.   They fly abroad and take to piracy.   Godwin lands in Kent and is joined by " all the Kentish men, and all the boatmen from Hastings, and everywhere thereabout by the sea-coast, and all the men of Essex and Sussex and Surrey, and many others besides.   Then said they all that they would with him live or die." [1]   They sail up the Thames to London and win over the burgesses.   The king's men are "loth to fight with their own kinsmen"; the Norman bishops run for their lives; and the national movement is victorious, but only for a time.   It was not to be expected that Rome or Normandy would take this provocation lying down.   The price was paid in 1066, when William, with an army of Norman, French, Breton, Flemish, and other adventurers, and the blessing of Pope Alexander II, slew Harold Godwinsson at Hastings, ravaged the country, and made the English a subject people under French-speaking lords.

It is interesting to note the reaction of contemporaries to this event.   The Anglo-Saxon chronicler is visibly torn between his feelings as a patriot and as a monk.   For most Englishmen the Conquest meant mere misery.   " Ever since has evil increased very much. . . . The king and the head men loved much, and overmuch, covetousness in gold and silver. . . . He recked not how very sinfully the stewards got it of wretched men, nor how many unlawful deeds they did. . . . Castles he let men build, and miserably swink the poor," and " extorted from his subjects many marks of gold, and many hundred pounds of silver; which he took of his people, for little need, by right and by unright."   The Domesday survey, which to modern historians is an invaluable record of the condition of England at the time, is to the chronicler a disgraceful inquisition.   " It is shameful to tell, though he thought it no shame to do it."   And yet (and for the chronicler it is a very big yet) " he was mild to the good men that loved God. . . . On that same spot where God granted him that he should gain England, he reared a mighty minster, and set monks therein, and well endowed it.   In his days was the

[1] *Anglo-Saxon Chronicle*, 1052.

great monastery in Canterbury built, and also very many others over all England." [1]

Another English monk, Eadmer of Canterbury, notes William's exclusion of Englishmen from all preferment, but at the same time his determination to be master in his own house and to allow no papal intervention (such as that to which he owed his crown) to be invoked against himself. For in those days Gregory VII was over-reaching himself and claiming temporal supremacy over emperors and kings—thereby in the end alienating his Norman protectors in Italy and dooming himself to die in exile.

The Norman chroniclers for their part, while proud of William's services to the Church, do not attempt to hide the miserable condition of the people under him and his sons. Like the English chronicler, they tell a monotonous tale of extortion. But for them, as for monkish writers generally, the corporate interests of the Church come first. William of Malmesbury, who wrote about 1120, censures a certain bishop of Wells and abbot of Bath for having manumitted the abbey serfs on his deathbed, " setting his successors an example not to be imitated." [2] Yet Malmesbury owns that the papal court, to which the Church is subject, is utterly corrupt, " trading justice for gold, selling canon law for a price." [3] Such was the delectable racket which nowadays we are asked to revere as the fountain of freedom and civilization.

The third enterprise in which the Normans played a leading part was the First Crusade and the consequent establishment of Norman or French rule in Syria and Palestine. Once again popular history gives an inadequate and misleading account of events. We are asked to believe that the Crusades were the outcome of high-souled zeal for the recovery of the Holy Sepulchre from the Moslems. Now the Moslems had been in possession of Jerusalem and its dubious " holy places " for over four centuries, during which the West had shown no interest whatever in their recovery. The Moslems were not intolerant. Jews and Christians could live at peace under

---

[1] *Anglo-Saxon Chronicle*, 1066, 1085, and 1087.
[2] Malmesbury, *Gesta Regum*, IV, 340.   [3] Ibid., 351.

their empire on payment of a tax; and pilgrimages to the
Holy Land continued without interruption.   True, Jerusalem
had passed in 1071 from the hands of the Fatimite caliphs into
those of the Seljuk Turks.   No doubt the Turks were rougher
and ruder than the Arabs, but they were not more bigoted.
Only in modern times, when Europe began to encroach on
the Ottoman Empire, did the Turks take to massacring their
Christian subjects.   The sufferings of pilgrims under the
Seljuks were such as anyone might expect who insisted on
travelling in a strange country in unsettled conditions.   Something more is needed to account for the mass movement
which swept western Europe in 1095-1096.   It is to be found
in the internal condition of the West rather than of the East.

The western peoples were in a condition of indescribable
misery.   We have already seen the state of England after the
Norman Conquest.   France was in no better case.   The
Normans and other feudal robbers had picked their prey to
the bone; and there were not, as in England, even the beginnings of a strong monarchy to moderate their brigandage.
The wretched country was swept by private war, pestilence,
and famine.   Its serfs had every inducement to escape if
they could; its lords every inducement to find some new
country more worth plundering.   No wonder that when
Urban II, answering an appeal from the emperor of Constantinople, proclaimed a plenary indulgence for all who
would enlist in a holy war against the infidel, a motley mass
of emigrants, mobilized by wandering preachers and tales of
a land flowing with milk and honey, promptly set out east-
ward.   "It was like the rush to the gold fields in modern
times, but undertaken with far denser ignorance and under a
more blinding glamour."[1]   Taking Urban a little too
literally, they began the war on the infidel by massacring
some ten thousand Jews in the trading towns of the Rhine-
land, and were themselves massacred by the Turks as soon as
they set foot in Asia.   They were followed by better-
equipped French and Norman adventurers, no doubt equally
in need of a plenary indulgence, and moreover bent on the
more serious business of carving out principalities and king-

[1] Cunningham, *Growth of English Industry and Commerce.*

doms for themselves in the opulent East. They fought their way through Asia Minor to Antioch and Jerusalem, stormed the city, massacred seventy thousand Moslems without respect to age or sex, burnt the Jews alive in their synagogue, and ended a perfect day by falling with tears of joy before the Holy Sepulchre which they had come to liberate. Such was what a contemporary abbot and historian, Guibert of Nogent, called a " new way of salvation."[1]

The fourth and last sphere of Norman prowess was Ireland. Ireland had never been part of the Roman Empire, and in spite of St. Patrick and its reputation as the "isle of saints," until the twelfth century it was only semi-Christian. Indeed, the Irish saints usually made a point of quitting their homeland for some country where saints could live. The mass of Irish were not far removed from savagery. They lived in village communities under petty lords owning allegiance to local kings and ultimately to a " supreme king " whose supremacy was seldom more than nominal, and, despite a veneer of Christianity, were essentially pagan in their way of life. Even if we dismiss as prejudiced the statement of a Norman chronicler that "most of them had as many wives as they would, and were wont to have even their own sisters to wife,"[2] there is no doubt that pagan marriage customs prevailed. Worse still from the point of view of the Church, they paid no tithes and baptized their children without the assistance of a priest. So when Pope Alexander III gave his blessing to Henry II's conquest of Ireland, Strongbow and his fellow-filibusters could say that in helping themselves to Irish lands they were serving Holy Church. After all, it was no more than their ancestors had done in England a century before. In 1171 at the Synod of Cashel the Irish clergy acknowledged Henry their temporal sovereign and the Pope their supreme director in faith and morals. In Ireland, as in England, Italy, and Palestine, the Normans turned their orthodoxy to profitable account.

If the test of orthodoxy (as Vincent of Lerins thought) is

---

[1] Guibert, *Gesta Dei per Francos*, quoted by Gibbon, *Decline and Fall*, LVIII.

[2] *Gesta Henrici Secundi*.

that a belief shall have been held " everywhere, always, and by all," no article of the Creed can be called orthodox. From the very beginning of Christianity there has been diversity of belief. Throughout the Middle Ages, despite all attempts to dragoon men and women into submission to the vast vested interest which was the Catholic Church, there were heresies. The East, where Christianity had first arisen and where Islam now disputed its monopoly, was a fertile nursing-ground of heresy. Before the rise of Islam, as early as the sixth century, and thereafter in the eighth and ninth, we find in Armenia a sect whom the orthodox named Paulicians, after Paul of Samosata, the heretical third-century bishop of Antioch. In reality they were an *omnium gatherum* of outcasts of various origins—Marcionites, Manichæans, followers of Paul of Samosata, Iconoclasts who objected to image-worship, and others—driven by repression to the confines of the empire and welded into one by common opposition to the persecuting orthodox Church. Their numbers ran to many hundreds of thousands. From the point of view of Constantinople, to leave them in Asia, where they might and often did side with the Moslem enemy, was dangerous. The most ferocious persecutions failed. So in the eighth and tenth centuries the Byzantine emperors deported more than two hundred thousand of these sectaries from Armenia to the Balkans to hold the frontier against the Bulgars, thus introducing their heresy into Europe. The transplanted heretics, instead of fighting the Bulgars, fraternized with them and converted them. From the Balkans the contagion spread in all directions along the trade routes, by the eleventh century had reached Italy and France, and in the twelfth Germany and England. As they spread westward, the heretics acquired many different nicknames. In Slav countries they were known as Bogomils (" God-prayers," " devotees "); in Italy as Patarenes (" ragmen ") because they were found mainly among the poor of the Italian cities; in France as Tixerands (" weavers "), Albigenses from Albi in the territory of Toulouse, where they were strong, and Bulgars, from their supposed country of origin —a name soon corrupted into a low term of abuse. Their name for themselves was Cathari, " the pure."

In the Cathars the Catholic Church was confronted by a resistance movement, linked together by secret correspondence between Armenia and Bulgaria, between Bulgaria and western Europe. Our knowledge of them is derived almost wholly from their enemies. By the time when chroniclers begin to notice them, their tenets have crystallized along certain well-defined lines. Not God, but Satan, is the creator of this world; and mankind are his slaves. God sent Christ to free mankind from slavery. Christ was not God, but an angel in human form who became Son of God by merit. We may become free by avoiding the pleasures of this Satanic world. The dominant Church, with its Pope, priests, monks, sacraments, and relics, is unchristian. Infant baptism is unscriptural; the Mass a superstition; the worship of crosses, images, and relics idolatry. In the true Church there are no priests, and the only distinction of rank is between the " perfect "— the *bons hommes* as they were called in France, the few men and women who have renounced the world, including sex, flesh food, and any kind of violence, and become to all intents and purposes Christs—and the " believers "—the many who live a normal life and are not yet " perfect," but hope to become so, and may profit by the prayers of those who are. Most Cathars not unnaturally deferred admission to the ranks of the " perfect " until their death-bed. Yet they believed that all mankind, if not here and now, nevertheless in some future incarnation, would become perfect and free from the prison of the world.

How was it that what seems to us an arid and depressing creed, which treated the whole visible world as the domain of the devil and saw perfection in the negation of natural instincts, could find adherents and martyrs by the hundred thousand in the East and in the West? The answer is that Catharism was a protest against the corruption, oppression, and hypocrisy of the official Church, whether Greek or Latin. The official Church, East and West, had become a vested interest, the auxiliary policeman of Byzantine, Frankish, or Norman rulers, and itself the greatest landowner and serf-owner of the Middle Ages. Hundreds of thousands of simple Christians believed that in so doing the Church had compounded with Satan and betrayed its trust. They turned away from it to an anti-Church whose ministers, even if they set up standards impossible for average human nature to fulfil, at least themselves fulfilled them and did not, under a cynical pretence of holiness, feather their nests at the expense of common men and women. They held that Satan was the creator of the world, because the world in which they lived was in fact Satanic—a world of brutal anarchy, a Dark Age. They held that they could escape only by renouncing life, because no other way was in fact yet open.

There is something moving in the description by an enemy, the contemporary chronicler William of Newburgh, of the Cathar mission to England in the reign of Henry II and of its suppression in 1166 by Henry, who, though not a very good Catholic, did not want to be accused of heresy in the middle of his trouble with Becket.

" There were a little more than thirty men and women who, dissembling their error, entered hither as it were peaceably to spread this plague, the leader being one Gerard, to whom they all looked as teacher and chief. For he only was in some sort lettered : the rest were unlettered and ignorant, altogether unpolished and rustic, of German race and language. . . . They could not hide themselves long, but, when certain men by diligence discovered that they were of an alien sect, they were tracked down, arrested, and held in a public prison. The king, unwilling to let them go or punish them untried, commanded that a synod of bishops should assemble at Oxford. . . . Pressed with divine proofs taken from holy scripture, they answered that they for their part believed as they had been taught, but that they would not dispute concerning their faith. Admonished to do penance and be joined to the body of the Church, they spurned all sound counsel. Threats also (held forth with godly intent that they might repent, even were it from fear) they laughed to scorn, misusing that saying of the Lord : ' Blessed are they that are persecuted for righteousness' sake, for theirs is the kingdom of heaven.' Then the bishops, seeing to it that the poison of heresy should creep no further, publicly pronounced them heretics and handed them over to the Catholic prince for bodily chastisement. He commanded that a mark of heretical infamy should be branded on their foreheads and that they should be beaten with rods and driven out of the town in the sight of the people, straitly forbidding that any should receive them into his house or presume to help and comfort them in anything.[1] Sentence being given, they were led rejoicing to a most righteous punishment, their teacher going before them with light steps and singing : ' Blessed shall ye be when men shall hate you ' . . . He who held first place among them suffered in token of his office the shame of a double branding on the forehead and about the chin. With garments cut away up to the girdle, they were publicly flogged and cast out of the town with resounding stripes, and unable to brook the cold (for it was winter) and no one showing them the least mercy, they perished miserably."[2]

Catharism on the continent was a more formidable affair. In Italy and southern France, the trading towns, enriched by traffic with the Moslem world, were but lightly attached to the faith. Denunciations of the wealth and worldliness of the clergy found a ready echo in such cities as Milan and Lyons, and even for a time in Rome itself, where in 1143 the temporal power of the Pope was overthrown and only restored in 1154 by the intervention of Frederick Barbarossa. This movement does not seem to have been actually heretical, though its spokesman, Arnold of Brescia, was hanged and burnt.[3] Southern France gave the Papacy far more trouble.

[1] All sheriffs, barons' stewards, knights, and freeholders were obliged to swear that they would not harbour any Cathar. Assize of Clarendon, article 21, cited by Stubbs, *Select Charters*, part IV.

[2] Newburgh, *Historia Rerum Anglicarum*, II, 13. These facts dispose of the eccentric theory of Hugh Ross Williamson in *The Arrow and the Sword* that Henry and Becket were crypto-Cathars.

[3] Gibbon says that Arnold was burnt alive (*Decline and Fall*, LXIX). But Villari (*Encyclopædia Britannica*, article " Rome") and Alphandéry (article " Arnold of Brescia ") agree that he was hanged first.

The people were attached to the ascetic *bons hommes*, and preferred them to the grasping Catholic clergy. A great part of the southern nobility protected them. Far from being summoned before episcopal synods, the Cathars were able to hold synods of their own undisturbed. By the end of the twelfth century it looked as if the south of France were lost to the Church. In 1207 Pierre de Castelnau, legate of Pope Innocent III, excommunicated Raymond VI, Count of Toulouse, for aiding and abetting heresy. In 1208 Raymond had Pierre assassinated. Thereupon Innocent resorted to the ultimate weapon of the Papacy: he proclaimed a crusade against Raymond and invited the whole Catholic nobility of France to invade and occupy his lands. Raymond had no stomach for the fight, and submitted at once. But the crusade was not called off. Cupidity and bigotry had their way. Let Gibbon sum up.

> " The visible assemblies of the Paulicians, or Albigeois, were extirpated by fire and sword; and the bleeding remnant escaped by flight, concealment, or Catholic conformity. But the invincible spirit which they had kindled still lived and breathed in the Western World." [1]

The thirteenth century is the turning-point in medieval history. Thenceforth the " kingdom of darkness," as Hobbes calls the Catholic hierarchy, is forced on to the defensive. The grave-diggers of feudalism are already at work. In Italy, where ancient civilization had never quite died out, maritime communities like Venice and Genoa held their own through the darkest of the Dark Ages as free towns in a sea of barbarism, to be emulated later by Milan (the meeting-place of transalpine trade routes), Cremona, Mantua, Pisa, Florence, and many another centre of thriving civic life. The Crusades brought prosperity to Italian merchants by opening up the East. With trade came impatience of feudal and clerical domination. The rivalry between the Pope and the German emperor for supremacy in Italy enabled the cities, by playing off one against the other, to make themselves independent of

[1] *Decline and Fall*, chap. LIV.

both. "The city of Milan," writes Matthew Paris, "was a refuge and asylum of all manner of heretics, Patarenes, Luciferani, Paulicians, Albigenses, and usurers." Frederick II, who was at lifelong loggerheads with both the Papacy and the Lombards, sarcastically "wondered that the lord Pope was in any wise favourable to the Milanese, seeing that it behoved him to be the father of the godly and the hammer of the ungodly."[1] The Popes had, in fact, financial reasons for favouring the Lombard cities. Their merchants were bankers to the Holy See. Moreover, they were doing very profitable business in economically backward countries, such as England, for example, then was, and provided that the profits (which might amount to sixty per cent) were shared with the Pope, were allowed to dodge the canon law against usury. For such considerations the Papacy was ready to wink even at heresy. In the absence of such reasons the newly established Inquisition was set ruthlessly to work to ferret out and burn the enemies of the Church.

It was the cruelty of fear. A Papacy which did not respect its own canon law could not hope to retain the respect of Europe. Dante's bitter lines to a Pope—one of those whom he puts in hell—are worth quoting:

> I pray thee tell me now how great a treasure
> Our Lord demanded of Saint Peter first,
> Before he put the keys into his keeping?
> Truly he nothing asked but "Follow me."
> Nor Peter nor the rest asked of Matthias
> Silver or gold, when he by lot was chosen
> To fill the place the guilty soul had lost.
> Therefore stay here, for thou art justly punished,
> And keep safe guard o'er the ill-gotten money . . .
> And were it not that I am still forbid
> By reverence for the keys superlative
> Thou hadst in keeping in the gladsome life,
> I would use words to thee more grievous still;
> Because your avarice afflicts the world,
> Trampling the good and lifting the depraved.
> The Evangelist you Pastors had in mind,
> When she who sitteth upon many waters
> Was seen by him to fornicate with kings . . .
> Ye have made yourselves a god of gold and silver:

[1] Paris, *Chronica Majora*, 1236.

How differ ye from the idolater,
Save that he worships one, and ye a hundred?
Ah, Constantine! of how much ill was mother
Not thy conversion, but that marriage dower
Which the first wealthy Father took from thee![1]

The Italian cities, though rich and free, could never make common cause; and there was no strong power to impose union on them. The emperor was too far off, and the Pope too discredited. " My Cæsar, why hast thou forsaken me?" cries Dante in his vain quest for a monarch.[2] But in France and England new nations were forming. In both countries the king found the towns useful allies and sources of revenue in his struggle with the feudal lords—England in this matter being slightly ahead of France. In 1191, in the absence of Richard I on his Crusade, London won at last the right to elect its own sheriffs and mayor—much to the discontent of churchmen, who quoted the proverb: " A corporate town means a fat people, a fearful king, a feeble priesthood."[3] Paris had its charter about the same time from Philip Augustus, the first great king of France since Charlemagne—the same who took Normandy from John. Nominally under France, but linked with England by their dependence on its wool, were the Flemish cities, Bruges, Ghent, Ypres, and their lesser sisters.

In the thirteenth century the towns increased greatly in wealth and importance. Henry III, a pious puppet in the hands of the Papacy, could see in the citizens of London only " serfs who were sickeningly rich and masqueraded as barons."[4] He paid for his extortions and insults when London and other towns, defying a papal bull, sided with Simon de Montfort and were for the first time invited to send members to sit with the lords spiritual and temporal in the Parliament of 1265. For this temerity London, after Evesham, forfeited its charter for five years. But Edward I understood the signs of the times better than his father had done and made Simon's innovation permanent.

---

[1] Dante, *Inferno*, canto XIX.   [2] *Purgatorio*, canto VI.
[3] Richard of Devizes, *Chronicle*, cited by Stubbs, *Select Charters*, part V.
[4] Paris, *Chronica Majora*, 1248.

In France it was not until 1302 that Philip IV, in order to have the nation behind him in resisting Boniface VIII, called together the States-General—clergy, nobles, and bourgeois. In the following year Philip's councillor, Guillaume de Nogaret (a man of bourgeois origin and, it is said, the son of a condemned heretic), went to Italy and with the aid of Boniface's Roman enemies took him prisoner at Anagni. There are few more contemptible figures in history than this Boniface. He was reported, probably with truth, to be an infidel at heart. In the thirteenth century Greek philosophy, through the medium of Arabic and Latin versions, was permeating learned circles in the West with revolutionary effect. Yet Boniface had the hardihood to revive, a hundred years too late, the overweening claims of Gregory VII and Innocent III to suzerainty over secular rulers. The French intended to bring him to France and compel him to summon a General Council which would depose him for heresy. He was rescued, but in little over a month was dead of chagrin and shock. In 1305 a French Pope was elected and the Papacy removed to Avignon. Thus the first meeting of the French States-General heralded the end of the glory of medieval Rome. In the far future a more famous meeting was to herald a greater Revolution. England in 1265 and France in 1302 seem to begin rehearsing their dramas of four or five centuries later.

In the last two centuries of medieval history we hear the rumble of the coming storm of the Reformation. In the womb of feudal society, in Italy, in France, in Flanders, in England, and as far afield as the Baltic countries, bourgeois society already exists in embryo, and the time of delivery is in sight. Flemish weavers, to escape French domination, take themselves and their industry to England, with the result that in 1337 England stops exporting wool to Flanders and begins to foster home industry instead. The Flemish cities, bereft of their trade, transfer their allegiance from Philip VI to Edward III. This, rather than Edward's flimsy claim to the French throne, is the real cause of the Hundred Years' War.

But the war would not have lasted, on and off, for a

hundred years for that alone. In the middle years of the fourteenth century the miserable, underfed populations of Europe were swept from south to north by bubonic plague, known in those days as the Black Death. On a sober estimate a quarter of the population must have died; contemporary estimates are much higher, but we need not take them literally. As the mortality was naturally greater in the poorer classes, feudal economy was dislocated. In England, "such a lack arose of serfs and servants, that there was none who knew what he should do. . . . Much corn perished in the fields for lack of a reaper. . . . And so all necessaries became so dear, that that which in past time had been worth a penny was at that time worth fourpence or fivepence." Consequently " the great men of the realm, and other lesser lords who had tenants, remitted part of the rent, lest the tenants should depart for lack of serfs and for dearth of things." [1] In a word, the diminished labouring population could not carry on their backs the feudal superstructure which hitherto had rested on them. The lords had to recoup themselves in other ways. One was to plunder foreign countries and hold their nobles and knights to ransom. The Hundred Years' War was prolonged by the fact that, to lords and gentlemen impoverished by the Black Death, war was a means of keeping up their state and employing retainers who otherwise would have been turned off. Hence even after the peace of Brétigny in 1360 " free companies " went on ravaging France until they could be induced to transfer their depredations to other theatres of war.

But war had the disadvantage of paying only the winners. Having in a few years lost most of their gains in France, the gentlemen of England had to think again. The whole feudal system was beginning to stink. Already in 1356–1358 the French States-General, led by Étienne Marcel, had tried to seize power by applying the financial screw, and French peasants had risen against the nobles in the Jacquerie—movements anticipatory of 1789, which failed through lack of cohesion, and ended in the murder of Marcel and the massacre of great numbers of peasants. Already, since 1360 or there-

[1] Knighton, *Chronicle*, 1348.

abouts, John Ball, the "mad priest," had preached in Essex and Kent the dangerous doctrines that "tithes should not be paid to parsons, unless he who paid were richer than the vicar or rector who received them";[1] that they should be withheld altogether from priests of evil life; nay, more, that there should be "no villeins nor gentlemen," and that if men "laboured or did anything for their lords, they would have wages therefor as well as other."[2] And from 1374 John Wycliffe, without going so far as Ball, argued that an unrighteous clergy had no title to property and might justly forfeit it to the civil power. This was popular doctrine. Many of the nobility sided with Wycliffe, perhaps the better to head off Ball. The citizens of London ("of all races in the world," says the monk Walsingham, "the proudest, most arrogant, most covetous, and most unbelieving in God and the traditions of their fathers; upholders of the Lollards, slanderers of the religious, withholders of tithes, and impoverishers of the common people "[3]) were overwhelmingly with Wycliffe.

The Papacy, for seventy years a French puppet, was no longer respected in England or in any country with national interests opposed to those of France. Some English lords, the chronicler complains, "believed that there was no God, that the sacrament of the altar was nought, that there was no resurrection after death."[4] In 1377 Gregory XI, alarmed lest Italy should revolt, left Avignon for Rome. The result was the Great Schism of 1378, when the Italian cardinals elected one Pope and the French another. For forty years the West was split between a Roman and an Avignon Pope. Most of the Italian states, England, Germany, and central Europe supported Rome: France, Scotland, Spain, and Naples supported Avignon. In strict theology half the bishops and priests ordained during that period were without valid orders,

---

[1] Walsingham, *Chronicon Angliæ*, 1381.
[2] Froissart, *Chronicle*, chap. 381. The view that Ball advocated community of goods seems inconsistent with these passages.
[3] Walsingham, *Historia Anglicana*, 1392. Notice the charge of exploiting the people. Already the feudal pot calls the bourgeois kettle black.
[4] Idem, *Chronicon Angliæ*, 1381.

half the Masses said were blasphemous parodies, and half western Christendom went unshriven to eternal damnation. The truth was that the new nations of western Europe refused to submit to the dictation of a power which, nominally spiritual and above nationality, was in fact as materially and secularly minded as themselves. The temper of the masses was manifested during the English revolt of 1381, when Wat Tyler's men, threatened by Simon of Sudbury, archbishop of Canterbury, with a papal interdict, replied that they feared neither interdict nor Pope, and struck off his head.

There is the presage of a new age in the chroniclers' accounts, all bitterly hostile, of the Peasant Revolt. It is as if the writers were forced in spite of themselves to acknowledge the existence and to give us a glimpse of that underworld on which their decadent feudalism rested. The vernacular English of Ball's propaganda to the peasants breaks into the monkish Latin of the chronicles like a breath of fresh air into a stuffy cloister.

> "John Shepherd, some time St. Mary's priest of York, and now of Colchester, greeteth well John Nameless, and John the Miller, and John Carter, and biddeth them that they beware of guile in burgh, and stand together in God's name; and biddeth Piers Ploughman go to his work, and chastise well Hob the Robber, and take with you John Trueman and all his fellows, and no more, and look sharp you to one head and no more."[1]

The Peasant Revolt in England, like the Jacquerie in France, was drowned in blood. The great lords were so frightened that they withdrew whatever support they had given to Wycliffe. But lesser folk did not. In England Wycliffe's followers, the "poor preachers" or Lollards, with their vernacular denunciations of the wealthy and worldly upper clergy and their plea for evangelical poverty, found a ready welcome among the smaller gentry, merchants, artisans, and peasants, and had spokesmen even in Parliament, until Church

---

[1] Walsingham, *Chronicon Angliæ*, 1381. The English has been slightly modernized.

and king forced through the statute *De Hæretico Comburendo*, burnt the more outspoken of them, and drove the rest underground. The modern Freethinker will gladly recognize in this movement a forerunner of his own. John Badby, who went to the stake in 1410 for saying that the consecrated host was "inferior to a toad or a spider, which are at least living animals," was a fifteenth-century Paine or Bradlaugh. In central Europe Wycliffe's doctrines were taken up by John Huss, who had the Czech nation behind him against papal rapacity and German encroachment.

That the Catholic Church survived the Great Schism was due to the action of secular rulers who could not dispense with it as an instrument of government. While Henry IV and Henry V crushed the English Lollards, the German emperor Sigismund had the Council of Constance convened to settle the schism. It was high time; for the two Popes had now become three. The Council started work in 1415 by luring Huss to Constance under an imperial safe-conduct and burning him alive. On that the whole hierarchy could agree. Further, it deposed all three Popes and elected its own man, terminating the schism. But the medieval Papacy never recovered its lost prestige. Power in the West had definitely passed to national rulers; and the rising merchant class cared less than nothing for these unconvincing Vicars of Christ.

Nothing so completely illustrates the subordination of the Church to secular politics as the case of Joan of Arc. In 1431 this peasant girl, who had put heart into the French people and led to victory troops whom the chivalry of France had led only to defeat, was handed over by the English (who were in occupation of northern France) to the Inquisition and burnt at Rouen as a heretic and a witch. The court which condemned her was composed of French clergy. If it be pleaded that they acted under duress, the fact remains that neither Charles VII and his counsellors, nor the Church in unoccupied France, nor Pope Eugenius IV lifted a finger to save her or to prevent the prostitution of the Holy Office to secular ends. Twenty-five years passed. The tide of war turned; Burgundy changed sides; England was thrown out of Paris,

Normandy, and Guienne, and left with nothing but Calais to show for the Hundred Years' War. Then in 1456, to oblige the victorious Charles, Calixtus III solemnly revoked the sentence on the woman whom, a quarter of a century before, king, Church, and Pope had abandoned to the flames. The proceedings in the one trial were as regular as in the other, and the motives no higher. The main difficulty in getting at the history of Joan is that the facts have to be distilled from the interested evidence tendered at one or the other of these two trials.

We are at the end of the Middle Ages. Three material inventions combined to bring the period to a close and to usher in the modern world. In each case the actual origin of the invention is a matter of dispute. The mariner's compass seems to have been introduced into Europe by Italian traders at the time of the Crusades, and to have been used in the later Middle Ages by English merchants voyaging to Iceland. Gunpowder was known in the thirteenth century, but was first put to warlike use by the Florentines early in the fourteenth. The printing-press was invented in the first half of the fifteenth century, probably by Lourens Coster of Haarlem, who seems to have been prior to Gutenberg of Mainz. Of these three inventions, the work, not of monks or knights, but of traders and burghers, the first made ocean navigation possible, the second ended the military domination of the feudal lords, and the third gave the quietus to the clerical monopoly of learning. Without the first two it is unlikely that the new civilization of the West, jammed between Islam and the Atlantic, would even have survived. Without the third its survival would have been culturally sterile.

The advance of the Osmanli Turks forced the West to rely on its new assets, and more especially on the mariner's compass; for in guns Islam was a match for Christendom. Superiority in artillery gave Constantinople to the Turks in 1453. The only way in which western merchants could recoup themselves for the eastern trade lost by Turkish conquests was by opening up a maritime highway to countries of Asia only precariously accessible by caravan. During the fifteenth century Portuguese explorers gradually made their way southward along the coast of Africa. Others, relying on the arguments of ancient geographers for the sphericity of the earth and on travellers' tales of "fortunate islands" in the west, planned to reach Asia by sailing in that direction. Columbus, the Genoese, was not the first engaged in this quest. In 1480, twelve years before his great voyage, John Jay, a merchant of Bristol, fitted out two ships to sail west in search of the legendary "island of Brazil." They were driven back by storms; but discovery was in the air. When Columbus, after vainly offering his services to John II of Portugal and Henry VII of England, at last managed to interest Ferdinand and Isabella in his schemes and to land in the New World, and when six years later Da Gama discovered the Cape route to India, the West had burst its prison, and the modern world was born.

CHAPTER XIII

MODERN HISTORY

THE materials for the history, I do not say of the world or even of Europe, but of any one country in Europe since the sixteenth century are so abundant that it is too much to expect even a specialist to master them all. The most that a non-specialist can reasonably hope is to make himself at home among contemporary sources for one or two selected periods—preferably periods of crisis in which the forces making for change are more manifest than at other times—and to rely for the general background on books of reference and on the works of scholars who have heroically pre-digested for the general reader material which it would take him more than a lifetime to sort out for himself.

For these reasons I shall deal in this chapter only with two periods of English history and one of French. The Tudor Reformation, the English Revolution of the seventeenth century, and the French Revolution of the eighteenth are all periods answering to the description above given. Each is illuminated by a wealth of contemporary authorities well worth reading for their own sake; and on each period later historians have spent and are spending a labour of research to which there seems to be no end.

For the sixteenth-century European background Preserved Smith's *Age of the Reformation*, and for the Tudor background in particular Green's *Short History of the English People*, Cunningham's *Growth of English Industry and Commerce*, Ashley's *Introduction to English Economic History and Theory*, and Creighton's *Cardinal Wolsey* and *Queen Elizabeth* are among the books which will be found useful. From them we get a general picture of the revolutionary century which immediately followed the discovery of the New World and of the sea route to the Far East.

First, Europe's economic centre of gravity shifts from Italy to the Atlantic seaboard: pepper and other luxuries are brought to the West no longer in Venetian, but in Portuguese ships. Venice, bereft of her eastern territory and trade, falls into decay. Even her Italian possessions would have been partitioned had the Pope, the emperor, and the French been able to agree over the spoils. England for a time is kept out of the New World by the Spanish and Portuguese monopoly, but never recognizes it: patents of exploration are granted from the first by Henry VII to the Cabots and other Bristol navigators. Protected or half-heartedly restrained by the Tudor monarchs, merchant adventurers are becoming a power in England—a power ready to ride roughshod over any vested interests, domestic or foreign, which bar them from a place in the sun. Even before the Reformation wealthy clothiers rented tracts of land to raise wool for their workshops, and set up workshops where they would, regardless of guild rules and town charters, which were now no longer necessary for the protection of trade. As Catholic writers often attribute such developments to Protestant avarice, it is as well to note that from the beginning of the fifteenth century, under the stimulus of the wool trade, the county of Norfolk was studded with villages where weavers worked wool into cloth for export by the great clothiers of the city of Norwich; that John Tame of Cirencester rented extensive sheep-runs at Fairford and bought lands for the same purpose all over the country, as early as 1480; and that as early as 1489 Henry VII's Parliament had to take notice of the enclosure of arable land for pasture and the consequent decay of people and townships.

Inevitably the rising bourgeoisie chafed at their dependence on local feudal lords and on the greatest feudal landowner of all, the Catholic Church and its monastic orders. The evictions by sheep-raising landowners in the fifteenth and sixteenth centuries at any rate meant the end of serfdom. What the insurgent peasantry had failed to effect, the bourgeoisie in their own interest brought about. For three centuries before the Reformation the burghers of Reading had fought the local abbot for the right to elect their own

mayor and appoint their own constables; and for two centuries the men of Lynn—Bishop's Lynn as it then was—had
fought the bishop of Norwich for similar freedoms.   We
find London on the very eve of the Reformation complaining
of the privileged competition of aliens in its midst (the Hanse
merchants settled at the Steelyard) and on the "evil May
Day" of 1517 carrying its protest to the point of rioting,
which led to fourteen luckless citizens being hanged, drawn,
and quartered.   A society torn by such conflicts was tinder
to the flame which Luther was soon to light.

With this background in mind we can turn to our contemporary sources.   First among these is the *Utopia* of Sir
Thomas More.   More, a London citizen by birth and yet
(owing to the Tudor policy of promoting new men) high
in the service of Henry VIII, embodied in his own person
the contradictions between the dying medieval order and the
forces which were destroying it.   In 1516, when he published *Utopia*, the future martyr for papal supremacy was
an ardent reformer, in matters of religion professing not
only toleration, but even indifference.   He depicts with
an eloquent pen the misery caused by the conversion of
arable land into pasture, and in doing so does not spare the
Church.

   " Your sheep, that were wont to be so meek and tame,
   and so small eaters, now, as I hear say, be become so great
   devourers and so wild that they eat up and swallow down
   the very men themselves; they waste and unpeople fields,
   houses, and towns.   For in whatsoever parts of the
   realm grows finer wool, and therefore more precious,
   there do noblemen and gentlemen, yea and some holy
   abbots also (not content with those rents and yearly
   fruits which were wont to accrue to their fathers from
   their farms, nor satisfied that they live at ease and deli-
   cately, and profit the commonwealth nothing, if indeed
   they do not hinder it) leave nothing for tillage, but
   enclose all for pasture, put down houses, and destroy
   towns, leaving perchance the church to sty their swine;
   and as if forests and parks of deer wasted not enough of

your land, those good men turn all habitations and corn-
land everywhere into a wilderness." [1]

More doubtless exaggerates the extent of Tudor enclosures. As
we might expect, they affected most the south-eastern counties
(the centre of the wool trade) and the north and west much
less. But so far as they extended, More's account accords with
other evidence. The stying of swine in the church is confirmed by Dugdale's *Antiquities of Warwickshire*, published in
1656, which mentions that in 1494 enclosure and depopulation
led to the stabling of cattle in the church of Stretton Baskerville
in that county. The general picture is borne out by contemporary legislation, which vainly tries to stem the evil.

From More we may pass to contemporary chroniclers,
and first and foremost to Edward Hall, lawyer and member
of Parliament, whose work in its present form extends to the
death of Henry VIII. We are now in the age of English
chronicles. The stream of monastic Latin dwindles to a
wretched trickle during the fifteenth century; and its last
representatives are not worth reading. The rise of a new lay
educated public created a market for English books which
the printing-press was able to supply. Hall's *Chronicle* may
be recommended as a corrective to anyone who believes the
Catholic story that the English Reformation was an accident
due to Henry VIII's adulterous passion for Anne Boleyn.
In London and other towns Lollardy had simmered since
the age of Wycliffe. In 1514, three years before Luther
nailed to the church door at Wittenberg his ninety-five theses
against indulgences, and when Anne Boleyn was yet a child,
the bishop of London induced Wolsey to quash proceedings
against the chancellor of the diocese for the murder of Richard
Hun (a merchant tailor accused of heresy for refusing to pay
a mortuary, who had been found hanged in his cell in the
Lollards' Tower at St. Paul's) on the ground that Londoners
were "so maliciously set in favour of heretical pravity, that
they will cast and condemn any clerk, though he were as
innocent as Abel." [2] Luther's theses fired a train already laid
in every trading city of north-western Europe.

[1] More, *Utopia*, 39.   [2] Hall's *Chronicle*, 6 Henry VIII.

From Hall, too, we learn of the deep hatred inspired by Wolsey. It was not only the feudal nobility who detested the upstart. They hated him, indeed, as an agent of Tudor despotism and a repressor of the private lawlessness which had run riot during the Wars of the Roses in the previous century. But because great men hated him, smaller men did not therefore love him. The game of power-politics which he played in Europe alternately against France and against the emperor Charles V led to heavy war taxation, and that in turn in 1523 to resistance by the House of Commons, and in 1525 to a revolt in Norfolk and Suffolk. Hall's account of this rising throws light on the social changes, already noted, which the growth of the wool trade had brought about in East Anglia. Charles Brandon, Duke of Suffolk, Henry's brother-in-law, was appointed commissioner for levying the tax in Suffolk. Thereupon—

"The rich clothiers . . . called to them their spinners, carders, fullers, weavers, and other artificers, which were wont to be set a work and have their livings by cloth making, and said, 'Sirs, we be not able to set you a work, our goods be taken from us, wherefore trust to yourselves, and not to us, for otherwise it will not be.' Then began women to weep and young folks to cry, and men that had no work began to rage, and assemble themselves in companies. . . . The people railed openly on the Duke of Suffolk and Sir Robert Drury,[1] and threatened them with death, and the Cardinal also, and so . . . there rebelled four thousand men, and put themselves in harness, and rang the bells alarm, and began to gather still more. Then the Duke of Suffolk, perceiving this, began to raise men, but he could get but a small number, and they that came to him said that they would defend him from all perils if he hurt not their neighbours, but against their neighbours they would not fight. Yet the gentlemen that were with the Duke did so much that all the bridges were broken, so that their assembly was somewhat letted."

[1] A local landowner.

The Duke of Norfolk, who was sent to levy the tax in that county, had no better success. A spokesman of the insurgents, one John Green, addressed him thus:

" My lord, since you ask who is our captain, forsooth his name is Poverty. . . . For all these persons and many more live not of ourselves, but we live by the substantial occupiers of this country; and yet they give us so little wages for our workmanship that scarcely we be able to live. . . . And if they, by whom we live, be brought in that case that they of their little cannot help us to earn our living, then must we perish and die miserably. I speak this, my lord: the clothmakers have put away all their people, and a far greater number, from work. The husbandmen have put away their servants and given up household; they say the king asketh so much that they be not able to do as they have done."

The two dukes, pleased at Wolsey's discredit, took this lesson in elementary economics in good part and promised to intercede with Henry.

" Then the demand of money ceased in all the realm, for well it was perceived, that the commons would none pay. . . . Now here is an end of this commission, but not an end of inward grudge and hatred, that the commons bare to the Cardinal, and to all gentlemen which vehemently set forth that commission and demand." [1]

The descendants of slaves and serfs are learning to act together as freemen. A century or so later the great-grandsons of the spinners and weavers who resist Wolsey will man Cromwell's army and lay the foundations of English democracy.

No wonder, then, that when Wolsey fell in 1529 he had no friends. It is impossible to feel pity for this proud, greedy, lecherous churchman—the very incarnation of the vices which throughout the Middle Ages had brought the Catholic hierarchy into hatred and contempt, and were now dashing it

[1] Hall, op. cit., 17 Henry VIII.

to its fall. The pseudo-Shakespearian lines in the play of *Henry VIII* delineating Wolsey are taken almost word for word from the chroniclers:

> He was a man
> Of an unbounded stomach, ever ranking
> Himself with princes; one that by suggestion
> Tied all the kingdom: simony was fair-play:
> His own opinion was his law: i' the presence
> He would say untruths, and be ever double
> Both in his words and meaning: he was never,
> But where he meant to ruin, pitiful:
> His promises were, as he then was, mighty;
> But his performance, as he is now, nothing:
> Of his own body he was ill, and gave
> The clergy ill example. [1]

After which the reminder that he was "a scholar, and a ripe and good one," and the founder of Christ Church, Oxford, falls rather flat.

Once it was known that Wolsey had fallen and that Henry had broken with Rome over his divorce, a long-pent-up anti-clerical storm swept the House of Commons. Hall tells us what the main grievances were—the mortuaries or customary offerings payable to priests from the estates of dead persons, the probate dues payable to bishops, the enormous landed property in clerical hands, the competition of abbeys in the wool trade, the pluralism and non-residence of the clergy. "These things before this time might in no wise be touched nor yet talked of by no man except he would be made an heretic, or lose all that he had." It was for refusing a mortuary, as we saw, that Hun had been accused of heresy. The passage by the Commons of bills limiting mortuaries and probate dues drew from John Fisher, bishop of Rochester (since canonized as a saint), the famous outburst: "Now with the Commons is nothing but 'Down with the Church,' and all this, meseemeth, is for lack of faith only." [2] Nothing could have so neatly exposed the material basis of medieval Catholicism as these words of Fisher. By remitting Henry's debts to the city of London, the Commons procured his aid

---

[1] *Henry VIII*, Act IV, scene ii.   [2] Hall's *Chronicle*, 21 Henry VIII.

in forcing their bills through the Lords. The first step in the English Reformation was taken. Then in 1531 followed the recognition of Henry as Supreme Head of the English Church, in 1533 the prohibition of appeals to Rome, in 1534 the excommunication of Henry by the Pope, in 1535 the execution of Fisher and More for refusing the oath of supremacy, and in 1536 the beginning of Henry's great revolutionary act, the dissolution of the monasteries and the confiscation of their property.

It is usual to treat these measures as the acts of a despotic king, endorsed by a servile Parliament which had degenerated into a mere rubber-stamp for ratifying his will. This view is utterly unhistorical. The Lords, indeed, might fairly be called servile. The old nobility had for the most part exterminated one another in the Wars of the Roses; the survivors and the new creations depended on the king; and the Reformation reduced the Church to a like dependence. But the Commons, who provided the driving-force of the Reformation, represented something more than the royal will. They represented, not indeed the people, but the rising merchant class and the smaller landowners, and between them they provided the spearhead of the revolution which was to destroy feudalism and the Catholic Church in England. If they supported the king, they did so in their own interest. They had shown independence enough in 1523, when they opposed Wolsey's war taxation. They should not be accused of servility for supporting Henry from 1529 onwards in carrying out a policy which they had desired for over a hundred years.

Certainly we need have no illusions about the Reformation Parliament. It was the Parliament of a class, and in dealing with the common people it showed itself class-bound. Nothing could be more brutal than the act of 1530 which threatened vagrants (reduced to vagrancy by expropriation from their holdings, or by the rapid rise in prices due to discoveries of silver in the New World and to Henry's debasement of the currency) with whipping at the cart's tail " until the blood streamed from their bodies "; or than the act of 1536 which provided that " valiant beggars " should for a first offence be whipped, for a second have their ears cropped, and for a third be hanged. We may compare the act of 1531 (passed after a bad case of poisoning and more than once enforced) under which poisoners were boiled alive. The idea of a scientific treatment of crime, poverty, or anything else had not yet dawned. But brutal as the Reformers were, in breaking the power of the Catholic Church they did work which had to be done. We need not be sorry for the monasteries. In the Middle Ages they had been as fiercely tenacious of their feudal rights and as savage to insurgent peasants and burghers as any lord of the soil. The worst that we can say of their dissolution is that it was carried out by grasping men not for the people's enrichment, but for their own. What manner of men these were we can gather when we read, in Grafton's continuation of Hall, of the abolition in 1536 of a number of Catholic holidays, the better to assist the "gathering in of corn, hay, fruit, and other such like necessary and profitable commodities";[1] and when John Leland in 1542 tells us that Malmesbury abbey has been bought by "one Stump, an exceeding rich clothier," who has filled it with looms and "intendeth to make a street or two for clothiers in the back vacant grounds of the abbey."

Our next chronicler is Richard Grafton, a London printer who was concerned in bringing out the Great Bible of 1539 and the first English Prayer Book of 1549, and sat in Parliament under Mary and Elizabeth. He completed and published Hall's *Chronicle* and later wrote one of his own, taking in the reigns of Edward VI and Mary. It was a dangerous time for public men; and if we cannot admire, we cannot altogether blame the care with which Grafton kept on the side of the government of the day. Besides his work, we have the *Chronicles* of his junior contemporary, Raphael Holinshed, of whom personally much less is known, but who gives many details omitted by Grafton.

The men who had shared out the loot of the abbeys were now firmly in the saddle without even Henry to restrain them. Their first act under Edward was to raid the property of the craft guilds by confiscating to the crown any revenues

[1] Hall's *Chronicle*, 28 Henry VIII.

devoted to religious purposes. At the same time they tried
to deal with the vagrant problem by an act punishing vagabonds with slavery and branding, and their children with
forced apprenticeship until the age of twenty-four. This
act evidently proved unworkable, for it was repealed the
following year and replaced by Henry's old prescription of
whipping, ear-cropping, and hanging. Meanwhile enclosures of land for parks or pasture continued, despite repeated
legislation and despite the denunciations of Hugh Latimer
and the proclamations of the Protector Somerset; debasement of the currency continued to raise prices; and labour
combinations to raise wages or reduce hours were prohibited
by an act of 1549.

We need not be surprised that in that year the people,
chastised formerly with Catholic whips and now with
Protestant scorpions, rose in rebellion in many different parts
of the country. In Cornwall, where the Celtic language was
still spoken, Catholic squires managed to divert the movement from its social objects to a demand for the abolition of
the English Prayer Book and the restoration of the old religion.
They besieged Exeter, were beaten off by the Protestant
citizens, and were finally crushed at Clyst St. Mary by Lord
Russell (one of the new lords who had thriven on the spoils
of the abbeys) at the head of three thousand German mercenaries. It is significant that foreigners had to be employed.

The most formidable rising was that led by Robert Ket in
Norfolk. By piecing together Grafton and Holinshed we
get a very vivid picture of this revolt. It was a movement
against enclosures, and had nothing to do with religion.
The Catholics were weak in eastern England : in fact, when
Stephen Gardiner, back in power under Mary, wanted to
disparage Somerset's administration, he called it "Ket's
government." The revolt began with the peasantry forcibly
unfencing enclosed lands at Attleborough, Wymondham, and
other places in Norfolk. Then Ket, a tanner and landowner
of Wymondham, whose own fences had been thrown down,
deserted his class and was chosen leader of the peasants. The
sheriff proclaimed them rebels, but to no purpose. They
marched on Norwich, and pitched their camp on Mousehold

Heath, where Ket administered justice under the "Oak of
Reformation," and lawyers, with " a pair of fetters upon their
heels, to keep them safe, when they had them, from stepping
away," were compelled to function as counsel in the rebels'
court.[1] The "meaner sort of the citizens of Norwich"
joined them; so, "sore against their wills," did the mayor
and "divers honest men."   "Firing of beacons and ringing
of bells" raised the peasantry of Suffolk.   Everywhere hedges
were thrown down and commons unfenced. Matthew
Parker, vice-chancellor of Cambridge University, the future
archbishop of Canterbury, was allowed to preach to the rebels,
but was interrupted by a "lewd fellow" who cried: "How
long shall we suffer this hireling doctor, who being waged
by gentlemen is come hither with his tongue, which is sold
and tied to serve their appetite?"   Another replied to a
summons to surrender "that he and the rest of the rebels
were earnest defenders of the king's royal majesty, and that
they would either restore the commonwealth from decay,
into the which it was fallen, being oppressed through the
covetousness and tyranny of the gentlemen; or else would they
like men die in the quarrel."   At length, after one royal army
had retired with loss, John Dudley, Earl of Warwick, marched
against them with a force including two thousand German
mercenaries who had served in the west, and put them to
flight. A bloody assize followed. Ket was "hanged in
chains upon the top of Norwich castle, and William Ket his
brother on the top of Wymondham steeple, in which town
they had both dwelled."   The squires' thirst for blood had
to be restrained by Warwick, who asked them: "What
shall we then do? Shall we hold the plough ourselves, play
the carters, and labour the ground with our own hands?"[2]
Other local risings were soon put down.

So ended Ket's rebellion. Its first political repercussion
was to bring down the Protector Somerset, who had tried to
enforce the law against enclosures. We cannot help being
sorry for Somerset. He was ahead of his time in his popular
sympathies, his desire for religious toleration, and his dream

[1] Grafton, *Chronicle*, 3 Edward VI.
[2] Holinshed, *Chronicles*, 3 Edward VI.

of an amicable union between England and Scotland; but he was powerless against the hard-faced men who had done well out of the Reformation—the Russells, Herberts, Dudleys, Wriothesleys, Pagets, and others who fattened on abbey lands and packed the Privy Council. That Somerset should even wish to do justice to the peasantry was enough to damn him; and he went to the Tower and then to the block—the only Tudor statesman to be genuinely mourned by the people.

In the case of Warwick, at least Nemesis was swift; for in 1553, when as Duke of Northumberland he proclaimed Lady Jane Grey, the men of Norfolk and Suffolk, his victims of four years before, rallied to Mary (not for love of her religion, but from hatred of the men in power) and marched with her on London, which received her royally. They were scurvily rewarded. With the sole exception of Northumberland, who was beyond pardon, the gang of the new rich who had lorded it under Edward continued to lord it under Mary. In 1554 a bull of Pope Julius III dispensed them from restoring the abbey lands. In return for this concession Lords and Commons knelt before Cardinal Pole for absolution from the sins of heresy and schism, voted the revival of the statute *De Hæretico Comburendo*, and in three years allowed nearly three hundred men and women to be burnt at the stake. Of these the largest number were Londoners, and most of the rest were people of those eastern counties which had done so much to put Mary on the throne.

For the reign of Elizabeth, which saw the final victory of the Reformation, our best contemporary witnesses are Holinshed's *Chronicles*, which he brought down to 1578, and which other hands continued to 1587; his collaborator William Harrison's *Description of England* published in 1577; and our last Latin chronicler, William Camden, who wrote his *Annals* under James I. Later, but nevertheless indispensable authorities are D'Ewes' Parliamentary journals, Fuller's *Church History*, and Strype's *Annals of the Reformation in England*, which last, though written in the eighteenth century, contains priceless transcripts of contemporary material. The modern authorities mentioned earlier are also useful.

From these sources we learn that the developments operating under the earlier Tudors continued on a greater scale under Elizabeth. She broke with Rome for the realistic reason that her title to the throne depended on it and that, as she told the Spanish ambassador, "she could not let her subjects' money be carried out of the realm by the Pope any more." [1] To effect the breach she had to evict all the bishops but one from their sees. The lower clergy were more compliant. D'Ewes puts the number of recusants at fourteen bishops and one hundred and seventy-seven others out of a total of nine thousand four hundred clergy. Strype, citing a Catholic authority, puts the whole number, including bishops, at about two hundred and fifty; Creighton at one hundred and ninety-two. The famous Vicar of Bray was evidently a common type. But zealous Protestantism was confined to London, the industrial areas, and the seaports. Catholic exiles claimed that more than half the nobility and gentry, and as much as two-thirds of the whole population, were with them; and though this, no doubt, was wishful thinking, the Reformation was incontestably the movement of a class. The Protestants, however, were reinforced by a stream of refugees flying from persecution in the Netherlands and France. As early as 1560 the Spanish ambassador reported to Philip II that ten thousand immigrants from the Low Countries were in England. In the same year Elizabeth, who was far from regarding all Protestants as brethren, tried to stem the inflow of unwelcome visitors by ordering Anabaptists to quit the realm within twenty days on pain of imprisonment and confiscation of goods. She, like her father, intended to halt the Reformation at a point convenient to herself.

The weak point of Elizabethan, as of earlier Tudor policy, was its indifference to the interests of the masses, whom conciliation might have converted into staunch supporters of the new order, but whom neglect often made ready instruments of Catholic counter-revolution. The enclosure of arable land for pasture continued to manufacture paupers. "Idle beggars," says Harrison, "are such either through other men's occasion, or through their own default. By

[1] Creighton, *Queen Elizabeth*.

other men's occasion, when some covetous man doth find
means to wipe many out of their occupyings, and turn the
same into their private gains." Prices continued to rise
through the importation of silver, while wages were frozen
by Act of Parliament. "Such a price of corn continueth,"
says the same writer, "that the artificer and poor labouring
man is not able to reach unto it."[1] Elizabethan England
was no doubt merry enough for the newly ennobled rich,
who took shares in Hawkins' slave-trading ventures and drew
dividends sometimes of sixty per cent. But for most Englishmen it was anything but a merry world.

It is no wonder that, in the closely-fought struggle between
the old order and the new, high-handed methods were used
to turn the scale. In 1569, when the north of England (still
feudal and Catholic) rose under the Earls of Northumberland
and Westmorland against Elizabeth's counsellors, the Privy
Council forestalled the rebellion by rounding up "thirteen
thousand masterless men" who might otherwise have
joined its forces.[2] This ensured its speedy collapse. In-
surrections in Suffolk and Norfolk "against the multitude
of strangers and foreign artificers" who were displacing
native labour were stifled by the same means. There
followed in 1570 the bull of Pius V excommunicating
and deposing Elizabeth, "the pretended queen of England,
with whom the worst enemies of mankind have found asylum,"
and who had ousted the old nobility of England from her
Council and "filled it with low-born heretics"—such men
as William Cecil, a yeoman's grandson, soon to be Lord
Burghley, to whom "gentility," in his own phrase, was
"nothing but ancient riches."[3] Elizabeth and Cecil replied
to Pius by a policy of terror, of which Catholics were not the
only victims. Their hand lay heavy on "sturdy beggars"
(many of them disbanded retainers of the northern earls and
potential recruits to a rebel army), whom Parliament in 1572
ordered for a first offence to be "apprehended, whipped, and
burned through the gristle of the right ear with a hot iron
of one inch compass," for a second to be adjudged felons,

[1] Harrison, *Description of England.*
[2] Strype, *Annals of the Reformation in England.*   [3] Ibid.

and for a third to be hanged.[1]   It lay heavy, too, on Anabaptists and other advanced sects, against whom from 1575 onward, despite John Foxe's plea for mercy, the stake and faggot were revived.

These facts do not discredit the Reformation.   On the contrary, they show how much greater was the Reformation as a movement than any of the limited, and often blind and brutal rulers who carried it out.   However much Henry, Elizabeth, or their continental contemporaries might wish to arrest it, the mass movement surged forward.   The Anabaptists carried the Protestant Reformation to lengths inconvenient to princes, courtiers, and courtly divines, but agreeable to peasants and artisans whose life was almost equally hard under the old feudalism and the new capitalism.   They varied among themselves on points of doctrine.   Carrying private interpretation of the Bible to its logical limits, some denied the Trinity, others the Incarnation; others preached and practised community of goods.   But all agreed that existing governments were unchristian and that Christians could not lawfully serve them as magistrates or soldiers, or take oaths in their courts; and all rejected infant baptism as unscriptural. Except for the attempt (provoked by years of cruel persecution) to set up the kingdom of heaven by force at Münster in 1535 the Anabaptist attitude to the State was completely negative.   Anabaptists first reached England from Holland under Henry VIII, who sent many of them to the stake.   In spite of proclamations, they continued to percolate into the country under Elizabeth.   In 1575 "two Dutchmen Anabaptists were burned in Smithfield, who died in great horror with roaring and crying." [2]   Anabaptism is important chiefly as a stepping-stone to Freethought.   In the middle years of the sixteenth century a mercer, Hendrik Niclaes, who had been mixed up in the Münster revolt, founded at Emden a sect known as the Family of Love, which passed from the private interpretation of scripture to a discreet denial of its authority.   We are told that the Familists "attenuated all

[1] Holinshed, *Chronicles*, 14 Elizabeth; Cunningham, *Growth of English Industry and Commerce*, II, 49.
[2] Holinshed, *Chronicles*, 17 Elizabeth.

scriptures into allegories, and made them airy, empty nothing ";[1] that some, more extreme, "questioned whether there were an heaven or an hell, but what is in this life," and "believed that all things come by nature"; that from 1574 onward the sect numbered many "weavers, basket-makers, musicians, bottle-makers, and such other like" in eastern England;[2] and that they avoided persecution by outward conformity to the established Church.

Not all East Anglian sectaries were so cautious or so fortunate. The glories of Elizabeth's reign are dimmed by the martyrdom of several of these simple men who dared to think beyond the bounds prescribed by Tudor statecraft. In 1579, while Francis Drake was plundering the Spanish Main on his way round the globe, Matthew Hamont, a ploughwright, was burnt at Norwich for calling Christ "a mere man" and the New Testament "a mere fable."[3] In 1583, while Philip was beginning to think of an expedition to smoke out the English wasps' nest, one John Lewes was burnt at Norwich for heresies similar to Hamont's, and two artisans were hanged at Bury St. Edmunds for circulating the tracts of Robert Browne against the right of the State to prescribe worship. In 1588, the year of the defeat of the Armada, Francis Ket, a Cambridge fellow, was burnt near Norwich for "divers detestable opinions against Christ our Saviour."[4] But repression did not quell heresy in the eastern counties, and their sectaries were to play a notable part in the revolution of the next century.

The Tudor Reformation, while solving one problem, created another. The fetters of feudalism and Catholicism were cast off, and an era of enterprise inaugurated which opened the oceans to English trade, and thereby paved the way for modern industrialism. But the price paid for this undoubted progress was a mass of misery which poisoned the body politic. In 1591, at the funeral of George Talbot, sixth Earl of Shrewsbury (husband of the redoubtable "Bess of

[1] Fuller, *Church History*.
[2] Strype, *Annals of the Reformation in England*.
[3] Continuation of Holinshed, 21 Elizabeth.
[4] Strype, *Annals of the Reformation in England*.

Hardwick" and sometime gaoler of Mary Stuart), so many thousands of beggars besieged Sheffield Castle for the customary dole that many were killed or injured in the press. In 1596 a Somerset magistrate, Edward Hext, wrote to Burghley a hair-raising report on the condition of the people in his county. Of particular interest is Hext's revelation of the sympathy of ordinary people for the outcasts. In that year forty "vagabonds and rogues" had been hanged in Somerset, thirty-five burnt in the hand, and thirty-seven whipped. Others, acquitted or released, were "for the most part desperate and wicked persons, and must of necessity live by spoil. . . . For none will receive them into service. And, in truth, work they will not; neither can they, without most extreme pains, by reason their sinews are so benumbed and stiff through idleness, as their limbs being put to any hard labour, will grieve them above measure. . . . The fifth person that committeth a felony is not brought to trial: for they are grown so exceeding cunning, by their often being in the gaol, as the most part are never taken. If they be, and come into the hands of the simple man that hath lost his goods, he is many times content to take his goods, and let them slip; because they will not be bound to give evidence at the assizes, to his trouble and charge. . . . In which default of justice many wicked thieves escape. For most commonly the most simple country man and woman, looking no further than to the loss of their own goods, are of opinion that they would not procure any man's death for all the goods in the world. . . . Others there be, and, I fear me, emboldened by the wandering people, that stick not to say boldly, *They must not starve, they will not starve*. . . . Which may grow dangerous by the aid of such numbers as are abroad, especially in these times of dearth: who no doubt animate them to all contempt both of noblemen and gentlemen, continually buzzing into their ears, that the rich men have gotten all into their hands, and will starve the poor."[1]

Such was the condition of England when, following the defeat of the Armada, merchant adventurers like James Lancaster were rounding the Cape, challenging the Iberian

[1] Strype, ibid.

monopoly of commerce in the Indian and Pacific Oceans, and obtaining in 1600 Elizabeth's charter for the "Company of Merchants of London trading into the East Indies." Tudor statesmen had to take notice of such social symptoms if their new mercantile commonwealth was not to sink under them. The Poor Law of 1601, which prescribed for the first time the levy of a compulsory poor-rate in every parish for the provision of work for those who could do it and relief for those who could not, was an attempt, not a moment too early, to drain the pool of destitution which had been increasing ever since capitalist sheep-farming had begun to break up the feudal manor. Thus underpinned, the new social structure could grow without immediate danger of collapse.

Let us now jump forty years and look at the next great epoch of change, that which opened with the meeting of the Long Parliament in 1640. For a general picture of this period Gardiner's great *History*, extending from the accession of James I down to the Commonwealth and Protectorate, is indispensable. It should be supplemented by Cunningham for economic history, Firth's *Stuart Tracts* and *Cromwell's Army*, and Gooch's *English Democratic Ideas in the Seventeenth Century*.

In the first forty years of the seventeenth century the men who had won wealth and power under the Tudors embarked on new enterprises. They obtained concessions for draining the Cambridgeshire and Lincolnshire fens, and were rewarded with thousands of acres of reclaimed land—much to the discontent of the fenmen, who, like the victims of Tudor enclosures, objected to the loss of their common rights. Enclosure continued to be resented, and provoked riots in the midlands in 1607. But the high price of corn attracted new capital into agriculture and supplied a corrective. Meanwhile the ruling class made a beginning of oversea colonization by the conquest of Ireland (a ruthless process of devastation and massacre, which sowed a hatred that three centuries have not sufficed to uproot) and by the settlement of Virginia.

But the immediate profit of such enterprises went to enrich a small class of monopolists—peers, courtiers, or rich mer-

chants—who obtained patents from the crown, and were
by no means popular with lesser landowners and traders or
with the nation generally. Depending as they did on the
royal prerogative, the monopolists favoured an absolute
monarchy propped by a subservient Church, while the middle
classes as a whole were for a strict limitation of royal and
episcopal power. The Tudor alliance between the monarchy
and the middle classes had begun to weaken even before the
death of Elizabeth. Under the opinionated James it was a
thing of the past. Church government, trading monopolies
in the most necessary commodities such as coal (granted,
revoked under protest, and granted again), and arbitrary
taxation became vexed questions on which the king and his
bishops and placemen were ranged on one side, and the
squires and burgesses who filled the House of Commons on
the other. One indirect result of the new struggle was the
cessation of burnings for heresy. The last execution of a
heretic (Edward Wightman at Lichfield in 1612 for " blas-
phemies against the Trinity ") provoked such a riot as to put
the fear of the people into James and his bishops; and they
never attempted the like again. A people whose fathers had
seen the fires of Smithfield brooked ill James' leaning to an
alliance with Popish Spain and his son Charles' marriage with
a French Catholic princess. " The City," wrote the courtier
and monopolist, Sir George Goring, " is so infested by the
malignant part of this kingdom, as no man that is moneyed
will lend upon any security, if they think it to go the way
of the court." [1] The quarrel was embittered by Charles'
attempt for eleven years to govern and levy taxes without a
Parliament—as his brother-in-law, Louis XIII, was already
doing with the help of Richelieu in France. By 1640, when
bankruptcy forced Charles to call a Parliament, the great issue
was who was to be master in the State, the king and his
court, or Parliament and its electors—who, though not
representative of the people, at least constituted a bigger
class than the court and the monopolists.

Let us now see how it struck contemporaries. Our first
witness shall be Edward Hyde, barrister-at-law and member

[1] Gardiner, *History of England*, chap. LX.

of Parliament, counsellor to Charles I and Charles II during years of civil war and exile, and in later life Lord Chancellor, Earl of Clarendon, and author of the *History of the Rebellion*. We do not expect impartiality from anyone so involved on the royal side as Clarendon. Nevertheless he should be read, and not only for his style. It is just his partisanship which makes his work live. His limitations are those of a learned, but narrow member of the ruling class of Stuart England. If he fails to understand the great revolutionary struggle of which he writes, and if posterity has reversed his verdict on many issues, that is the common lot of losing sides. We can at least use his testimony to refute the romantic rubbish written by modern admirers of the Stuarts who understand even less than he what it was all about.

Clarendon, for example, lends no support to the view that Charles was a popular monarch trying to protect his people from a gang of rich rascals who wanted to steal the common lands. Read his story of the enclosure of Richmond Park in 1636.

> "The King . . . had a great desire to make a great park for red as well as fallow deer between Richmond and Hampton Court, where he had large wastes of his own and great parcels of wood . . . : but as some parishes had common in those wastes, so many gentlemen and farmers had good houses and good farms intermingled . . .; and without taking in of them into the park, it would not be of the largeness or for the use proposed. His Majesty desired to purchase those lands, and was very willing to buy them upon higher terms than the people could sell them at to anybody else . . .; and so he employed his own surveyor and other of his officers to treat with the owners. . . . The major part of the people were in a short time prevailed with, but many very obstinately refused; . . . and the King being as earnest to compass it, it made a great noise, as if the King would take away men's estates at his own pleasure."

Archbishop Laud, Juxon, bishop of London, and Lord Cottington, Chancellor of the Exchequer, tried to dissuade

Charles from his impolitic design, till Charles " grew very angry " with Cottington " and told him he was resolved to go through with it, and had already caused brick to be burned, and much of the wall to be built upon his own land, upon which Cottington thought fit to acquiesce. The building the wall before people consented to part with their land or their common looked to them as if by degrees they should be shut out from both, and increased the murmur and noise of the people who were not concerned as well as of them who were, and it was too near London not to be the common discourse." [1] Did Naboth's vineyard afford a favourite text that year to Puritan preachers who could elude the vigilance of Laud?

Clarendon brings out the intimate connection between the policy of the Long Parliament and the interests of the City of London. The citizens would lend no more money to Charles, but they would lend to Parliament, provided they were assured that Parliament would not be suddenly dissolved and their money lost. This was made clear in 1641 during the debates on the impeachment and attainder of Strafford—the first revolutionary act of the Long Parliament. Strafford had tried to be an English Richelieu. Between him and the Parliamentary leaders there could be no truce : it was his life or theirs. London knew it. During the proceedings against Strafford Westminster and Whitehall were beset by mobs of sober citizens demanding the Earl's head as a guarantee of freedom. The City made any further loan conditional on the passage of an Act prohibiting the adjournment, prorogation, or dissolution of the existing Parliament without its own consent. " Which," says Clarendon, " was within a short time (less than an hour) brought into the House, and immediately twice read and committed (an expedition never before heard of in Parliament) and the next day, with . . . the contradiction of very few voices, engrossed and carried up to the Lords." According to Gardiner, Hyde, who at that date was not yet committed to the king's cause, himself voted for the bill. Perhaps not unnaturally Clarendon says nothing about this. After a show of resistance, " the Lords, in that

[1] Clarendon, *History of the Rebellion*, I, 208–210.

hurry of noise and confusion when the people were abroad, kindly consented likewise to it : and so, . . . in the agony of the other despatch, the king was induced to include that bill in the commission with the Act of Attainder, and so they were both passed together." [1]

Clarendon shows a candour about the class character of the English Revolution which succeeding historians have not always emulated. Parliament, he says, was "followed and submitted to principally by the meanest of the people. And though some persons of quality and estates . . . followed their party, yet the number of them was not great." [2] This, of course, does not mean that the Roundheads were a party of peasants or workers. To Clarendon, coming from a landed family and bred to the genteel profession of the law, the category "mean" included all walks of life below his own —all that we denote by the term "middle class." He describes as "horrible" a petition addressed to the House of Commons early in 1642 by "many thousands of poor people in and about the City of London," praying that Lords and Commons should "sit and vote as one entire body." [3] This would have made short work of the Lords' veto. Indeed, shortly before the London petition Pym had carried a motion that the Commons, "being the representative body of the whole kingdom, and their Lordships being but as particular persons," might if necessary override the Upper House. Clarendon tells us that by the beginning of the Civil War "there was not left a fifth part of the House of Peers at Westminster, and . . . I do not believe that there was near a moiety of the House of Commons." [4] Later, in 1644, we learn that of eighty-five peers sixty-three were with Charles or in his service, and only twenty-two in London. Of a Lower House of some four hundred only one hundred and eighteen were with the king. In Yorkshire, we are told, "there were very few gentlemen, or men of any quality, . . . who were actively or factiously disaffected to His Majesty; and of those the Lord Fairfax, and his son, Sir Thomas Fairfax, were the chief, who were governed by two or three of inferior quality,

[1] Clarendon, *History of the Rebellion*, III, 210.   [2] Clarendon, *Life*.
[3] *History of the Rebellion*, IV, 267, 269.   [4] Ibid., V, 333.

more conversant with the people, who were as well known
as they."[1]   But "Leeds, Halifax, and Bradford, three very
populous and rich towns (which depending wholly upon
clothiers naturally maligned the gentry) were wholly at
[Parliament's] disposition."[2]   In Somerset, "though the
gentlemen of ancient families and estates . . . were for the
most part well affected to the King . . . yet there were a people
of an inferior degree, who, by good husbandry, clothing, and
other thriving arts, had gotten very great fortunes, and by
degrees getting themselves into the gentlemen's estates, were
angry that they found not themselves in the same esteem and
reputation with those whose estates they had; and therefore,
with more industry than the other, studied all ways to make
themselves considerable. These from the beginning were
fast friends to the Parliament, and many of them were now
entrusted by them as deputy-lieutenants in their new ordinance of the militia."[3]   In general, "the common people
. . . were in all places grown to that barbarity and rage against
the nobility and gentry (under the style of *Cavaliers*) that it
was not safe for any to live at their houses who were taken
notice of as no votaries to the Parliament. . . . The poorest
and lowest of the people became informers against the richest
and most substantial. . . . They further appointed that the
fines, rents, and profits of archbishops, bishops, deans, and
chapters, and of all delinquents who had taken up arms against
the Parliament . . . should be sequestered for the use and
benefit of the commonwealth."[4]

In short, the picture of the English Revolution painted by
Clarendon is a great deal more like the later French Revolution than is suspected by those to whom English history is
one long tale of "freedom slowly broadening down from
precedent to precedent."   Clarendon is confirmed by a witness
from the other side, Sir Simonds D'Ewes, a Suffolk squire

---

[1] *History of the Rebelliion*, V, 446.   Fairfax explains what Clarendon here
leaves obscure.   The Commission of Array sent to levy forces for the king
in Yorkshire, says he, "exceeded their commission by oppressing many
honest people, whom they called Roundheads. . . . Many were forced
to come and entreat [my father] to join with them in defence of themselves
and country."   Cited by Firth, *Stuart Tracts*.

[2] Ibid., VI, 261.   [3] Ibid., 5.   [4] Ibid., 36, 55.

and antiquarian, who sat for Sudbury in the Long Parliament and with some misgiving threw in his lot with the Puritans. " Great was the calamity everywhere," he writes in his diary, " of those counties in which His Majesty's forces or ours came, neither side abstaining from rapine and pillage; and besides, the rude multitude in divers counties took advantage of those civil and intestine broils to plunder and pillage the houses of the nobility, gentry, and others, who were either known Papists, or being Protestants, had sent or provided horses, money, or plate to send to the King, or such as being rich they would make malignants."[1] " The whole land was in confusion," he told the House late in 1642. " No man would pay his rent. As the House had passed an ordinance to tax the subjects, it would be well to pass another to compel tenants to pay their rents. . . . It would soon be a crime to be rich."[2]

The Long Parliament in fact had raised forces which it could not control. The city merchants and their friends at Westminster could vote resolutions against Charles, but they could enforce their resolutions only by arming and drilling common men whose interests were by no means identical with theirs. The Grand Remonstrance of 1641, in which the Lower House stated their case to the nation, had complained, among other things, of the appropriation of " large quantities of common and several grounds " without the owners' consent, under colour of improvement. On the outbreak of civil war the fenmen of Hatfield Chase, York-shire, had taken the Commons at their word and re-flooded the fens. As the struggle went on, this cleavage of interests became more acute. The minority of peers who took the Parliamentary side (such men as the half-hearted Edward Montagu, Earl of Manchester, and his like), and the richer members of the House of Commons, already alarmed by the no-rent campaign in many counties, saw with dismay the promotion from the ranks of Cromwell's " plain, russet-coated captains, who knew what they fought for and loved what they knew," and who assuredly did not fight to make

[1] Cited by Gardiner, *History of the Great Civil War*, chap. I.
[2] Ibid., chap. IV.

England safe for the nobility and gentry. The upshot was the creation in 1645 of the well-paid and well-disciplined New Model army with Cromwell's East Anglian cavalry as its nucleus. Many grandfathers or great-grandfathers of the men of the New Model must have been out with Ket in 1549.

It needed only the defeat of the king to bring the quarrel to a head. On May 5, 1646, the day when Charles surrendered to the Scots at Newark, over two thousand people of Hertfordshire and Buckinghamshire petitioned the House of Commons for the abolition of tithes. They found no supporter. Those who wanted to be quit of tithes, said some members, would soon want to be quit of rent—a dismal prospect for a House in which squires predominated, and in which many were waxing fat on the confiscated estates of Cavalier magnates. A month later John Lilburne, summoned to the bar of the House of Lords for speaking ill of Manchester, denied that " peers, merely made by prerogative, and never entrusted or empowered by the Commons of England," could sit in judgment on a commoner.[1] " What were the lords of England," asked the men of the New Model, " but William the Conqueror's colonels, or the barons but his majors, or the knights but his captains?"[2] Democracy, dead since ancient Greece, was reborn in Puritan England.

Clarendon, who left England in 1646 and did not return till 1660, is not a good authority on events which took place in his absence and which he sees with the warped vision of an émigré. Exiled in Jersey, Paris, the Hague, Madrid, Cologne, or Bruges, he receives bitter news of " common soldiers, as well as the officers," nay " women as well as men," preaching to the people in " all churches "; of his royal master carried off by Cornet Joyce, " one of the agitators in the army, a tailor," and others who indeed (more tolerant than the Parliament) allow him to have such chaplains as he wishes, but will soon clamour for his trial as a " tyrant, traitor, and murderer "; of " great numbers of the lowest and most inferior people " flocking to Parliament " with petitions with reference to religion and to the civil government "; of " liberty of

[1] Gardiner, op. cit., chap. XLII.

[2] *Reliquiæ Baxterianæ*, cited ibid., chap. XXXV.

conscience" becoming "the great charter"; of "Anabaptists and Quakers" growing "very numerous"; and of
" the nobility and gentry . . . totally neglected, and the most
inferior people preferred to all places of trust and profit." [1]

For a close-up view of Clarendon's nightmare we must
go to the State Papers of John Thurloe, Secretary to the
Council of State and to Cromwell; to the diary of John
Evelyn; to the early part of Burnet's *History of His Own
Time*; and to other contemporary papers preserved by
Gardiner, Firth, and Gooch. Invaluable, for example, are
Fairfax's *Short Memorials of Some Things to be Cleared during
my Command in the Army* (written after the Restoration and
included in Firth's *Stuart Tracts*). Fairfax was a first-rate
soldier, but no politician. His wife was a Royalist, and his
position difficult. He had taken up arms in sympathy with
the "honest people" of the West Riding oppressed by the
king's commissioners, rather than with any understanding of
the wider issues at stake. When in 1647 the army under his
command transformed itself into a political party, it was
plainly too much for Fairfax. The men's petition to Parliament for their arrears of pay (amounting to £331,000),
and for pensions for widows and orphans of the fallen, was
just, and seemed so to him. Until those demands were met,
the men would neither disband nor go to Ireland, of which
they had the option. But they put forward their demands
in a way more suggestive of a trade union than an army;
and that Fairfax did not like. In March the House of Commons made his position impossible by rejecting the petition
and voting its promoters enemies of the State. From that
time on the army took the bit between its teeth. The matter
of arrears and pensions became mixed up with demands for
abolition of the king's and Lords' vetos, liberty of conscience,
dissolution of trading monopolies, law reform, and separation
of Church and State.

The story of the movement is told in the contemporary
Clarke Papers, freely quoted by Firth. In April, after their
rebuff by Parliament, delegates of horse and foot regiments
(the famous "agitators") again approach Parliament through

---

[1] *History of the Rebellion*, X, 79, 90, 106, 175; XI, 1.

their generals. At the same time, we know from Gardiner, overtures are made to the beaten king. In vain Parliament again in May orders the army to disband. Fairfax finds it beyond his power to restrain the men. Cromwell, more wily, swims with the stream in order to control it, and sends Joyce to secure Charles. For a short time the army acts as a unit. In June officers and men together register a " solemn engagement " not to disband until they obtain satisfaction for the past and security for the future. Parliamentary emissaries offering payment of £10,000 on account are met with cries of "Justice, justice!" Security is to be obtained by the dissolution of the Long Parliament (which had too well deserved its name) and the election of a more representative House for a fixed term. But on the nature of that security and that representation the army fatally splits. All are agreed on an extension of the franchise, a redistribution of seats, biennial Parliaments, and a measure of religious toleration. (Clarendon considers even this "ruinous to the Church and destructive to the regal power.") But whereas the "agitators" and some of the officers, influenced by Lilburne and other democrats outside, would have manhood suffrage (Cavalier "delinquents" only excluded), the abolition of the monarchy and the House of Lords, and the recognition of absolute freedom of conscience as a "native right" of all Englishmen, Cromwell, Ireton, and most of the officers would limit the vote to landowners and "those in corporations in whom all trading lies," would exclude Catholics from unconditional toleration, and are prepared to keep Charles if he will only accept their terms. The thing is debated. Colonel Rainborough pleads that "the poorest he that is in England hath a life to live as well as the greatest he "; and Ireton replies that "godliness and honesty and peace " are more important than "birthright." So it goes on.

Meanwhile Charles tries to play off his enemies one against another. Nothing will induce him to agree to liberty of conscience. "Religion," he writes, "is the only firm foundation of all power; for when was there ever obedience where religion did not teach it?" But with typical Stuart kingcraft he is ready to use the quarrel of Parliament and army to master and destroy both. In this he is favoured by what we can only call the amazing forbearance of his captors. Although a prisoner, he is not closely confined; he is allowed to give audiences, and has no difficulty in negotiating with the Scots lords for an invasion of England and the suppression of "blasphemy, heresy, and schism." By November some of the army, like Thomas Harrison, are alive to the game and calling for his trial as "a man of blood." In the middle of their debates he escapes from Hampton Court and makes for the coast, and although soon again a prisoner at Carisbrooke, is still so loosely guarded that he is able in December to conclude and sign his "engagement" with the Scots for a new civil war.

The New Model has to pull itself together. We need not wonder that Cromwell's resort to martial law to suppress the Levellers meets with temporary acquiescence, that even Rainborough submits, that even Lilburne rallies to the common cause. Nor need we wonder that in 1648, as they go to meet the Scots, officers and men are in regicidal mood; that on returning victorious (but poorer by the loss of Rainborough and other comrades) they demand of Parliament not only constitutional reform, but justice on Charles and an end of hereditary monarchy; and that when Parliament temporizes, the answer is Pride's Purge, the abolition of the House of Lords and the monarchy, and the axe and block before the Banqueting House in Whitehall on January 30, 1649.

That year 1649 was a year of ferment. Before the king's head falls, the fatal rift between the army council and the Levellers reopens. The Levellers stick out for manhood suffrage and absolute liberty of conscience; the "grandees," as Cromwell and his friends are called, boggle at both. In February Lilburne and others, in a manifesto entitled *England's New Chains Discovered*, go farther than they have yet gone, demanding annual Parliaments, abolition of tithes, law reform, full religious liberty, and work or a comfortable maintenance for the poor and impotent. The Council of State ask John Milton to reply to the Levellers: he refuses. "You must break these men," Cromwell tells the Council, "or they will break you"; and in March they commit Lilburne to the Tower on a charge of treason. Petitions in his favour pour into the House of Commons, one from London, one from Essex, one signed wholly by "well-affected women"—whom the House tells to go home and wash dishes. In April orders to certain regiments to proceed to Ireland lead to a mutiny in London and to the shooting of its leader, Robert Lockyer. He tells the court that "God will make his blood speak liberty to all England." Thousands follow his funeral. Meanwhile news comes that other Levellers are digging and sowing common land at St. George's Hill, Surrey. They turn out to be no more than twenty. Their leaders, Gerrard Winstanley and William Everard, when brought before the Council of State, refuse to bare the head to Fairfax, saying that he is but their fellow-creature, and that God is about to restore to the people the freedom to enjoy the fruits of the earth, which was lost by the coming of the Conqueror six centuries ago. In a pamphlet published soon afterwards they denounce landed property as theft and call on the landlords to "let Israel go free" and "make the earth a common treasury." In May another mutiny in the army is suppressed at Burford in Oxfordshire, where a cornet and two corporals are shot. During the summer Lilburne in the Tower, while disclaiming sympathy with the "Diggers," continues writing pamphlets against Cromwell and inciting the army to rise; and in September there is another abortive rising at Oxford. Lilburne is prosecuted for treason, but in October is acquitted by a London jury, the verdict being greeted by "loud and unanimous" shouts lasting half an hour.

Meanwhile Cromwell has taken his army to Ireland, and so removed it from all temptation to make trouble in England. Drogheda and Wexford are a tale of horror. According to the estimate of William Petty, who served as physician in the English army, one-third of the Irish "perished by the sword, plague, famine, hardship and banishment" in this war of reconquest. In November the Diggers are ousted from St. George's Hill by the military—Winstanley indignantly telling Parliament that it has betrayed the people who ventured their blood in the quarrel with the king. "At this very day poor people are forced to work for 4d a day, and corn is dear. . . . You jeer at the name of Leveller. I tell you Jesus Christ is the head Leveller." [1]

The Levellers remained a numerous party; but that year of shipwreck ended their chance of achieving anything. Lilburne continued to attack what he believed to be corruption in high places, and in 1652 was banished by the Rump Parliament. In the same year Winstanley published his *Law of Freedom*, which may be considered the earliest English Socialist manifesto, advocating as it does co-operative production, universal education, and the separation of Church and State. With the defeat of the Levellers the life went out of the English Commonwealth. It degenerated into something very like a racket in the interest of members of the Rump, who trafficked in confiscated Cavalier estates, hundreds of which were seized after the battle of Worcester and sold to meet the cost of the Dutch war. So greedy were they of the sweets of power that they refused to dissolve on any terms until in 1653 Cromwell himself grew sick of them, marched his musketeers to Westminster, and "put an end to their prating." For a moment the hopes of the Levellers revived. Lilburne returned to England, prepared for reconciliation with Cromwell, but was at once arrested and again tried for his life. It was his last hour of glory. Multitudes in London and the adjacent counties petitioned for his release. Cromwell kept three regiments under arms to prevent a rescue; and when "freeborn John" was again acquitted, the very soldiers shouted and sounded their trumpets. But Cromwell dared not release him. He was detained in successive prisons without trial until, becoming a Quaker, he renounced politics and was set free. Both Lilburne and Winstanley died in the Society of Friends.

The last years of Cromwell's life were spent in vain attempts to give a semblance of regularity to the absolute power which he was forced to assume. By killing the king, against his instincts and to content his army, he had estranged the

[1] Winstanley, *A New Year's Gift for the Parliament and Army*, cited by Gooch, *English Democratic Ideas in the Seventeenth Century*, chap. VII.

landowning class to which he belonged, and by crushing the Levellers he had estranged the common people, including many of his own soldiers. He could count on no one except those officers whom he had promoted and enriched with land in England, Scotland, or Ireland. Even they followed him with less enthusiasm and more jealousy as his power increased. He must find a broader basis for his rule; but where? In the Instrument of Government, which set up the Protectorate, he tried (as his son-in-law Ireton, whom he had lost in Ireland, would have advised him to do) to vest power in the middle classes, excluding from the franchise on the one hand active Cavaliers and Catholics and on the other hand persons with less than £200 in property. He tried to make Parliament more representative of the middle class as a whole by disfranchising small boroughs which had decayed to the point of rottenness and giving more members to counties and growing towns—a measure which even the hostile Clarendon finds worthy of commendation. The result was a House in which the landed class had less, and the trading class more, influence than ever before in the history of Parliament, or than they ever would again until the Reform Act of 1832. But Cromwell's position was no easier for that. The Levellers and republicans, who still had support in the army, petitioned and plotted; and the men of property, terrified of the Levellers, did not feel really safe without a king. Cromwell was more concerned to propitiate these last than the men whom he had led in the Civil War. Under the Protectorate profitable enterprise went ahead. The draining of the fens was completed (many square miles of reclaimed land going to Cromwell's immediate circle) and the monopoly of the East India Company was protected against interlopers. In 1657, on the motion of Christopher Packe, " one of the most wealthy aldermen of the city of London,"[1] the House petitioned Cromwell to assume the crown. Counter-petitioned by his officers, he refused the name, but accepted the reality in the shape of power to create peers and to nominate his successor. Down to his death in 1658 he had more to fear from disaffected

---

[1] Clarendon, *History of the Rebellion*, XV, 41.

artisans and Fifth Monarchy Men (determined " to have the Protector suffer at Whitehall Gate as the late king did, because that the Protector had a hand in putting the king to death, and now acteth the same things that the king did "[1]) than from the disarmed and impoverished Cavaliers who on what was left of their estates waited, without much hope, for better times.

Within a few months of Oliver's death the army, now again militantly republican, dashed the Protectorate from the hands of the insignificant Richard Cromwell and sent Lords and Commons about their business. But on how to replace them there was the same fatal cleavage between higher and lower ranks in 1659 as in 1647. Finally they recalled the Rump, not from any love of that body, but because they could agree on nothing else. That made the Restoration only a matter of time. While Oliver's son-in-law Fleetwood and his colleague Lambert fumbled for power which they knew not how to wield, Monk, who seems to have been preparing for years for this situation, marched on London with an army carefully purged of republican enthusiasts. He was welcomed by the gentry and trading classes everywhere, and met no opposition. The Commonwealth had given its soldiers nothing to defend: they said they would " not fight, but make a ring for their officers to fight in."[2] Monk's entry into London, the annulment of all acts of the Rump, the election of a new Parliament on the old franchise, and the recall of Charles II followed as a matter of course.

For events from the Restoration to the Revolution of 1688 the best modern authority is G. N. Clark's *Later Stuarts*. Cunningham, as usual, is good on the economic side. Macaulay's *History of England* may be read with pleasure and profit, but is an inadequate guide unless checked by other sources. Arthur Bryant's *Letters of King Charles II* and other works may please those who desire a Tory counterbalance to Macaulay's Whiggery. For a contemporary picture of the period the diaries of Evelyn and Pepys and Burnet's *History of His Own Time* are all indispensable.

[1] Report of a spy in Thurloe's *State Papers*, March 17, 1656.
[2] *Clarke Papers*, cited by Firth, *Cromwell's Army*.

When Charles II entered London on May 29, 1660, the pious Evelyn " blessed God . . . for such a Restoration " as " was never mentioned in any history ancient or modern, since the return of the Jews from the Babylonish captivity." [1] But there were things which could never be restored. Charles owed his return not to the valour of the Cavaliers, but to the opportunism of some Cromwellian leaders and the divisions of the rest. He came back at the price of a promise, made to Parliament and the city of London in the Declaration of Breda, that the questions of the disposal of estates which had changed hands during the interregnum, of an amnesty for offenders, and of a religious settlement should be left entirely to Parliament. The Parliament convened by Monk handled these matters in a spirit of compromise. The Act of Indemnity and Oblivion passed that summer restored crown lands, Church lands, and those confiscated from their owners, but not those which their owners had sold to pay Commonwealth taxes. So many Cromwellian purchasers thus remained in possession of their gains that disappointed Cavaliers dubbed the Act one of indemnity for the king's enemies and of oblivion for his friends. The only persons excepted from the indemnity were those who had sat in judgment on Charles I or been otherwise concerned in his execution. They had dared to lay hands on a king, and had failed so to rally the masses as to crown their daring with success. Of those who failed to escape abroad, ten were hanged, drawn, and quartered late in 1660—the genial Pepys going " to see the first blood shed in revenge for the King at Charing Cross," and recording the sight in his diary. [2] Three were kidnapped in Holland and brought to London for execution in 1662. "They all looked very cheerful," says Pepys; " but I hear they all die defending what they did to the King to be just; which is very strange." [3] Strange to Pepys; not so strange to us. Twenty-five were imprisoned for life. In some important matters Parliament adopted policies initiated by the Commonwealth : for example an embargo on the export of wool, imposed in 1648 in the interest of the

[1] Evelyn's *Diary*.   [2] Pepys' *Diary*, October 13, 1660.
[3] Ibid., April 19, 1662.

textile industry, was perpetuated in 1660; and the Navigation Act, passed in 1651 to foster English shipping, was confirmed and strengthened in 1661.

But compromise by no means suited the Cavaliers, who romped into Parliament on the tide of reaction in 1661. They had twenty years of defeat, impoverishment, and humiliation to avenge, and hastened to make hay while the sun shone. To this end they passed at once an act excluding from borough corporations (which elected a majority of members of Parliament) all who would not renounce the use of force against the king, another in 1662 depriving of their livings all clergy who would not use the authorized Prayer Book, and (these measures having led to an insurrection in the Puritan West Riding) two further acts in 1664 and 1665 forbidding the expelled clergy to conduct services anywhere or to live within five miles of a corporate town.

This policy of repression, as well as the disgraceful and disastrous war with Holland (undertaken to oust the Dutch from the African slave trade, in which Charles and his brother James were financially interested), led to a reaction against the court which we may trace in the pages of Evelyn and Pepys, king's men though they were. Already in 1661 Pepys finds "the Clergy so high that all people that I meet do protest against their practice." [1]   In 1662 " the discontent is great," [2] and strong guards are posted in the City to prevent riots over the ejection of Puritan clergy.[3]   In 1666, after the Dutch war, the Cavalier majority begins to crumble: the slogans at by-elections are " No courtier " and " No Court pimp." [4]   By 1667 Pepys' circle are talking what in 1660 they would have voted treason.

> " At dinner we talked much of Cromwell; all saying he was a brave fellow, and did owe his crown he got to himself as much as any man that ever got one." [5]

> " It is strange how everybody do nowadays reflect upon Oliver, and commend him, what brave things he

[1] Pepys' *Diary*, August 31, 1661.   [2] Ibid., August 15, 1662.
[3] Evelyn, August 20, 1662.   [4] Pepys, October 21, 1666.
[5] Ibid., February 8, 1667.

did, and made all the neighbour princes fear him; while here a prince, come in with all the love and prayers and good liking of his people, who have given greater signs of loyalty and willingness to serve him with their estates than ever was done by any people, hath lost all so soon, that it is a miracle what way a man could devise to lose so much in so little time." [1]

In harrying the Puritans the Cavalier Parliament were barking up the wrong tree. The Cavalier way of life was far more threatened by an enterprise of which some of their own friends were among the promoters. On the neutral ground of the Royal Society (which had taken shape under the Commonwealth, though it derived its charter and title from Charles II), John Evelyn, William Petty, Robert Boyle, and later on Isaac Newton met periodically to investigate theoretical problems suggested by the practical needs of the society around them. The needs of navigation suggested problems in astronomy, optics, and mechanics; of industry in physics; of trade and finance in economics; of calculation in mathematics. Certain experiments on atmospheric pressure conducted before the Society by Boyle (at which Charles II " mightily laughed, for spending time only in weighing of air and doing nothing else since they sat " [2]) paved the way for the invention of the steam engine and the industrial revolution of the next century. Meanwhile, though such was not the intention of Evelyn, Boyle, or Newton, the progress of experimental science accustomed educated men to take a materialistic rather than a miraculous view of natural processes and insensibly undermined established theology and the " divine right of kings," of which it was a prop.

The new opposition which gradually grew up under Charles II—the " country party " or, as they came to be called, the Whigs—resembled their Puritan predecessors in everything but piety. Like the Roundheads, they represented money rather than land, were suspicious of the royal prerogative, and were " heartily for the Protestant religion, and

---

[1] Pepys' *Diary*, July 12, 1667.   [2] Ibid., February 1, 1664.

for the interest of England " [1] against French competition in industry and French influence at court. But their leading lights were such men as Anthony Ashley Cooper, Earl of Shaftesbury, author of the famous *mot* that " all sensible men are of the same religion," which " no sensible man tells "; and Algernon Sidney, whom Cromwell called a " heathen " and Burnet a deist. As the reign proceeded, the political struggle crystallized into a combat between, on the one hand, the squires, the parsons, and the monopolists, organized in the Cavalier, court, or Tory party; and, on the other hand, the merchants and middle classes generally, organized in the country or Whig party. Since throughout the seventeenth century successful merchants were buying land and founding county families, the opposition of interests was not rigid : it was easy for opportunist politicians to pass from one camp to the other even two or three times in the course of a career. But events did not allow the line of cleavage to become blurred. When Charles, already secretly a pensioner of his cousin Louis XIV, committed to an unpopular French alliance and reconciliation with Rome, in 1672 (prompted by his Catholic Treasurer, Sir Thomas Clifford), repudiated his debts to the City of London and ruined a multitude of creditors, he did as much as Shaftesbury ever did to recruit the future Whig party and ensure its triumph. In vain did Charles try to play off Nonconformists against Anglicans by a Declaration of Indulgence. His own Cavalier Parliament replied by the Test Act, which forced Clifford out of office. Thenceforward Charles' ministers could command a majority in the Commons only by corruption; and in the scare over the Popish Plot even corruption did not avail. Finally Charles, and after him James II, were reduced to governing without a Parliament and depending on Louis for their revenue, thus involving their dynasty in final shipwreck.

But the Revolution of 1688 was not a repetition of that of 1640. The landed and moneyed men who carried it through were careful not to arm the common people. In 1685 they held severely aloof from Monmouth's rebellion and left the yeomen, artisans, and Mendip miners who followed his

[1] Burnet, *History of His Own Time*, Book III.

standard to the tender mercies of Kirke and Jeffreys. In 1688, when their own time had come, when James had alienated the squires and parsons, and all was ready, they called in Dutch William not only to replace James, but to avert the danger of another Commonwealth. Burnet, who accompanied the expedition, relates how, when William was preparing to sail, the old Leveller John Wildman, who had acted with Lilburne in 1647 and was now in Holland, drafted a declaration indicting the arbitrary government of both Charles II and James II; and how the politicians (the Earl of Shrewsbury, Henry Sidney, Edward Russell, and the rest) who had called in William urged " that the prince ought not to look so far back as into king Charles' reign : this would disgust many of the nobility and gentry, and almost all the clergy." William, who cared nothing for democracy in England or anywhere else, but much for bringing England solidly into his coalition against Louis, agreed with them. " So the declaration was printed over again, with some amendments." After the landing at Torbay, says Burnet, " both the clergy and magistrates of Exeter were very fearful, and very backward. The bishop and dean ran away. And the clergy stood off, though they were sent for, and very gently spoke to by the prince. . . . We stayed a week at Exeter, before any of the gentlemen of the country about came in to the prince. Every day some persons of condition came from other parts." On the other hand, " the rabble of the people came in to him in great numbers. So that he could have raised many regiments of foot, if there had been any occasion for them. . . . After he had stayed eight days at Exeter, Seymour [1] came in with several other gentlemen of quality and estate "; [2] and then more and more, until James' army went over in a body. So the glorious Revolution was effected without resort to the disagreeable necessity of raising another New Model.

Transfer of power from king, court, and nobility, not to the people, but to a Parliament in which land and money in partnership predominated; abolition of some monopolies,

---

[1] Sir Edward Seymour, ex-Speaker of the House of Commons.
[2] Burnet, *History of His Own Time*, Book IV.

such as that of the Merchant Adventurers in the cloth trade with the continent, of the Eastland Company in trade with Russia, and of the African Company in negro slaves; abolition also of the Anglican monopoly in religion; foundation of the Bank of England and flotation of the National Debt; full speed ahead for enterprise and empire: that, on the face of it, is the English Revolution. Reactionaries who seek to blacken all progress naturally make the most of its negative side. But in the course of the struggle it gave birth to a democratic movement which, suppressed at the time, was to inspire men and women in later centuries to fight and destroy the corruptions and cruelties which the Revolution had allowed to survive.

And now, having crossed to France with James, let us advance a hundred years. As Spain in the sixteenth, so France in the seventeenth century was the lynch-pin of European reaction. To Bossuet, the leading French theologian of his day, England was a revolutionary country rebelling against Almighty God, and Cromwell a moral monster. Less than a century after the death of Bossuet we shall find Burke, the leading British orator of his day, denouncing France in much the same terms as Bossuet had denounced England. Robespierre and after him Bonaparte will fill for British reaction the same Satanic rôle which French reaction had assigned to Cromwell. The way in which the whirligig of time wrought this revenge merits examination.

Richelieu had established in France the royal autocracy which Laud and Strafford unsuccessfully initiated in England. But the French monarchy, in spite of its imposing show of absolutism, was in reality extremely inefficient. Feudal rights abolished in England under the Tudors continued in France until the eighteenth century. Instead of the protector of the people against feudal oppression, the monarchy became the apex of a bureaucracy exploiting the people in the interest of a parasitic clergy and nobility. After the English Revolution of 1688 the crazily financed France of Louis XIV failed to hold its own in war against the relatively efficient England of William and Marlborough, and saw its colonies and commerce diminish before British expansion. In the eighteenth century the French bourgeoisie, chafing under a régime which could no longer be credited even with ordinary competence, swallowed with avidity the writings in which Voltaire, Rousseau, and the Encyclopædists popularized for French consumption English science, English deism, and English political philosophy. It needed only a series of costly and unprofitable wars, ending in national bankruptcy, to produce the crisis of 1789 and to leave the States-General, resuscitated at long last, masters of the situation.

The literature of the French Revolution is so enormous, and continues so to grow from year to year, that only the merest selection can be mentioned here. Carlyle's *French Revolution* is still the best English work on the subject. Like Macaulay's *History of England*, it is a great story greatly told by a historian who is not ashamed to be an enthusiast. But Carlyle's history was published in 1837 and on matters of fact needs checking by other authorities. Naturally enough, most of the relevant authorities are French. Mignet and Michelet are excellent reading, but both wrote in the first half of the nineteenth century—too late to have been witnesses of the events they relate, yet too early to be other than ardent partisans. Aulard's *Histoire politique de la Révolution française* is perhaps the best history of the Revolution published in the present century. Other modern works will be found valuable in different ways. Individual biographies, such as Belfort Bax's and Castelnau's lives of Marat, or Hilaire Belloc's *Danton*, *Robespierre*, and *Marie Antoinette*, are worth reading to supplement the general history. Kropotkin's *Great French Revolution* tells the story from the point of view of a revolutionary Anarchist and, given his point of view, tells it well. Latreille's *L'église catholique et la Révolution française* states in a scholarly way the Catholic case against the Revolution. J. M. Thompson's *French Revolution* embodies the latest research on matters of fact in a form convenient to English readers.

But all histories of the French Revolution suffer from a common disability. The events, even at a distance of one hundred and sixty years, are too recent and the party lines then drawn are too persistent for anyone to be wholly impartial. Every Frenchman is a royalist or a republican, a Catholic or an anti-clerical, an individualist or a Socialist. Even Englishmen count themselves the political heirs of Pitt or Fox, Burke or Paine. The debate begun in the French Revolution continues; and as long as it continues, an impartial historian will be as rare as a blue moon. There is only one remedy, and that is to go back to contemporary sources. Contemporaries are biased; but at least we know their bias and can allow for it. That is not always so easy with the "impartial" modern. Contemporary sources such as speeches, memoirs, letters, despatches, newspapers, and police dossiers, if they do not give us objective history, at least show us history in the making. They show us events as they appeared, not to historians in the light of what came after, but to the always interested, always limited, often foolish, and often unscrupulous actors in them. By piecing such material together, provided that we read it in a critical spirit, we can build up a more faithful picture than by blindly following the story in some approved textbook. Memoirs especially need critical reading. Not only have we to bear in mind the proclivity of most memoir-writers to speak well of their friends and ill of their enemies, but we have to remember that memoir-writers are a select class. As Carlyle puts it, " it was not the Dumb Millions that suffered here; it was the Speaking Thousands, and Hundreds, and Units; who shrieked and published and made the world ring with their wail, as they could and should : that is the grand peculiarity." [1] Apart from memoirs, useful material of the above nature has been collected in Amic and Mouttet's *Orateurs politiques*, W. A. Schmidt's *Tableaux de la Révolution française*, Legg and Wickham's *Select Documents of the French Revolution*, Alger's *Paris in 1789–1794*, Hericault's *La révolution de thermidor*, and R. W. Postgate's *Revolution : 1789 to 1906*.

We may begin by comparing the French Revolution with its English predecessor. There are many points of resemblance. In both cases national bankruptcy compelled the assembly of a Parliament. In both cases the Commons, representing the bourgeoisie as opposed to the clergy and

[1] Carlyle, *French Revolution*, last book, chap. VI.

nobility, profited by the situation to make themselves masters in the State. There is an obvious parallel between Pym's claim to override the House of Lords and Sieyès's motion that the Third Estate, representing ninety-six per cent of the nation, should act as a National Assembly and legislate without waiting for the privileged orders. Despite this claim, neither the English House of Commons nor the French National Assembly had any thought of democracy. This is made abundantly clear in the memoirs of Bailly, the elderly astronomer who sat for Paris and presided at the famous sitting of June 20, 1789, when the Assembly swore not to separate until they had given France a constitution. "The Assembly," he writes, "was dominated by two classes: business men and barristers." Later he appeals to the English precedent. "We represent the men capable of volition. . . . If the English . . . have adopted property as the basis of representation, it is because they regarded property or wealth as a sort of measure of intelligence." [1] Only when the French, like the English before them, had to oppose force to the force wielded by the court did the question of democracy arise. The appeal to force came earlier in the French than in the English Revolution, because the condition of the people was more desperate. Four-fifths of the French people, the peasantry, endured a grinding misery unpalliated even by a Poor Law. Paris and a few large towns were just beginning to be affected by the industrial revolution from over the Channel. Behind the bourgeoisie, therefore, was a hungry army of workers and peasants easy to mobilize in defence of the Revolution. The result was that Louis XVI could not follow the precedent of Charles I and turn the struggle into a civil war. At the first sign of doing so he became a prisoner in Paris, with foreign intervention his only hope.

The French Revolution, like the English, was not at the outset republican. The Third Estate styled themselves His Majesty's "faithful commons" and asked only for Parliamentary control of taxation, its equitable distribution, the responsibility of ministers, and the security of individual liberty and property. What complicated the case was the

[1] Bailly, *Mémoires*, vol. I, pp. 51, 281.

bankruptcy of the country and the enormous wealth of the French Church. Owing to the defeat of the Huguenots in the sixteenth and seventeenth centuries, France in the eighteenth had to have her Reformation and Revolution in one. To pay off State creditors, the Assembly confiscated and sold Church property just as Protestant countries had done at the Reformation. They reorganized Church government on an elective basis, just as Calvin had done in Geneva and Knox in Scotland, and required the clergy to swear allegiance to the State, just as Henry VIII and Elizabeth had done in England. True, they disclaimed interference with doctrine: so had Henry VIII. But by appropriating Church revenues and making the clergy into State functionaries they broke with Rome as effectively as if they had abolished the Mass or the confessional. Moreover, by defending the seizure of Church lands on the ground that public utility is the supreme law, they set a precedent for attacks on other forms of property on the same ground. It might seem evident to the business men and barristers of the Assembly that corporate property and individual property were in different categories: it was not so evident to the land-hungry peasant or starving workman outside. It was open to Marat in his *Ami du Peuple* to ask whether it was worth while to have a revolution in order to gorge dishonest politicians with the patrimony of the poor.

As the English Revolution had its Levellers, so had the French. But until 1792 they were little regarded. It was the intervention of foreign powers in league with the court against the Revolution, and the necessity of arming the people to repel invasion, which gave power to the Jacobins and brought Louis XVI from the Tuileries to the Temple, from the Temple to the guillotine. From that point onward the analogy with the English Revolution breaks down. The National Convention, elected by manhood suffrage to frame a republican constitution, was a body without precedent in modern history. Neither the Swiss cantons, the Dutch Republic, nor the English Commonwealth, while it lasted, had produced anything comparable. Even the American States at this date had not adopted manhood suffrage. But the immediate task of the Convention was to win the war, which with the addition of England to the coalition had entered a critical phase. To that end drastic interference with the rights of property was necessary. The struggle between the Gironde and the Mountain turned mainly on that question. To the Gironde the purpose of the Revolution had been to free private enterprise from royal and feudal shackles : that once done, interference even in order to win the war, let alone in the interest of social equality, was to betray the Revolution and reopen the way to tyranny. To the Mountain, on the other hand, the main thing was to rally the people to the defence of the Revolution, and for that purpose strong measures were necessary. " The people," says Danton, " have only their blood, and they are lavish with it : wretches, be as lavish with your wealth ! " The enemy will pay later on : meanwhile the rich must pay, inflation must be stopped, distress relieved, the people armed, and traitors punished. Robespierre in stronger terms attacks the " bourgeois aristocrats who hate the sight of equality and are frightened for their property," and who by opposing palliatives set the people against the Revolution. The upshot was the ejection of the Gironde from the Convention by the Paris rising of June 1793, the delegation of power to the Committee of Public Safety, and the emergency régime known to history as the Reign of Terror.

This was in no sense a working-class dictatorship. The Terrorists were of the same social class which had led the Revolution from the start—barristers and other professional men, even an ex-noble or two. But they put the defence of the Revolution first and, with a war on their hands and a fifth column in their rear, took no chances. They had no intention of abolishing private property, but were ready to impose ruthless controls for the duration of the war, and had no mercy on men who divided France in face of the enemy. Evil things were done : no one defends the *noyades* of Nantes. But their régime will bear comparison with the Britain of that day, in which boys of fourteen were hanged for theft, men were flogged publicly for killing game between sunset and sunrise, poor children were drafted in cartloads to a living death in coal-mines or cotton-mills or as chimney-

sweeps, and a man was whipped through the streets of Edin-
burgh and banished from Scotland for taking part in a combination of Glasgow weavers against a reduction of wages.
Against that background the tirades of Burke about the
horrors of the French Revolution ring false and hollow.

Carlyle's judgment that " there is no period to be met with,
in which the general Twenty-five Millions of France suffered
less than in this period which they name Reign of Terror " [1]
is true to this extent, that it was during the Terror that the
first positive efforts were made to raise the condition of the
rural and urban masses. Confiscated lands were sold, not to
the bidder who could pay the fattest wad of *assignats*, but to
peasants in small lots. Feudal dues abolished in 1789 subject
to redemption were in 1793 swept away and the title-deeds
burnt. " The Contrat Social section," reports a police agent
in Paris early in 1794, " has just established a hospital where
pregnant women will go and find the broth and meat necessary in their condition. This has excited the emulation of
the other sections, and several already propose to imitate it." [2]
Abroad, the Convention abolished colonial slavery. Last,
but not least, it is to be noted that the war policy of the Committee of Public Safety was free from the aggressive imperialism pursued later by the Directory and Napoleon. Robespierre
had opposed the declaration of war in 1792, and to the end
was acutely aware of the danger of military dictatorship.
" Our aim," Billaud-Varenne told the Convention in 1794,
" is not conquest, but victory. We shall cease fire the moment
the death of an enemy soldier is no longer necessary to freedom. The experience of centuries has sufficiently proved
that a warrior nation forges a yoke for itself by imposing it
on others."

The Terror was bound to end with the emergency which
had called it into being. But its organizers did not know
how to end it. Robespierre has the reputation of a ruthless
dictator, but in reality he destroyed himself by timidity and
infirmity of purpose. He could tolerate a priest or an aristocrat, if they accepted the Revolution, but he could not

[1] Carlyle, *French Revolution*, last book, chap. VI.
[2] Alger, *Paris in 1789-1794*.

tolerate an atheist. For the last eight months of his life his speeches are one wearisome tirade against the atheism which is growing in Paris and other large towns. Moreover, the Revolution had undoubtedly thrown up a number of adventurers who speculated in confiscated lands and feathered their own nests. To Robespierre the difference between an atheist and a grafter is never very clear. The Terror is turned against the Left and against his colleagues of the Mountain, and becomes midsummer madness—a machine out of control—until Left and Right profit by his irresolution to join together and strike him down. But the Right, not the Left, reaps the fruits of Thermidor. Thenceforward the bourgeoisie are in complete control; concessions to the workers are withdrawn; projects of universal education are shelved; and starvation, aggravated by inflation, reigns in the midst of plenty. The abolition of feudal privilege has merely stripped the mask from capitalism. The Jacobins of the future will be Socialists. Between the devil of royalist reaction and the deep sea of working-class revolution, the French bourgeoisie turns to foreign conquest and to the guns of Bonaparte.

As in its beginning, so in its end, the French Revolution exhibits some similarities with the English. There are obvious parallels between the corruption of the Rump and the corruption of the Directory, between the dictatorship of Cromwell and that of Napoleon, between the two Restorations, between 1688 and 1830. But the parallels become less important and the divergencies more so as events develop. The French Revolution, far more than the English, was a world-event. Marvell's lines on the man who

> Could by industrious valour climb
> To ruin the great work of time,
> And cast the Kingdoms old
> Into another mould [1]

are far more applicable to Napoleon than to Cromwell. World history since the French Revolution has been its

[1] Marvell, *An Horatian Ode upon Cromwell's Return from Ireland.*

continuation. The questions which it put, questions of democracy, of Church and State, of the rights of property, of landlord and peasant, of capital and labour, are still being debated. To deal at any length with post-Revolutionary history would carry us into current politics and outside the province of this book.

CHAPTER XIV

SAGA OF CIVILIZATION

THE life of man is reflected in his art. The greater the artist, the more vivid the reflection. Art may mirror life in words, as in poetry and drama; or by wordless suggestion, as in music; or the two may be combined.

At the time of the French Revolution there lived and worked in Vienna one of the greatest of musicians, Wolfgang Amadeus Mozart. His life-story is the most scathing of satires on the claim of the old régime to have created and fostered great art. Musicians in the eighteenth century ranked among the menial servants of the feudal patrons who condescended to employ them. The son of a poor violinist and with no capital but his genius, Mozart throughout his short life suffered alternately the patronage and the insults of men unworthy to turn the leaves of his scores. The steadiest of his patrons, the emperor Joseph II, systematically underpaid him. We can hardly wonder that Mozart joined the Freemasons, who at that time formed a sort of underground opposition to the established order and played a notable part in preparing the programme of the French Revolution. In 1791, the last year of his life, when the French court and emigrant nobles were pestering the powers of Europe to intervene and crush the Revolution, Mozart wrote and produced The Magic Flute, in which the Freemasons (thinly disguised as priests of Isis) are glorified and the crusade against them rebuked. In Catholic Vienna Mozart's known Freemasonry undoubtedly had much to do with the neglect and starvation in which his life ended. While old Europe prepared its war for civilization, its brightest genius was buried at the end of that year in a pauper's grave.

War broke out. After one or two bad starts, France went over to the offensive, freed her frontiers, and under the

Directory and Napoleon turned the war into one of conquest. To European liberals in those early years Bonaparte represented the Revolution, the force which had smashed kings and nobles and inaugurated a new age in the history of the world. So it seemed to the master-musician on whom the mantle of Mozart had fallen, Ludwig van Beethoven—like him a poor man's son who knew by experience the beggarly lot of the artist in old Europe. In 1804 Beethoven wrote his *Eroica* Symphony, and put into it the storm and stress of conflict between old and new—the violence of battle, the tragedy of death, the joy of liberation, and in the great finale the emergence of a new humanity at one with itself.[1] It is well known that Beethoven meant to dedicate the work to the First Consul, and that on hearing that Napoleon had made himself emperor of the French he nearly destroyed the score in his anger.

Thus with the French Revolution came a revision of the philosophy of history accepted in the eighteenth century. The " age of reason " had hoped for the peaceful diffusion of principles of liberty, equality, and fraternity by such educative agencies as the Masonic lodges. Now men had come to see that progress could be won only through struggle. The transition in music from Mozart to Beethoven is symptomatic of the change from an epoch of apparent stability to one of world-shaking conflict. Although the Europe of kings and nobles was able to destroy Napoleon, it did so only by enlisting the new nationalism as an ally, and emerged from the fray damaged beyond repair. In the next thirty years the industrial revolution swept all before it in Britain and made progress in France, bringing in its train mass misery and intensified class struggles. Central Europe and Italy were as yet hardly penetrated by industrialism, but were shaken by revolutionary movements which saw in national unity and independence the first condition of progress. Both causes contributed to the upheavals of 1848.

In that year Richard Wagner, then conductor at the

[1] The main theme of the finale of the *Eroica* is taken from the ballet *Prometheus*, composed two years before on the subject of the Titan who formed men out of clay.

Dresden opera-house, was planning a music-drama on a theme drawn from Teutonic mythology. While so engaged, he was overtaken by the storm. The Revolution which dethroned Louis Philippe in France spread to Germany. Within a month Austria, Prussia, Bavaria, and other German States were rocked by movements demanding national unity and political democracy. Wagner threw himself into the fray and publicly appealed to the king of Saxony to anticipate the revolution by introducing universal suffrage and a radical social programme. The king having failed to rise to the occasion, Wagner in 1849 joined the active revolutionaries and had to escape arrest by flight, taking his operatic sketch with him. It was a penniless exile in Zürich who in 1852 finished the poem and began the music of *The Nibelung's Ring*.

The framework is mere saga. There is nothing original or, in the last analysis, even particularly German in the story of a ring which brings power, but also a curse, to its possessor, or in the enmity of gods and giants, or in the dragon-slaying hero, or in the self-immolating heroine. The novelty is not in the material, but in Wagner's handling of it. In his appeal of 1848 he had asked " whether man, that crown of creation," was " meant by God to serve in menial bondage . . . to sallow *metal*." [1] In 1849, immediately after his exile, he writes: " Our god is gold, our religion the pursuit of wealth." [2] Plainly in the poem which took up the two following years he was thinking of no mere fairy ring, but of the money-power which was beginning to conquer Europe and to subdue human life to the rhythm of an industrial machine.

This is borne out by the music-drama itself. We need not be musical critics, we need only read and listen to realize that the curse lies not only on the possessor of the ring, but on the whole world (" he who shall hold it and he who shall not " [3]), and that the power of the gods is itself but a transmuted form of the power of gold. In his prose writings of that time Wagner looks forward to " a free

[1] Wagner, *Prose Works*, vol. IV, *The Vaterlandsverein Speech*.
[2] Ibid., vol. I, *Art and Revolution*.   [3] *Rhine Gold*, scene IV.

mankind, delivered from every shackle of hampering nationality " [1] by " revolution . . . from below, from the urgency
of true human need." [2] In the music-drama deliverance is
to be won by a fighter who flouts what others revere, who
owes nothing to the powers that be, and who for that very
reason can do what they cannot—even though he pays with
his life.

But contemporary history did not go as Wagner hoped.
European revolution was crushed by European reaction.
France, the fountain-head of revolution, voted the clericals
into power and Napoleon the Little on to the throne of his
uncle. Wagner, ill and depressed, read Schopenhauer and
became convinced that mankind, in bondage to illusion,
was for ever doomed to frustration and that only by renouncing
struggle could we attain inward happiness. In this mood he
continued and, after long interruption and many vicissitudes,
finished *The Ring*, though he never entirely purged it of
the revolutionary ideas of 1848 and therefore never rendered
it internally consistent. A thorough-going treatment of
the theme of renunciation was reserved for his last work,
Parsifal.

Every thoughtful student of history is confronted by these
alternative interpretations. Is there discernible in history
taken as a whole anything which we can call progress, or is
the record one of an aimless struggle among a species of
higher apes, in which any apparent gain is offset by equal
or greater loss? The idea of automatic progress must be
ruled out at once. No one is so naïve as to maintain that
from the mathematics of Egypt and Babylon to the philosophy
and art of Greece, the jurisprudence of Rome, the theology
of the Middle Ages, and the science and social conscience
of the modern world runs a continuous line of advance in
which each segment represents a clear gain on the last.
On the contrary, it is evident that the emergence of
Greek civilization from the background of ancient Asia,
the appropriation of the Greek achievement by Rome, the
decline and fall of Rome before Gibbon's " barbarism and

[1] *Prose Works*, vol. I, *Art and Revolution*.
[2] Ibid., *A Communication to My Friends*.

religion," [1] and the overthrow of medieval Catholicism by modern commercial civilization were in each case attended by cruel struggles, and in each case created problems which the succeeding order could not solve without creating new ones in their place.

Nor is it a sufficient answer to say that in every such struggle good triumphs over evil and enlightenment over obscurantism. We are apt to think so, but then in many cases we have only the winning side's account of the matter. There is no Persian history of the Græco-Persian wars. All pagan accounts of the victory of Christianity over paganism have perished. Where we have both versions, we see that virtue and enlightenment were not confined to one side. Luther was assuredly not more enlightened than Erasmus, nor Henry VIII a better man than More, nor Cromwell than Falkland, nor Napoleon than Pitt, nor Metternich than Napoleon. History is not a tale of the triumph of virtue over vice. If we say in any given case that the winning side was the better, it must be on some other ground than that.

Is there such a ground? To answer this question we must clear up our conceptions of good and evil. Once we repudiate the authority of so-called divine revelation, we cannot even pretend to apply those labels in any but a relative sense. Good can mean only what is good for so-and-so, evil only what is evil for so-and-so. If so-and-so is Everyman, so much the better : there will then be nobody to dispute his valuations. But usually so-and-so is not Everyman. Usually he is the average member of a social group strong enough to impose its views—a primitive tribesman; an Egyptian or Babylonian priest; a Greek or Roman citizen; a medieval cleric, baron, or burgher; a modern politician or press-lord. In such a case there is always somebody to dispute his valuations—an enemy tribesman, an ancient prophet or philosopher, a medieval heretic or peasant rebel, a modern reformer or revolutionary. It is useless to attempt to answer the question whether progress is discernible in history until we have decided *whose* good is to be the criterion.

We escape this difficulty as long as we confine our atten-

[1] Gibbon, *Decline and Fall*, chap. LXXI.

tion to scientific and technical progress. Here the criterion is simple. Obviously one country or one age has more knowledge of and command over nature than another. Archimedes represents an advance on the Egyptian priests, Newton on Archimedes, Einstein on Newton. But we need not here waste time on this criterion. It is the fashion now to decry scientific and technical progress, to ignore its obvious gains in the lightening of daily labour and the reduction of daily suffering, and to ask derisively whether discovery and invention are worth while if they have merely led us from the bow and arrow to the atomic bomb.

The people who decry science never for a moment contemplate doing without the daily advantages which they owe to it. Nevertheless, let us for the sake of argument ignore discovery and invention and consider only what is called moral progress. We are immediately up against the difficulty of the relativity of moral values. For example, we take for granted that the abolition of slavery is moral progress. Plato and Aristotle would have called it moral retrogression. We take for granted that a society which does not burn heretics has advanced morally on one which does. Thomas Aquinas would have called it sinful indifference to the welfare of souls. We look back with horror to the days when people flocked to public executions. Dr. Johnson defended public executions. " Sir, executions are intended to draw spectators. If they do not draw spectators, they don't answer their purpose." [1]   Now Plato, Aristotle, Aquinas, and Johnson were not morally insensitive. Their moral standards simply differed from ours. And though practically all of us disagree with them on the issues stated, it would be possible to name other issues which divide man from man today just as deeply as these divide us from the sages of the past.

It will be easier to answer our main question if we consider why we differ from these distinguished men on such issues. If we ask why we disagree with Plato and Aristotle about slavery, the answer is that we are able to do without it. Greek and Roman citizens could not do without it: they

[1] Boswell, *Life of Johnson*, Everyman edition, vol. II, p. 447.

were dependent on it for all those things which to them made life worth living. In consequence practically no one proposed to abolish slavery. The many were frankly regarded as means to a good life for the few. In course of time, owing to causes mentioned earlier in this book, their descendants were forced to do without slaves—first, to substitute for gang-slavery the less rigorous system of medieval serfdom, and in the end to abolish that too. When slavery ceased to be the rule in Europe, public opinion began to condemn it, and finally became strong enough to enforce its abolition in tropical and sub-tropical climates where it was still the rule. In the United States the North, which knew that it could provide itself with the amenities of life without slavery, forced abolition on the South, which believed that it could not. The economic change preceded the moral. The average man is as humane as circumstances allow him to be, but no more.

If we ask why we differ from Thomas Aquinas about the burning of heretics, the answer is that we do not, as he did, see in heresy a mortal danger to mankind. To Thomas a heretic was a murderer of souls, a cancer in the body of the Church to be cauterized without mercy. We do not consider religious conformity vital to our temporal and eternal welfare, and therefore do not take a serious view of its infraction. To say that we have an invincible objection to burning people alive, when competent authority thinks necessary, would be unduly complacent in a society which in war uses flame-throwers and jellied petrol and obliterates cities with high explosive, incendiary, and atomic bombs. Once again, the average man is as humane as circumstances allow him to be, but no more.

If we ask why we differ from Johnson about public executions, the answer again is that we find we can do without them. In the eighteenth century, when mass poverty of a degree now unknown in this country led to a crime rate now also unknown, the propertied classes who controlled Parliament thought it necessary to their security to punish hundreds of offences with hanging and to terrorize potential offenders by making it a public spectacle. Various causes contributed to the reformation of our penal code. Juries drawn from a less limited class than members of Parliament refused to send people to the gallows for petty theft and so brought the law into disrepute. Parliament itself was reformed and opened to a wider class than before. The abolition of hanging for certain offences, being followed by no increase in those offences, led to its abolition for others with the same negative result. Finally it was found that public executions, far from being a deterrent to crime, actually by attracting degraded and hardened characters to the spot contributed to its increase. Today we do without public hangings and, if we were confident that total abolition would lead to no increase in murder, should probably do without hanging at all. Here again the average man is as humane as circumstances allow him to be, but no more.

That being so, to expect history to reveal an automatic increase in the moral stature of individuals is as unreasonable as to expect it to reveal an automatic increase in their physical stature. As the physical stature of man is conditioned by his natural environment, so is his moral stature by his social environment. As giants or dwarfs may occur in the one case, so may saints or criminals in the other; but they are not typical. The only kind of moral progress for which we may legitimately look in history is social development of such a kind as to reduce the frictions which make for unsocial behaviour.

The view which denies the fact of progress is as shallow as that which regards progress as automatic and inevitable. Those who see in human history a mere continuation of the struggle for existence which reigns in the animal kingdom have to explain away the unaccountable fact that they can entertain the idea of progress, even to reject it—that they can look at the struggle and pronounce it vain. Man alone among animals has evolved a critical faculty; and the fact that he has evolved it suggests that it serves some useful purpose. Plato and Aristotle approved of slavery, but at least they thought it worth arguing about. To that extent they represented an advance on the warriors and kings who took slavery for granted. No philosopher of the present day defends slavery even in argument. To that extent we have advanced on Plato and Aristotle. Nor does any writer of world repute today advocate the death penalty for heresy. There are Catholic authorities on canon law who do; but the majority even of their co-religionists have never heard of them, and but for the researches of Mr. Joseph McCabe and Mr. Avro Manhattan we might be unaware of their existence. To that extent we have advanced on Thomas Aquinas. Nor does any one now say a word for the penal practice of the eighteenth century. To that extent we have advanced on Dr. Johnson.

But that is not the root of the matter. Age cannot be compared with age by measuring the stature of their intellectuals. The criterion of progress in history is, when we think it out, the well-being of men and women in the mass, for the simple reason that without men and women in the mass there would be no intellectuals. To those who argue that the masses are a mere means for the production of an aristocracy of artists, poets, and thinkers, the answer is that the masses support artists, poets, and thinkers, and not *vice versa*; that if the masses withdraw their support, the game will be up; and that there is no reason why they should support artists, poets, and thinkers except in return for benefits received. History is the saga of men and women like you and me; of our age-long struggle to win a living from nature; of discovery and invention; of ignorance and superstition; of benefactors and betrayers; of exploiters and liberators; of defeat, the stepping-stone to victory; and of victory, the starting-point of new struggle. That the struggle is unending does not prove it vain. The very fact of struggle implies the existence of evil: in that sense evil is an ingredient of life itself. But the enemy which we fight is never evil in the abstract, but always some particular evil in the concrete. To those who combat it, the conquest of any particular evil is good. Good, therefore, is no less than evil an ingredient of life.

No one who reads the history and other literature of the ancient world in which the majority were slaves, or that of the medieval world (as distinct from modern romance about it) in which the majority were serfs, can doubt that the mass of men and women in our world have gained in concrete well-being more than they have lost. That gain is none the less a fact because the successful struggles of the past have left us face to face with new devils to fight—the devil of mass poverty where it still exists, the devil of mass ignorance and superstition, and the devil of total war with its weapons of mass destruction, to name no others. History should teach us that what man has done, man can do—that as men and women like ourselves fought and overcame their ancient and medieval oppressors, so we, their children and heirs, have it in us to carry on the fight, to refuse to be destroyed by the work of our own hands, and to bequeath to our descendants new tasks to face and new worlds to win.

INDEX